Other Books by Mickey Mantle
THE QUALITY OF COURAGE
THE EDUCATION OF A BASEBALL PLAYER
WHITEY AND MICKEY (with Whitey Ford)

Other Collaborations by Herb Gluck
EVEN BIG GUYS CRY (with Alex Karras)
JERRY LEWIS: IN PERSON

The Mick

MICKEY
MANTLE

WITH HERB GLUCK

Doubleday & Company, Inc.
Garden City, New York
1985

DESIGNED BY WILMA ROBIN

Library of Congress Cataloging in Publication Data
Mantle, Mickey, 1931–
   The Mick.
   1. Mantle, Mickey, 1931–   . 2. Baseball players—
United States—Biography. 3. New York Yankees (Baseball
team) I. Gluck, Herb. II. Title.
GV865.M33A35   1985   796.357′092′4 [B]
ISBN: 0-385-19456-0
Library of Congress Catalog Card Number 85-2000

To Merlyn, who has put up with me for thirty-three years.
To my mother, who made everything possible.
And to my father. I wish he could read this book.

I just recently read about a poll of all-time popular people and it said I was the working-class people's favorite. That made me very happy. This book is dedicated to everyone who ever yelled to me, "Hey, Mick, how you feelin'? How's your legs?" From New York City cabbies to Okie farmers to presidents of corporations that I see in my travels . . .

This book is for you. I hope I got it right.

I love you all.

Thanks a lot.

The Mick

Chapter 1

Let's start here. April 15, 1951, my first season as a Yankee. I'm on a train headed for Washington. Opening Day against the Senators. And I'm saying to myself, "What am I doing anyway? I don't even have a contract. What's going to happen now? Where do I fit in? I know I can play minor league ball, yet all the talk—'Another Babe Ruth,' 'Another Joe DiMaggio'—who's kidding who?"

A sudden wash of rain across the window, pinpoint lights of Washington getting nearer and nearer. Casey Stengel is at my shoulder, saying, "C'mon, I want you to meet Del Webb, Dan Topping, and George Weiss. They're waiting for us in the smoking lounge."

I'm just the new kid and the top guys—the two owners and general manager of the team—want to talk to me.

I say, "All right," hesitating to add, "Casey, can you tell me something? Am I going to play in Beaumont this year?"

He winks. "I think you'll stay with us." Then he says, "When we get back there, just be quiet and I'll do the talking." We move from car to car toward the lounge. Then my first glimpse of the big brass. And Casey says, "You all know Mickey . . ." Webb and Topping beam flashy smiles, congratulating me for the fine job I've done in spring training. Whereupon Casey tells Weiss I'm ready for the Yankees.

Weiss mutters, "I think he's too young."

"I don't care if he's in diapers," says Casey. "If he's good enough to play for us on a regular basis, I want to keep him."

Now it's Webb's turn. He tells Weiss soothingly, "George, they've been writing so much stuff about Mickey, I feel we have to keep him."

Topping agrees. "The thing is, George, we're not opening in

New York, we're opening in Washington. After two or three games under his belt, I think he'll be all right."

Casey nods and goes a step further. "Bet your ass he'll be all right. In fact, I'm so sure the kid's gonna make it"—looking straight at Weiss—"I want you to give him twenty-five hundred above the minimum."

The minimum, I know, is $5,000. After making $225 a month playing in the minors at Joplin, it sounds like a fortune. I have to bite my tongue to keep from saying, "I'll take it!" before the haggling even begins.

Weiss cradles his chin for a moment with an expression of unmistakable annoyance. He says, "It's not the money, Casey. The boy needs more farm club experience. Besides, our roster is loaded with outfielders." He ticks off the names on five pudgy fingers. "DiMaggio, Woodling, Bauer, Jensen, Mapes—I can't see a place for Mickey in that lineup. I'd rather see him playing every day in the minors than have him sitting on the bench up here."

"What are you worried about?" says Casey. "There's room on the ball club. Let the kid stay. If he carries his weight, pay him the seventy-five hundred. If he doesn't, we'll send him down and you'll only have to give him the minimum. You've got nothing to lose, George."

Weiss folds his arms, stares at the ceiling, lets out a big sigh. "Okay."

So I float out of that smoking lounge on the New York–Washington Express like I'm in a dream. I had just signed my first major league contract, easily the biggest moment in my nineteen years.

Back in my seat, I look out into the rain and I'm far away, back home at the real beginning of it all. I remember my dad walking down the street in Commerce, Oklahoma. He's coming home from work in the lead mines, smiling wearily. I peer into his lunch bucket for the piece of cupcake that he always saves for me. And I've brought along my glove and a tennis ball for the game that we play every evening until dark.

Out loud, I hear myself say, "Everything will be better now." It sure will be. I wish there was a way to let my dad know. But I can only hope he'll read about my signing in the papers tomorrow.

If you look at a map of Oklahoma, you can see the towns where I grew up all crushed together in the northeast corner of the state: Commerce, Picher, Cardin, tiny towns that used to be the hub of the Oklahoma mining district. The Missouri state line is just ten miles east and Kansas is just five miles to the north.

My grandfather, Charlie Mantle, was raised near there, same as my mom's folks. They all lived in Spavinaw, about thirty-five miles southwest of Commerce in Mayes County, near one of the big lakes that feed the Tulsa water supply. People from Tulsa used to take vacations on the lakeshore nearby; they still do.

Spavinaw is an Indian name. As a small boy living in Commerce, I heard many stories about the Cherokees, the Chickasaws, the Creeks, and the other Oklahoma tribes, stories told mostly by my dad's friends who remembered driving their wagons over muddy roads past sorry-looking Indian cabins and afterward pulling into town, hitching their horses and watering them at troughs smelling of sulfur. When the Picher mines first opened, it was like the Alaska gold rush, everything booming: towns filled with dollar-a-day hotels and people arriving by the dozens. The companies expanded left and right, making millions, while the workers dug at the most valuable zinc and lead fields in the world.

On the day they finished the last section of paved highway connecting Chicago and Los Angeles—Route 66—at the Kansas–Oklahoma state line, they say the Cherokees came down to watch, squatting along the highway, wrapped in blankets, silently gazing at the construction site with glum faces. Years later, reading up on Indian history, I began to understand more. Until then it never occurred to me that the Indians made a forced march from Southern prison camps, that hundreds died of starvation during the journey into Oklahoma. Their Trail of Tears. They didn't teach that in school, so I didn't know.

When my mother was a little girl, she asked her mother where she was born and her mother replied, "In Indian Territory, the Cherokee Nation. Take your pick, child." If someone asked me now, I would say likewise. Proud of it, too.

For the record, though, our family bloodlines run mainly to English beginnings, with a sprinkling of Dutch and German. We go back about five generations in America. As for the proof of this or that ancestor, I only know I had grandparents who lived with their parents, who eventually settled in Spavinaw, had their own families, and worked the best they could scratching out a livelihood, as long as it was honest.

My mother was a Richardson. Her father got his schooling strictly through experience and ambition. As a young man, he was a carpenter. Mom says he was really good at it. He could draw up plans for all types of buildings without using a blueprint and he never went wrong in his calculations. He married a girl named Annie Laurie Thomas. In February 1904, she gave birth to my mother, Lovell. Actually, Mom grew up to be a pretty catch herself; tall, slender, light gray eyes, and reddish-blond hair. I guess she should have waited a while, but at seventeen she ran off and married William Theodore Davis, a farm boy from Craig County, despite Grandpa Richardson's strong objections. She tried to make a go of it. But after bringing two children into the world—my half brother Theodore and half sister Anna Bea—there was a divorce. Mom came home, saying nothing about what happened except, "We had a bad misunderstanding."

Dad was the first of four children. Born Elvin Clark Mantle, starting with his cradle days everybody called him Mutt. Dad's second brother, Eugene, hung on to the nickname Tunney, after the old heavyweight champ Gene Tunney. Family legend has it that Uncle Tunney once put a man's eye out with a shovel. Dad claimed that they were at a dance in a small town near Spavinaw. A fight broke out and the Mantle boys were outnumbered. So Tunney just picked up the nearest weapon and let some guy have it. Uncle Tunney was *tough.*

Next came Aunt Thelma, followed by Emmett, the youngest child.

Unfortunately, a week after Emmett was born Grandma Mantle developed pneumonia and died. Emmett was sent on to an aunt and uncle. Through it all, Grandpa Charlie braved it alone. He worked as a butcher in Spavinaw, did house chores at night, and made sure the other kids had proper food on the table. Troubles or no, he somehow managed. The one thing I'm sure of, in all the time I was around Grandpa, he always smiled, even when there was little to smile at.

Working and saving and scrimping. To what end? I guess Dad instinctively felt there was a need to pitch in and help. So he quit school and got a job grading county roads. As fate had it, the Mantles and Richardsons lived on the same block. Every once in a while Dad would drop by their house and visit my mother's youngest sister. Nothing heavy, just a few laughs—innocent, so to speak.

One spring night he knocked at the front door. Mom opened it. Whatever happened after that, fifty-five years passed before she finally let out the reason why she married my father, saying at a surprise party in Oklahoma City—on her eightieth birthday —that he was tall, handsome, and a real gentleman under the rough exterior.

I was born on October 20, 1931, in a two-room, unpainted hilltop house on the north edge of Spavinaw. We had no streets leading there, only a narrow dirt road winding up past fields of corn and wheat. This was during the Great Depression, when Oakies were getting kicked off their land—broke, hungry, rattling along Route 66 toward California in Model Ts. Dad was darn close to driving me and Mom out there too, having lost the grading job. Instead, he took his chances as a tenant farmer. For two years he plowed eighty acres, turning up bumper crops. After each harvest the man who owned the farm went to market and was paid next to nothing a bushel.

Hard times for my dad, but I was just a little boy then and, thank God, I am spared the memory.

As clear as yesterday, though, I remember one incident from that period. We were sitting on the front porch; I must have been four years old. In those days they used to haul water and ice to us on a truck. It would come by with a bucket for our use. A tank sat on two beams on the bed of the truck and these two beams stuck out. I jumped up and grabbed one of the beams, rode the underside of the truck for about a half a block, thinking I was really doing something great.

When I got back to our yard, Dad was so mad he was shaking. He looked around for something to hit me with and all he could find was a piece of baling wire lying in the ditch. So he picked up that piece of baling wire and gave me five or six good licks across the ass.

It was just about the only time he ever whipped me. Was about the last time he ever *had* to whip me, too.

Around that time we moved to Commerce. Dad became a shoveler for the Eagle-Picher Zinc and Lead Company. They had mines operating in every hole and corner of the tri-state area. You could go twenty miles from where we lived, all the way to Joplin, Missouri, and get there underground. That's how far the veins stretched. They laid car tracks, had mules pulling cans of ore, while the miners chopped day and night at walls of rock. The mule skinners took care of the mules and hauled the cans over to the shafts; others hooked the cans to be hoisted. The so-called screen apes broke big boulders into rocks with sixteen-pound sledgehammers and the shovelers scooped up the rocks and deposited anywhere from two to three hundred pounds of them into the cans. My dad worked each of those jobs until he finally became a ground boss. When somebody got sick, he'd fill in as a shoveler or hooker or whatever all over again. When he came to the surface, he'd ride up on that hook, standing in one of the cans, his face blackened, eyes blinking at the glaring light.

They called the spent ore "chat." Giant piles of it towered over our town. During warm summer evenings I would climb to the top and look down at the little sand-scarred houses. Blocks and blocks of them with patched roofs and raggedy weeds in the front yards. My house at 319 South Quincy Street was stuck among the rest.

Baseball was a very big factor in my dad's life. It didn't matter how tired he was, he still managed to play semi-pro ball on weekends. The family would drive down from Commerce and he'd join the Spavinaw team against Salina, Jay, Grove, and

Vinita, and other such teams around Mayes County. I sat in the stands, thinking he was Pepper Martin, Mickey Cochrane, and Dizzy Dean all rolled up in a single package. I mean, he ran, pitched, fielded most any position, batted both ways, hit for distance, had a shotgun arm, and threw strikes. I thought he was the best damn ballplayer in the territory. Only the professional scouts never saw him play. They never got a glimpse of him. There's no doubt he would have made a fine major leaguer if given the chance.

But he gave that chance to me.

Before I was even born he had a name picked out. Mickey—after Mickey Cochrane, the great-hitting catcher who spent his entire career in the American League. Yet Dad was a lifetime St. Louis Cardinals fan. He practically lived and died with them while I was growing up, so the best I can figure is that he must've singled out Cochrane because of his qualities. Brash. Fiercely competitive. A sure winner. Guess Dad thought that someday I'd step into Cochrane's shoes.

Near every house that we lived in, Dad would establish some area where we could play ball. In Commerce, when I was five or six, there was a battered tin barn that leaned close to our house. I spent countless hours there, hitting tennis balls off the roof or into the trees on the adjoining lot. Dad would pitch to me right-handed and I'd bat lefty; Grandpa pitched lefty and I'd bat righty. That's how they taught me to switch-hit. Every once in a while I would hit one over the house. Often as not, the next pitch would knock me down. Wherever I hit 'em, my brothers Roy and Ray would chase them.

I'm told that Mom cut my toddler clothes down from Dad's baseball uniforms. He'd bring home broken bats from his semi-pro games and whittle them for me, taking five inches from the barrel and shaping the handle so I could hold it. There was a backstop set up behind our garage and I'd play out there every day, swinging nonstop at the ball. Every Christmas he bought me a glove, a good one, getting larger ones for me each year as I grew. We had no money to speak of and the gloves were expensive. I used a Bill Doak model. Spittin' Bill, who was a Cardinals pitcher then. Anyway, all through my early childhood, Dad kept drumming it in: "Practice, practice, practice." Which I did, attacking each pitch, whether it was thrown underhand, sideways, or over the top. Sometimes he really let go. The garage and the house withstood a lot of punishment, I'll tell you.

Dad worked with me every day. And the practice paid off. By the time I reached second grade, I was hitting them pretty good from the right side. But Dad also wanted me to bat lefty, which I hated. When it got dark and supper was ready, Dad would turn me around, from righty to lefty. "Your belly can wait," he'd say. Then he'd start pitching again. He believed that any kid could develop into a switch-hitter if you taught him early enough.

More to the point, he had this uncanny instinct and actually predicted that someday in the not-too-distant future we'd find just about every big league manager platooning his players; right-handed batters facing southpaws and vice versa, depending upon the situation. The year I joined the Yankees is when Casey Stengel started to platoon. So Dad was a prophet in his own way long before the system became an accepted part of the game.

But as a boy, who could see that far? In fact, it's a wonder I didn't rebel against baseball, from having it spoon-fed down my throat every day of my life. But somehow Dad always made it seem like fun. And I didn't play ball all the time. To break the pattern, sometimes I'd sneak off, looking for a new adventure. Like climbing fences or simply walking up the street to LeRoy Bennett's house. My first real friend. Also Nick Ferguson, whose house was on Vine Street, about eight blocks from mine. To me that was downtown. A different world. So Nick usually met me at LeRoy's house. If I stayed there too long, a yell would go up: "Mickey Charles!" My mom, reminding me that I had better be starting home. The more this happened, the more Nick and LeRoy tagged along. Pretty soon we were playing baseball all the time, in one form or another, such as Pitch and Catch, Annie Over, and Major League . . . when we pretended to be the genuine article. I would bat for the Cardinals, LeRoy for the Boston Red Sox, and Nick for the New York Yankees. The real team's batting order had to be followed. I'd hit righty as Marty Marion, left-handed as Enos Slaughter, righty again as Terry

Moore, left-handed as Stan Musial, my idol. The rules went this way: a ground ball that was caught was an out. Ground balls that hit the house were singles, while flies that hit the house were doubles. If you hit the roof, you had a triple. Anything over the roof was a home run. We kept track of each game, from inning to inning, over a whole season, recording all the statistics— batting averages, etc.—until we reached the "final standings" in our invented eight-team race to the championship.

Then one summer we claimed a spot near an abandoned mine shaft. It made a perfect baseball field, smooth and firm. The foul lines were laid out with a stick and we used old gunny-sacks for bases, nailing them to the ground. One bad feature, though, was the outfield. An endless plain of alkali. You couldn't see a ditch or a fence or anything that would slow the ball. I guess it's the main reason why I became an infielder. I hated chasing after base hits when they skipped past and rolled half-way to the next town before I could flag them down. And whenever the wind came howling in, it carried gray clouds of alkali dust, the gritty particles that swept over the field and burned into our eyes nearly blinding us. End of game. We'd cough all the way home.

Chapter 2

During the early forties, LeRoy, Nick, and I joined a bunch of other kids who played for a sandlot team in Dauthat. We hiked there, covering the three miles in the afternoon. No big deal. We would've hiked a hundred miles to show up and practice. But the real excitement came on Saturdays and Sundays when our gang played a team from Picher or a team in some other town in the mining district. The kids ranged in ages from twelve to eighteen. Strictly amateur, although you'd never know it from the size of the crowds. A whole mob used to drive out, mostly mining people and their families. You'd see the dust coming up on the road and dozens of old cars honking by. What a sight! They formed a circle around the field. Picnic baskets, egg crates, and whatnot would be dragged out of the backseats, pints of whiskey in back pockets too; everybody laughing and hollering, then settling down to watch us play, so attentive, so respectful you'd think they were actually paying their way into the World Series.

Well, many of the old hard-packed diamonds are gone now. Like the one in Commerce. Today it's a caved-in hole surrounded by piles of chat. Under a leaden sky the whole area looks as barren as a wasteland: desolate, forgotten, nobody within hailing distance. You ride through the mining area in an eerie silence and discover a graveyard of rocks, stunted trees, rotting shafts, the earth dry as bone.

But extending in any direction away from the town, you'll pass beautiful countryside and see cloud banks over the hills, wild flowers, wooded land and ploughed fields, the twin rivers known as Spring and Neosho, which come together at Grand Lake; the little bridge is close by and the basin to go swimming . . . I remember that rickety bike of mine, imagine myself riding on it, peddling down to the Neosho, Nick and LeRoy and Bill Mosely on their bikes—"Let's go to Steps-Ford bridge to swim."

I remember an afternoon at that swimming hole. A bunch of us kids were pushing off a log on a sandbank. Somebody yelled, "There's a girl looking at us!" She was across the river and there we were, naked as jaybirds. I let go of the log and panicked because I could barely dog-paddle out of there in the first place. Bill Mosely came back and got me. That was it. No more "swimming" for me.

I always wished my dad could be somebody other than a miner. I knew it was killing him. He was underground eight hours a day. Every time he took a breath, the dust and dampness went into his lungs. Coughed up gobs of phlegm and never saw a doctor. What for? He'd only be told it was "miner's disease." He realized that if he didn't get cancer he'd probably die of tuberculosis. Many did before the age of forty. "So what the hell. Live while you can," he'd say and light another cigarette. A confirmed chain-smoker; I hardly remember him without one stuck in the corner of his mouth.

Years later, when I was getting started with the Yankees, I signed a contract to endorse Camel cigarettes. Yet I couldn't understand how anyone could derive pleasure by inhaling smoke into his lungs. Meanwhile the Camel people kept giving me a free carton every week, which I promptly mailed home. Dad would then take the carton to the grocery store to trade it for a carton of Luckies. I heard later that the grocer would brag to his customers, "See these Camels? They came straight from Mickey."

In 1944, with me in the ninth grade, Grandpa Charlie got very sick. He had Hodgkin's disease, a form of cancer that attacks the lymph nodes and eventually penetrates the bone marrow.

I was just a kid then. I didn't understand death and sickness very well. Even now I don't remember the order of events from that time in my life. It just seemed that all my relatives were dying around me. First my Uncle Tunney, the tough one, then

my Uncle Emmett. Within a few years—before I was thirteen—
they had died of the same disease. I knew Uncle Emmett had it
because the doctor had to cut the lymph nodes out of his rav-
aged body for nearly a year. To no avail.

Grandpa suddenly became old and feeble, almost overnight.
My father would help him out of bed, support his wobbly legs
that used to stride along South Quincy Street with so much
vigor. What I'm absolutely sure of is that Dad was worried sick
over Grandpa's condition. He began looking for a place in the
country, as far away from the mining area as Grandpa could get.

He died shortly after we moved. I never forgot that moment,
standing beside the casket with my little twin brothers Ray and
Roy, the three of us looking down on him, and my father whispering, "Say goodbye to Grandpa . . ."

You probably can't imagine what we were up against after we
moved from our house in Commerce. Dad had swapped it for
some cows, a horse, a tractor, and the right to sharecrop 160
acres of land five miles out in the country on Dr. Wormington's
farm. We were more like caretakers. There was a great big lawn
and one of our duties was to mow the grass. I played a lot of ball
out there, all kinds of games with my twin brothers and sister
and youngest brother Butch, who was three at the time. I would
make them play football; usually me and Barbara and Butch
against Ray and Roy. Or we'd get into a game where anyone
who threw the ball over the house had to start running the
moment it was caught on the other side. For example, if I threw
the ball and Roy made the catch, he would speed around the
house while I turned tail in the opposite direction, hoping to
avoid being smacked with the ball. Also, I used to get out two
pairs of socks, stuff them with two or three more pairs, put them
on Butch and Barbara, say, "Butch, you're Joe Louis and, Barbara, you're Billy Conn . . ." and I'd make them fight. I liked to
tease the kids, especially Barbara. But she could take it, really.
In her own way I guess she enjoyed the fun as much as us boys,
though she occasionally threatened to leave home. She finally
did one day, saying she would never come back. I had to run
after her, shouting, "I didn't mean it, Barbara! I didn't mean it!"
Butch wasn't happy about the prizefighting either. Once in a

while the socks on Barbara's hands fell off and he'd get punched in the face with her bare knuckles. She had very hard knuckles, I can tell you.

On the farm Dad seemed happy just getting up in the morning to be outdoors. Early spring we planted oats, wheat, and a field of corn and milked the cows, bringing the filled buckets to our house, where Mom separated the milk from the cream. A milk truck would stop by and she sold him whatever we didn't need; this way my parents could afford a few extra groceries.

On warm sunlit days I'd ride my horse Tony to school and tie him to a hitching post. Then the times when I'd see the shoot-'em-ups at the Saturday matinees, come out and go down the street to the Black Cat café, where I'd have the blue plate special—a hamburger, a bowl of chili, and a soda pop, all for a quarter. And the biggest thrill of my life was when Dad took me to a Class C baseball game—Joplin against Springfield. We were watching this Springfield player hitting line drives at batting practice. Bullets. Dad pointed. "See that guy? He's going to be a major league star." He's pointing at Stan Musial, soon to be my first baseball idol.

It was just before harvest; the crops were ready to be put into the barn. Dad never got the chance. A torrential rain, which lasted for days and days, flooded everything. The creek behind our house swelled from the backwaters of the Neosho River and ran over the bank. It wiped us out. We took four trips in our wagon to move our furniture and belongings to Whitebird, a tiny village on the edge of Commerce. It was a terrible blow and nobody felt it harder than Dad. He realized he would have to work the mines again. Probably the lowest ebb of his life; he sat in the wagon, jaws clenched, his eyes just staring at the road.

One winter, years later, I brought Billy Martin out to see that little shack in Whitebird. We had been in Tulsa for a Diamond Dinner, sponsored by A. Ray Smith, who owned the Oiler baseball team. It was a dilapidated, primitive shanty, abandoned by then. Only a jar of pickles sat on top of the icebox. Billy couldn't believe it, couldn't understand how anybody had ever lived there. And to tell the truth, the rusted tin barn next to our house on South Quincy Street looked a lot better than the house in Whitebird.

There were seven of us bunched together in our Whitebird home, with no inside plumbing. A small kitchen was built onto the house later. Mom would heat the water on a wood-burning cook stove, then pour it into a No. 3 zinc tub so we could take a bath. She also washed our clothes in that tub.

I shared a bedroom with my parents and Barbara. The twins and Butch slept in the adjoining bedroom. Well, Oklahoma winters are generally cold—not too much snow, but the northwind comes howling across the plains; bleak, gray, the fields covered with frost. Some nights those winds whistled through little cracks in the wall so fierce they'd lift the linoleum right off the floor. You had to be careful or you'd step on the rising billows and crack the linoleum.

At dawn I'd brace myself, jump out of bed, and feed the stove kindling wood. As soon as it threw out enough heat, everybody would gather around the stove, trying to keep warm.

Then summer, when it would get stifling hot, the sun burning into the land. Mom used to flap towels around the house to chase the flies that swarmed through holes in the screen door. A losing battle. If one of the kids left the door open, they'd really swarm in.

Mom worked day and night, always giving. I don't think she had more than two dresses to her name. When Dad got paid on Saturdays, they'd go to the store and buy a box of groceries for the entire week. They never asked for a dime's worth of credit and the owner showed his appreciation by letting us kids choose a bag of candy as treats. Maybe ten or twelve all-day suckers or penny bubble gum, something to last a long while.

Surprisingly, with all the stress, I can't recall Mom and Dad having a serious argument. If they did, it wasn't so I could hear them. But if any punishment had to be dealt out to the kids, she usually did it. I took a couple of whippings off her. One time I went wading around in a caved-in hole near the Blue Goose mine. It had filled up with water after a heavy rain, forming a muddy pond about 400 feet deep and 50 yards across. People said those holes were like hidden whirlpools and warned us that

anything that fell in them would be pulled right to the bottom.
Bill and LeRoy and others would swim there anyway. I was just
wading around and slipped off to try some swimming. Mom
found me there and whipped my butt all the way home. She
said, "You know you can't swim. You could've drowned."

I said, "Momma, I was just trying to easy around the edges."

She said, "Mickey, I might not be the smartest woman in the
world, but one thing is certain and it's knowing that you can't
swim a lick in the first place."

Of course, I had my baseball and I loved football too. After the
eighth grade athletics meant everything. At Commerce High
I'd sit in class listening to the teacher, but half the time I would
gaze out the window and see myself scoring sensational touch-
downs in the Lucky Seven high school conference. The thing is,
I wasn't a very good student, but I passed my classes. I took easy
subjects—home economics, shop, gym, and so forth—and stag-
gered through the rest. In English class we had to memorize a
certain amount of poetry. And I remember an English teacher
by the name of Mrs. Jacoby who had us memorize the poem
called "Trees." I didn't get it quite right in class. But after school
she let me catch a glimpse of the page over her shoulder while I
recited to the empty classroom.

Mrs. Aldene Campbell taught journalism and I was one of the
editors of the school newspaper, *Tiger Chat*, mainly because I
knew so much about sports. Still, Mrs. Campbell wasn't too
impressed by my journalistic knowledge and one time—probably to embarrass me—she sent me to a local competition for
high school journalism students. Me and the star editor from
Tiger Chat, Mary Ann Howard, went up to Miami for a whole
day of tests. And wouldn't you know it, Mary Ann won the first
prize up there and I came in second! At my graduation, Mrs.
Campbell said, "I always knew you could do it if you tried." I
never found out whether she meant trying to be a ballplayer or
a journalist.

I graduated with Bill Mosely, who was my best friend at
Commerce High—a basketball and football hero, the best we
had. Bill went on to play football at Pittsburg State Teacher's
College in Kansas. I first met him in the seventh grade after he

moved from Picher to Commerce. He was with me the night I made Patty McCall angry. She was in my class and had invited three or four of us boys, along with several girls, over to her house. Four girls and us. My friends and I kept dropping things so that the girls would have to bend over and we could look up their skirts.

It seems pretty innocent now, but then it caused a big scandal. I guess Patty's folks told the principal and we were in for a big paddling the next day at school. My mother and father never knew, otherwise I would have gotten another licking at home.

Bill and I were friends from the beginning and we used to hang out together a lot. He lived with his mother. Sometimes after football practice I'd go to their house. See, if I missed the school bus it was a long walk to Whitebird, so I would ask my parents for permission to stay over. Many's the night I'd sit up with Bill and talk about sports, both of us dreaming of making the big time. Bill painted exciting pictures of football and somehow those pictures got to me. Because during my sophomore year I went out for the Commerce High team. Dad said it could bust me up for baseball and I think it almost broke his heart when I did get hurt. But until then, I was a pretty good halfback. I had good hands and I could outrun everyone.

One day we were practicing. I was carrying the ball when a tackler kicked me on the left shin. Bill Mosely and the coach helped me off the field. The coach said it looked like a sprain. That night my mother soaked the ankle in a bucket of hot water. Next morning my temperature had soared to 104 degrees and the ankle was swollen to twice its normal size. At that point, my dad drove me to the Picher general hospital. Our family doctor examined me and thought the injury was superficial. Still, there was the high fever, so he tells my dad, "We're gonna lance the ankle and put the boy in bed for a while." I laid there two weeks. They had liniments, sulfur, peroxide, plus more stuff like hot and cold compresses. But the ankle remained swollen. Meantime Mom walked a mile every day from Whitebird to catch the NEO (North East Oklahoma) bus to the

Picher hospital. Every evening, when Dad came to the hospital, she'd go home and fix the kids' dinner.

Then one weekend she's in consultation with the doctor. He kinda hems and haws and finally says, "The bone is badly abcessed. I'm afraid it's osteomyelitis. We may have to amputate the leg." And she says, "The hell you are!"

Remember the kid who ran across America—or tried to? The Terry Fox story, y'know. When he found out they were going to take his leg off, he went berserk. I can imagine how he felt because I would have rather seen mine rot off than have somebody cut it off without at least trying to find an alternative.

That afternoon my mother is at a lawyer's office in the neighboring town of Miami. He hears the problem and draws up papers that will transfer me to the Crippled Children's Hospital in Oklahoma City. A 175-mile trip and I remember my dad at the wheel of his big old wreck of a sedan—a 1935 LaSalle—thinking I'd never be able to play baseball again. And in the backseat I'm thinking of his wounded pride, the fact that he was taking me to a state hospital where they accepted patients who couldn't pay, knowing all the while that we were as poor as could be.

Nevertheless, we had something working in our favor. That same year the wonder drug penicillin came out. They gave it to me in Oklahoma City. An injection every three hours around the clock. Almost immediately the ankle showed improvement. Another good thing happened. During my confinement I listened to the 1946 Cardinals–Red Sox World Series—my man Country Slaughter tearing around third base with the winning run in the eighth inning of the seventh game. A few days later it felt terrific just to get out of the hospital, even if my half brother Theodore had to carry me.

I had a long way to go because I was down to 110 pounds.

It was a matter of daily rest and recovery at home, more or less to keep the infection under control, then ditching the crutches and finally getting into high school basketball games between flare-ups. The following summer I played sandlot baseball in Commerce, Picher, Miami, Baxter Springs, Treece, Neosho, and a dozen other flyspeck towns covering the northeast corner of the Kansas–Oklahoma–Missouri tri-state area. Wherever it was, I drove myself to get better and better, regardless of time and circumstance. I had to swing that bat and field my position better than any kid around. So that's all I did: *play, play, play.*

I had no other enjoyment. Nothing was more important.

Chapter 3

As you ride out of the mining fields, heading north on Highway 66, you're bound to see a sign that says: BAXTER SPRINGS—FIRST COWTOWN IN KANSAS. And here I first got to know Barney Barnett. He was a big force behind the Ban Johnson League. Though strictly amateur and not in organized baseball's jurisdiction, the league ranked a cut above sandlot ball, thereby attracting professional scouts who'd show up now and then to keep an eagle eye on anyone who looked like a good prospect. They scanned Barney's team the closest because it was the best around—the Whiz Kids of Baxter Springs.

Toward the tail end of the summer of 1947, I played second base for Miami. We were going against the Whiz Kids at their ballpark and evidently I impressed Barney with my hitting. When the game ended, he asked me if I would like to join them the following year. I jumped at the chance.

Certainly my best dreams had come true and over the winter months the thought of playing for Barney left little room for anything else in my mind. As I look back, it was one big long holiday full of exciting games and that great charge I got out of being a winner.

The Joplin *Globe* covered our games. We would draw between 200 and 250 people into the Baxter Springs ballpark. There were benches, chairs, buckets, blankets, or anything the fans could sit on behind our backstop and along the right and left field lines. The Spring River cut through, marking the outer boundary. It was some 400 feet to dead center field, where the river crooked in. We came ready to play: no locker rooms, no real conveniences, but we did have a fine lighting system. Barney purchased it a couple of years before I joined the team. I've been told it cost him $3,500. He felt it was worth every cent. He wanted night baseball. There were Sunday day games, of course. However, he couldn't start weekday games until five o'clock, after the kids came home from school and had their supper. So he bought the lights and set them up on stanchions along the foul lines with two in the outfield. The only problem was paying the electric bills. Fortunately, the fans contributed their nickles and dimes when the hat was passed around. No admissions were charged, just an appeal for whatever they could spare to keep the bills paid, plus a few extra dollars for replacement uniforms, balls, bats, and other essentials. Also, the umpires received five dollars apiece and if we collected twenty bucks a night it more or less covered Barney's expenses.

Barney was a big old Irishman with a bald head, shiny red nose, and a perpetual grin on his face. He loved kids, loved the game.

When I became an extra-special project of his, Barney said, "Mickey, the big leagues seem a million miles from here and out of reach for everyone, but if you work real hard they won't be out of reach for you."

Poor Barney. He didn't make it, getting only as far as Burlington in the Three-I League. He ended up like my dad, slaving in the mines. But the game never left his bones. It was his life.

He would work his shift as a ground boss at the Eagle-Picher mines, then devote the rest of his time promoting and booking our games. Things like calling around after a heavy rain to check on the condition of a particular field and having to load up and take the Whiz Kids to a field earlier than anticipated, besides talking with high school coaches and kids in an endless search for good ballplayers. That's how he found Ralph Terry, pitching against Commerce in our Lucky Seven high school conference. Barney had gone to see my cousin play—Max Mantle. And there was Ralph, throwing aspirins all day. He could thread a needle with his fastball even then. Threw the ball low and threw strikes. And Barney said, "Forget about Max. I want that kid Terry." Eight years later Ralph was brought up late in the season and became a Yankee teammate of mine.

But one summer—1948—there was a special night in Baxter Springs. I hit three home runs that got to the river, two right-handed and one left-handed. There were some 200 or 300 people watching and after the third homer somebody yelled, "Did you see that? Let's pass the hat for Mickey!"

When the game ended, they dumped it in front of me. Every Whiz Kid, including Barney, began counting. Fifty-three bucks in small change. More money than I had ever seen in one pile in my whole life. Well, you win a few and lose a few. Somebody called the Oklahoma Athletic Commissioner and he called the coach at Commerce High and said that if I didn't give the money back to the people I would be considered a professional and I wouldn't be eligible to play football for Commerce the next year. I gave it all back to Barney. He accepted it reluctantly, knowing my folks could've put the money to good use. What the hell, that kind of cash meant two weeks' wages for most people in those days. I mean, almost every kid I knew had a part-time job to help their families put bread on the table.

During my first year with the Whiz Kids, I had worked for a man named Harry Wells. He owned a cemetery business in Baxter Springs. Harry didn't look the type. You'd expect to find him behind a mahogany desk at Banker's Trust. Well, he had me out digging graves and erecting tombstones. Matter of fact, he had me going everywhere to bury the bodies. One day he called me into a room where he stored the vaults. He points to one and says, "We'll be using this to bury old Jonesy in. We're gonna get it up on the truck and drive to the cemetery." I said, "Harry, are you kidding? It's too heavy." The vault was made of concrete and reinforced steel; must've weighed over a ton. So he explained. "Mickey, we have cables. They lift the vault and let it down . . . understand?" I nearly quit the job until he explained the procedure.

That's Harry all over. A man of great patience. I remember when he bought a brand-new red Mercury convertible. He invited me and some of the Whiz Kids—Billy Johnson, Buddy Ball, and Jim Canega, I think—to take a ride all the way to St. Louis, a 300-mile trip. It was the end of our baseball season and Harry had secured tickets for a Cardinals game at Sportsman's Park. We left the night before and persuaded Harry to put the top down. It was colder than Siberia and Harry's shivering at the wheel while the three of us are in the backseat, laughing our heads off. At the same time other cars are darting to avoid us because we're chewing these big wads of bubble gum, then taking them out of our mouths and throwing them at the windshields of cars coming from the opposite direction on the old narrow highway going into St. Louis. Drove there in the middle of the night, then stopped off at the crack of dawn and restocked ourselves with candy, soda pop, and more bubble gum. When we finally strolled back to the car, Harry was wearing a frozen smile to match the icicles on his nose.

Those were great times.

But you also have to remember that back then there wasn't very much of anything going on for teenagers in Commerce. The main drag was only a few blocks, one end to the other; the city hall, the volunteer fire department, the Black Cat café, a bank, a movie house, one motel, a handful of stores, and the local pool room, where we used to hang out after school. I stayed there late one night and couldn't get a lift home. So I called in a fire on the telephone.

"Where at?" they wanted to know.

"In Whitebird," I said, then ran to the corner, jumped on the truck as it roared out of the firehouse, and hitched a ride home. As soon as the driver saw there was no fire in Whitebird, he started to turn back. I said that I might as well walk home from there—a few hundred yards—and I did. This is as exciting as it ever got. Usually it was enough just to be out seeing the lights, the store windows, and the people passing by.

There were four churches in Commerce. I must've been in all of them at one time or other. Yet nobody in my family took religion seriously. I suppose it was my dad's influence. He used to say, "Religion doesn't necessarily make you good. As long as your heart is in the right place and you don't hurt anyone, I think you'll go to heaven—if there is one." Mom felt the same way. She backed him no matter what he believed.

LeRoy Bennett's mother always had LeRoy attending Sunday school and prayer meetings, Bible study classes, and so on. I'd often go along with him. Maybe because we were buddies.

Whatever the reason, while the preacher gave his sermon I dreamed about playing baseball for the St. Louis Cardinals. Nearest I came to believing in saints.

I didn't have much of a social life. I was real bashful, especially when I found myself at those Saturday night Teentown dances they'd hold in a large room above the bank. Actually, I couldn't dance. The place had a juke box and I would stand by the wall, watching everybody else dance. One night a bunch of seniors talked a very pretty girl by the name of Claudine Sanders into asking me for a dance. I tried clomping around the floor with her, my face red as a beet, and she kept rubbing her body against mine. I could see the gang laughing at me. I'm thinking, "Goddamn! If I ever get away from here, I'll never dance again."

On days when I didn't take the school bus home or stay overnight at Bill Mosely's, I'd take the NEO bus to Cardin, exactly a mile away from my house in Whitebird, along a gravel road. The first part went right by the old Eagle-Picher mining offices. At night they were well-lit, but soon as you left those offices it got pitch dark. Blackbirds would fly up alongside the road, their wings flapping like mad, and I'd visualize all the ghost stories that came from the miners. Weird tales about murders, people being thrown into caved-in holes around the mills; a perfect spot if you wanted to commit a crime and bury the evidence without ever getting caught. Come to think of it, I didn't know of any actual murders. Why would anyone be killed in the first place? You couldn't rob anybody. Nobody had anything. Still, when I walked past the lights of the office buildings, I was scared to death of the dark. I must have ran that mile in less than four minutes—long before Roger Bannister thought of it. I didn't even feel my feet touch the ground until I reached home.

Then came a significant event, a milestone in my life. In 1948, at the age of seventeen, my sole ambition was to play professional ball. The where and how meant little, only the chance. Well, there's such a thing as luck and some of it rubbed off on me when Tom Greenwade came down the road from Springfield, Missouri, to scout prospects for the Yankee farm system. He was at the Baxter Springs ballpark, evaluating a kid named Billy Johnson, our third baseman. I wasn't on Greenwade's list. But whatever he saw in Billy, he apparently found something more to his liking after watching me switch-hit a couple of home runs into the river on one bounce. I also remember the rain; a big cloudburst, everybody ducking for their cars, when suddenly Dad steers me to his, saying there's a fellow in there who's dying to meet me. It's Greenwade, a reedy old guy with a nice friendly smile. He says, "How would you like to play for the Yankees?" I give him a look, totally flabbergasted. He says, "Well, I can't talk officially because you're still in high school, but don't sign with anyone else and the day you graduate I'll be back."

Dad says, "With an offer?"

And Greenwade smiles reassuringly. "We'll see what we can do."

Going home, I remember Dad explaining the opportunities I'd have in New York, feeling the excitement as he talked about Yankee Stadium, the Babe, Lou Gehrig, Joe DiMaggio—a royal tradition. "No question," he said, "we oughta wait on Greenwade."

The months dragged on. Things settled down. I listened to the radio, fiddled around, and read the Miami paper to know what was going on in the world. Meanwhile Greenwade's promise sorta faded. By midwinter high school basketball had swung into gear. I was no longer a peanut, though still smaller than most of my teammates. It didn't stop me from feeding Bill Mosely winning points at key games during the season. My folks were always involved. They loved every minute of it. And Mom used to rant and rave at those games, a sports nut through and through. If she objected to a referee's decision, you could hear her voice travel across the gym: "Where are your glasses, you bum!" Believe me, if the referee called anything against Commerce, she'd cuss him out like a sailor. It unnerved my father. He'd cover his head with his hands and sit a few rows behind her to get away from the shouting.

Years later, when my twin brothers were playing football at

Commerce High, she saw Roy make a spectacular leap in the end zone to knock the ball loose from the outstretched arms of an Afton High receiver. Last play of the game. The losing side angrily jumped on Roy, taking vicious swipes at him. Mom joined the fray, whacking Afton helmets with her pocketbook. Finally Roy wobbled to his feet, bruised but still in one piece. She walked off the field with him and the Afton boys gave her a wide berth.

When I graduated in 1949, Tom Greenwade showed up as he had promised. He even got me excused from the commencement exercises so I could play for the Whiz Kids that night. The game was in Coffeyville, Kansas. I had a good game—singled and hit a pair of home runs, connecting from both sides. You'd figure I had it made, yet Greenwade comes over to Dad after the game and says very solemnly, "I'm afraid Mickey may never reach the Yankees. Right now I'd have to rate him a lousy shortstop. Sloppy. Erratic arm. And he's small. Get him in front of some really strong pitching . . ." Then, without blinking an eye, he says, "However, I'm willing to take a risk."

He stuck a contract in Dad's hand. "All right, Mutt, I'm ready to give Mickey four hundred dollars for playing at Independence the rest of the summer."

Dad winced. "He can make that much playing Sunday ball and working in the mines during the week."

Greenwade started scribbling something on the back of an envelope. Finally he says, "Tell you what, we'll throw in an eleven-hundred-dollar bonus. How's that sound?"

The old ballyhoo—a foxy move to get around the possibility of having to offer a heckuva lot more. When I read the announcement about my signing, it quoted Greenwade as saying I would probably set records with the Yankees. Stuff like that. He did tell me later that I was the best prospect he had ever seen.

Chapter 4

Independence, Kansas. A Class D club in the K–O–M (Kansas–Oklahoma–Missouri) League. I remember going there with my dad to meet manager Harry Craft. He lived in the Darby Hotel. In his room, Dad said, "I've done all I can for Mickey. I believe he's a good ballplayer and I'm turning him over to you now." Craft nodded. At the door, before saying goodbye . . . "This is your chance, son. Take care of yourself and give 'em hell."

Oh sure. I had an empty feeling in my stomach. I was in strange surroundings, didn't know where I'd sleep or take my meals, and Dad wasn't going to be around anymore, saying, "Nice hitting. You're doing this right, you're doing this wrong . . ."

Harry Craft sensed my dismay. He stepped right in. "We have a decent bunch of kids, about your own age mostly, so I think you'll enjoy playing here. Just keep your nose clean and we'll find a place for you to stay."

I bunked with three or four other guys. One of them was first baseman Nick Ananias. We called him the Old Man. He was twenty-one. It seemed more like high school. Somebody always had a car. We'd pile in and shoot over to Pop's Place. Our big social hangout, near the busiest corner in town. We'd have a snack, then stand outside just talking and looking. Lou Skizas, our third baseman, would size up the local maidens, hoping they'd stray close enough so he could pick them off. What a character. The nervous Greek—a pre-fifties hippie from the streets and alleys of Chicago. He had a girl under his arm before and after every game. I recall a particular early afternoon when me and Skizas were killing time in front of the soda shop. We saw this older woman, obviously high-class and a real dazzler. Skizas bounded off the curb and introduced himself. "Excuse me, ma'am. By chance, do you have a passport? The reason why I'm asking, you appear to be lost."

She says, "I'm in town visiting Harry Craft. He manages the Independence Yankees. Do you know him?"

At which point Skizas takes a bow and says, "Of course. I'm his famous third baseman and this young lad here is our star shortstop."

Now about Harry Craft. As wonderful and great as he was with his players, nevertheless we'd find it hard to penetrate the inner workings of his mind. A very quiet, cold kind of guy. He spoke softly, with a Southern nasal twang. And he walked ram-rod straight; handsome, neatly dressed, in top physical shape. Another thing. Harry was separated and in the midst of divorce proceedings.

His wife would come through Independence now and then to see him and he'd be nice and polite to her while she was in town. To put it mildly, he was a bit of a ladies' man. If you saw a pretty girl in one of the six towns that we played in, chances were she was a friend of Harry's—or about to be. Us kids really looked up to him. We were kind of awed, I guess, but it sure didn't put off Skizas.

As I said, this gorgeous older woman (she may have been all of twenty-five) tells Lou that she's registered at the Darby Hotel. The desk clerk was a heavy-bosomed widow who (according to Lou) was already a member of Harry's group. He sent this one for a walk while the widow was on duty, trying to prevent a serious confrontation. Anyway, the woman immediately took to Lou. I got scared and left. Didn't know what to say to her in the first place. Me and my pimples versus Lou the Lady Killer. No contest.

The next day he told me what happened. They saw a movie, then did some wrestling in the park, but she wouldn't bend. That night at the ballpark there's a club meeting. Harry folds his arms and stares around the room. He says, "It has come to my attention that one of my young men has violated a sacred golden rule. What the rule is, only the young man who knows what I'm saying will understand. If it occurs again, I shall not go easy on him. You have my word."

We were approaching Bartlesville for a game against the Pittsburgh Pirates farm club there. I had been experimenting with a knuckleball pitch, having some success throwing it while at Commerce High. On the way over by bus, I was demonstrating the grip, what made it float, and so forth. And Lou kept saying, "Yeah, yeah, yeah." Now we arrive at Bartlesville and start warming up on the sidelines. Lou held up his glove, crouched down, and said, "Okay, let's see it, kid." I uncorked the knuckleball. Struck him right on the nose and sent him tumbling. He was out cold for two or three minutes. They rushed him to the Bartlesville infirmary. He had a broken nose and missed three days of baseball. Matter of fact, he still has a permanent lump on his nose.

That's how it is when you're seventeen and away from home for the first time. Pals or no pals, it takes a while before you can say, "I'm on my own—a professional." Once I got into the flow, I enjoyed the hell out of it. But the first week of the K–O–M season I seriously thought of giving up and going back to Commerce. I was wound tight, overanxious—sometimes after a strikeout, feeling frustrated and mad at myself, I'd trot off the field and let loose a vicious kick at the dugout water cooler. One time I kicked it so hard the damn thing sprang a leak. A gusher, four or five feet high, which emptied the bench. After that the guys called me King of the Broken Water Coolers.

I felt I had to be the best. I couldn't stand failure, didn't want to know the meaning of the word. That K–O–M League was a real test for me. Up to then, I'd outdistanced the other kids by a mile. But now I was a pro and the competition got a lot stiffer. I was surrounded by kids who had been stars in sandlot ball or whatever. And while hitting .300 was great in any league, I had to learn that I was going to make seven outs for every ten times I went to bat.

I also had a big problem playing shortstop. Even if the ball was hit right at me, I often threw it up in the stands. They had to put a chicken wire screen behind first base as a backstop to prevent somebody in the stands from getting killed. I set new records for wildness anyway.

Bless Harry Craft. He would see me sitting off by myself in

the dugout, just miserable. He'd come over, slap my leg, and say, "Forget the error. Get your head up off the ground and keep hustling."

Typical of the man. Under his direction, Independence kept winning and winning. I mean hot streaks of eight or nine games in a row before we lost. Then we were off on another tear.

We traveled by bus, bouncing along on black-topped roads to the various ballparks—Bartlesville, Carthage, Chanute, Pittsburg, Miami—long dusty rides with stopovers only to get out and have a bite, take a piss and climb right back again. At the rear of the bus there was a long seat. As a reward on getaway day, the winning pitcher and the star of the game would get to sleep on that seat. I remember sleeping away a lot of trips on the bus.

More often than not, a bunch of us would bring water guns aboard and we'd yell and scream and squirt those guns everywhere. Regular cowboys and Indians—and Harry would sit down front, not saying a word. But his jaw muscles would grind pretty good. He was used to it all, though you could hardly blame him for being sore whenever we had water fights in our hotel rooms. He'd come barging in, glaring daggers at us. You never heard a place get so quiet. Absolute stone silence and contrite faces each time he caught us. Nevertheless, Harry appreciated a joke as well as the next one. He liked his players and liked what he was doing, spending the best part of his life loving everything about the game of baseball.

For instance, our greatest rivalry was against the Carthage Cubs. Early that season they signed Rogers Hornsby, Jr., to a contract. Naturally the Carthage press made a big thing out of it.

We played our first game at Carthage on the day of Junior's debut. The stands were packed, late inning, the score tied, with me coming to the plate. I swung from the heels and hit a hard line drive to center field.

Junior turned his back to run after the ball, probably lost it in the lights, and it hit him in the back of the head. By the time they retrieved it, I had scored.

In the final week of that season, we won the K–O–M championship, beating the Pittsburg, Kansas, team for the title. After the game, as usual, we came home by bus, fantasizing about the marching bands and the parade through the streets, with the entire population of Independence turning out to greet us. We pulled up to deafening silence. Not a soul anywhere. The town looked like a morgue. Even Pop's Place was padlocked for the night.

Well, Harry gave a quick tug at his tie and said, "Okay, boys, if it's a celebration you want, let's have it now." Perfect. We climbed down from the bus and then right there on the main drag we all danced and yelled and did somersaults. Third baseman Lou Skizas climaxed the affair with a rousing rendition of "Long Gone Lonesome Blues," my favorite country song at that time.

Then the law stepped in. Dan Peters, a local cop, was about to bust Skizas over the head with his billy club. Harry said, *"Listen,* Dan, we won *you* the K–O–M championship tonight."

So Peters stepped back, smiling, and Skizas finished his song.

That season I hit .313 in 89 games, driving in 63 runs, while scoring 54. On the negative side, my fielding percentage was terrible—47 errors at shortstop. Still and all, I figured to climb up another notch or two in the Yankee chain.

After getting home from Independence I looked up my old friends. They said, "How did it go?" And I said, kinda low-keyed, professional-like, "I had a decent year."

"Oh really?" Before I knew it, they were telling me what I hit, how many home runs, stolen bases, sacrifice flies; hell, they knew more about my season than I did. At any rate, I spent a lot of time relaxing and hunting rabbits and quail out in the woods around Whitebird.

One Friday night I went over to Picher and saw a football game with Ivan Schouse and a few other friends. Ivan was dating Pat Johnson, a Picher High School majorette. Her sister Merlyn and another girl named Lavanda Whipkey were also majorettes. Well, during halftime I couldn't help noticing how pretty they all were. But I was too shy to ask for a date or even wave, so later on I got Ivan to arrange a triple date. We decided to go to the Spook Light.

Now the Spook Light is a minor mystery in that part of the world. There's just this ghostly light that seems to shine through the trees at a deserted spot near Seneca. If you park your car there and wait long enough, you're likely to see it. There were all sorts of stories, such as the one about an Indian holding a torch while looking for his head—or for somebody's wife. In any case, if you happened to be waiting at the Spook Light and if you happened to have a girl with you, it was a pretty good place for necking.

And I guess that's what we had in mind when we piled into my car, a bullet-nosed 1947 Fleetline Chevy with a vacuum shift that I'd bought with my bonus money.

I was paired off with Lavanda. A nice girl, but when I asked her to go out with me the next night, she said she'd be busy. I decided to try for Merlyn. On the way home, Ivan told me that she worked in the Picher High School office. I called her there and we made a date.

I took her to a movie. Sat there eating popcorn, slumped in my seat, wondering what I'd talk to her about after the show. So we leave the theater and I say, "You wanta go out again?" She says, "All right."

The next Saturday it's freezing out and we drive over to the movie theater again, angle into a parking space, hop out, lock the car doors, and go in to see the picture. Probably one starring Gene Autry and Champion . . . Who would have thought that years later Gene would become a good friend of mine.

Now we come out to see steam trailing from the tailpipe. The keys are in the car, the motor's running. I place a call to Dad. He gets on the phone. "Yes?"

"We're at the movies and the car is locked. How about coming down to get us? We'll be waiting in the back row."

Ten minutes later he taps me on the arm. Merlyn and I follow him out to the car. He looks at the exhaust, peers in the window, and sees the keys dangling from the ignition. "Well I'll be damned," he says, turns around, and drives off in the Eagle-Picher truck.

A local cop jimmied open the car window with a hanger wire while we watched, shivering in our boots.

From then on we saw a lot of each other. And where I lived, going steady was almost the same as being married.

Chapter 5

That fall I was earning extra money at the Eagle-Picher mines, working as an electrician's helper for the motor crew. I drove a pickup truck, delivering equipment. One day in November my dad came by the shop and handed me a postcard which stated I'd have to appear before the Ottawa County draft board. "Can't do any better than that," he joked, then looked away, frowning. And I'm going "uh-huh, uh-huh" and "I wouldn't mind it a bit," but I can already see myself trapped in one of those gigantic B-52 bombers flying across the Atlantic.

I drove down to the draft board with a set of X rays of my leg. They ushered me into this cubicle of a room, containing a Toledo scale, examination table, an eye chart, and a kindly old doctor. He gave me a once-over with his stethoscope, then probed at the scar on my left shinbone.

You have to understand that once you have osteomyelitis, you have it for good. If you join the Army and have it and get a flare-up once you're in there, they have to pay you a disability pension for life.

In early December I got the news. They classified me 4-F. I thought, "Well, I'm exempt and that's the end of it."

Meanwhile, between my job at the mine and seeing Merlyn on weekends, I hunted, scrimmaged with the Commerce basketball team, and did everything I could to stay in shape. It was January 1950 when I signed a contract to play Class C ball with the Joplin Miners in the Western Association. I knew Harry Craft would be there, also many of my teammates from Independence. The same old bunch. I couldn't wait to see them.

The whole Yankee farm system was training at Lake Taneycomo in the Ozarks. A big sprawling complex. Barracks everywhere. For morning practices they had us on a field doing calisthenics with two or three other teams while more minor league clubs worked out at another field—Class D right up to Triple A. I mean, there were literally hundreds of players taking batting practice, pepper, outfield wind sprints, sliding instructions, and so forth. Every afternoon they'd schedule intrasquad games. Joplin beat the pants off everybody. It didn't matter who, we even beat the Triple A teams as if they were amateurs.

I will never forget those off-hours when we used to hunt frogs and fish for bass. We had a guy named Red Crowder, a tall, barrel-chested relief pitcher from Seneca, Missouri. When he wasn't pitching, you'd always find him chewing nickel cigars and wearing his baseball cap turned backward.

Besides his love for the game of baseball, Red was obsessed with hunting and fishing. What beats me is that only a year or so later he drowned in a freak boating accident. Like most experienced fishermen, Red kept his wallet on the top of his head, under his hat. For some reason, his hat fell off, the wallet went after it, and he jumped out of the boat in pursuit of the wallet. As soon as poor Red hit that icy water, he had a heart attack and drowned.

I have some beautiful memories of those times with Red, of his funny ways, his simple nature, and how he taught me to catch frogs by shining a flashlight in their eyes with one hand and grabbing them from behind with the other. We'd bring along a cooler of ice cold beer and frozen tomatoes. Once we got a gunnysack full of frog legs, we'd eat them with the tomatoes, sipping beer and telling stories around a little fire on a bank by the stream; me and Skizas and Red and Carl Lombardi, Al Billingsley, Cal Neeman, Steve Kraly, Bob Weisler, Tommy Cott . . . the gang. At night we'd shine our flashlights over the lake and take a three-pronged hook, drop it with a rod and reel, and stare down at these big old bass laying on the bottom, fast asleep. When the hook drifted under them, we'd yank up the line and—I'm not kidding—it was one of the most fun times I ever had. Not a single care in the world from the middle of March until mid-April.

Then the season started.

The Joplin park was small and weather-beaten. It had lots of rocks in the outfield. Lou Skizas roamed it, having been shifted there from third base. I remember him making a ritual of plucking rocks out of the grass every inning, his nose skimming the ground like a mine detector. Behind right field you could see the upper stories of an orphans' home; tiny faces peering through the windows. During the course of a season, I stroked a number of home runs in their direction. One day a bedsheet appeared, with a message painted across: THANKS FOR THE BALL, MICKEY! They hung it under one of the windows I broke. I think the team eventually paid for it.

At the time I lived in an upstairs apartment of a two-family house not far from the ballpark. My roommates were Carl Lombardi and pitchers Bob Weisler and Steve Kraly. We paid $65 a month rent, split four ways. When I came up to Joplin, Harry Craft moved Carl over from shortstop to second base. We weren't the greatest keystone combination by any means, yet Carl took my miscues with a good deal of patience. We discussed the ins and outs of our positions at the apartment. Mostly, though, we'd be joking around or arm wrestling with Bob and Steve. It was family. We spent a lot of our time in hotel lobbies and played the pinball machine all night. Weisler was a magician. He would rest the front legs of a machine on top of his shoes and jockey that baby with his fingers, hands, feet, belly, tongue—you name it. Everything would light up. Buzzers went off, bells rang, and Weisler would win sixty-five games in a row, then walk out of the hotel with broken-down shoes.

Our utility infielder was Al Billingsley. When Billingsley got a base hit, nine times out of ten it had eyes. Always a hairline beyond the fielder's grasp. It seemed as though the Lord was looking down on Billingsley and smiling. So we called him Lord.

And Lord owned a convertible roadster. One morning he lent the car to Lombardi, who in turn drove it to our apartment, where he picked up me and Skizas, along with third baseman Muddy Waters and catcher Cal Neeman. So we're in the car, driving along Route 66. Suddenly Skizas has an idea and we all rise up, including Lombardi, who's behind the wheel, and put our heads through the canvas top. Can you imagine what the other motorists thought when they saw us? After the joy ride we returned the car to Lord. He was merciful, only charging us what it cost to replace the canvas top.

Still, payday came twice a month and that brief outing put a sizable dent in our food budgets for a while. That is, for everyone except Skizas. He saved every paycheck, first to last. The girls loved him. They took him out, bought his meals, his clothes, whatever he needed. He'd go to the ballpark, shower with his sweatshirt on, get dressed, go out on the town, and smell like a rose. As for the rest of us, I lightened the burden somewhat by winning free steak dinners at various restaurants in Joplin. I think one of them was a place called Wilder's. I know it was recommended by Duncan Hines. Anyway, these restaurants would sponsor our games on radio station KFSB and if a Joplin player hit a home run it was steak dinner for two—on the house. If I hit a pair, I'd have some of the guys eating at one steak joint that I couldn't go to because I was already eating at another.

I filled out while at Joplin. I wasn't exactly a giant, but I grew quite a bit. Picked up 10 pounds and gained an inch in height to five foot ten and a half, where I stayed for a while. My weight was 170 pounds. When I signed with the Yankees, I added 5 more pounds. In my third major league season, the Topps bubble gum people reported that I weighed 200 pounds and stood six foot tall. Boy, did I grow!

And with Joplin I *was* getting longer distance on the ball. The fans began looking for those shots. I hit one at Miners Park that went way out over the center field fence. Our equipment man, a veteran of bush league days, greeted me in the dugout. "Boy, that's the longest homer I've seen since Babe Ruth cleared Sportsman's Park roof back in the '28 World Series."

As we traveled around the Western Association, the fans yelled for more. Once in a while I'd come through and the papers would say it was a first, the only home run hit that far in St. Joe or Topeka or Muskogee—wherever. Besides, I was hitting close to the .400 mark most of the season. That's when they started to call me the Commerce Comet. And the word spread. The Yankee brass took notice, giving me their highest ratings for speed, throwing, and power. But it all came up to them through Harry Craft, who was still saying, "Put him in the outfield."

In baseball, the real secret of power is the strength you have in your wrists, forearms, and shoulders. I'm sure all my strength came from the early farm days, milking sixteen cows twice a day for two solid years. You know, Ted Williams was forever squeezing rubber balls to build up his wrists and forearms. With me it was the cows, plus the mines. We didn't have Nautalis equipment in my time. None of that scientific equipment existed. We conditioned ourselves gradually, doing a few jumping jacks, leg stretches, and other simple exercises.

I learned very early that timing is important too, whether you're hitting or fielding. That year I was no farther advanced as a shortstop than I was at Independence, invariably because of bad timing, an erratic pattern of throwing balls away or letting them skip through my legs. My biggest embarrassment was at an All-Star game in Muskogee. I made four errors. After the last error, our pitcher got a strikeout. So what happens? The catcher whips the ball to the third baseman and he starts passing it around the infield, first to me. The ball hit me right in the face. My fifth error. At that point, my timing really hadn't caught up with my strength.

The team at Joplin was so good we were far ahead of the pack halfway through the schedule, leading the nearest team by about twenty-five games. God, if we had kept going at the same pace, who would've come to see us? Fans around the circuit would think, "Why waste money? Joplin's unbeatable. Our boys don't have a prayer." Naturally, finances figure heavily in minor league ball. The majority of clubs barely hung on by their teeth, so the chance for a pennant meant good gates and extra dollars. In this case, league president Tom Fairweather split the season in two, ruling the first- and second-half winners would meet for the championship. Wouldn't you know, we lost the playoff.

I went into the last month hitting .400, then finished out with a Western Association batting title. I hit .383 and led in three other departments, scoring 141 runs with 199 hits and 326 total bases.

We were coming home from our last road trip, late at night. Harry Craft always sat alone, down front, keeping the adjoining seat empty. When I got on the bus, he called me over.

"Mick," he began in a level voice. "I wasn't going to tell you until later, but this is as good a time as any. The Yankees are bringing you up the day our season ends. You'll meet the team in St. Louis, then travel with them on their last two-week swing."

I looked straight ahead, saying nothing, but my heart was pounding. He says, "As for me, well, next year I'll be managing the Beaumont club."

"Really?"

"Yep. That's what I've been told." He gave me an affectionate grin. "If you get cut by the Yanks next year and want to play for me . . ."

"Harry, I'll play for you anywhere."

He chuckled, then started reading his copy of *The Sporting News.* I went back to my seat. Lou Skizas looked up. "What did Harry want?"

I said, "Nothing much. Just baseball talk."

I could hardly refrain from shouting, "Hot dog, I'm gonna be a Yankee!"

Chapter 6

It was Sunday, September 17, 1950, and I was at Sportsman's Park, moments before the Yankees–St. Louis Browns doubleheader. I can't imagine anyone being more scared. There was a big crowd and the noise kept building while the Yankees took infield practice. I watched, in awe of Phil Rizzuto. A human vacuum cleaner, going wide to his left or right, snapping balls into his glove with unerring quickness. They didn't give him the nickname Scooter for nothing. Don't forget, I wasn't too hot playing shortstop in the minors and now they were touting me as Rizzuto's eventual successor. Not only that, I knew manager Casey Stengel had released a statement saying I was the Yankees number-one prize. Just then I felt like their booby prize.

The rest is a maze . . . Working out for a while, watching Johnny Hopp's grand-slam homer beat St. Louis, hearing him being interviewed after the second game, everybody talking about the stretch drive and another Yankee pennant. Somehow I got through it all.

Next stop: Chicago. I met Moose Skowron, a college boy fresh from the campus of Purdue University. The following spring Moose went down to Binghamton in the Piedmont League and played shortstop. When he made it to the Yankees in 1954, they converted him to first base. He became a good one.

But on that Western trip we roomed together as nonroster players. We took batting and infield practice with the team. Chicago was his hometown, so he showed me the sights. We'd wander along Michigan Avenue and inevitably find ourselves on the Loop, staring at the bright lights of movie houses. I guess we saw every movie there, whether the show was good or bad. It didn't matter. When you're eighteen and suiting up at major league parks with your best days still ahead, every movie is good.

My first vivid impression of Moose is after we went off the practice field and took showers. He was sitting in front of his locker, ready to put his socks on. I couldn't help but notice his feet. They had been stepped on so much during his college football days that his toenails were mangled nubs. Later on I'd tease him, saying his feet smelled and that he had rotten toes. Of course, we were great friends by then and he'd kid me right back. "Yeah, Mantle, but at least I don't have crabs like you."

I kinda followed Moose's lead during our week's stay with the big team, such as waiting until he said something to the veteran players before I'd open my mouth. With Joe DiMaggio I couldn't even mumble hello. He had this aura. It was as if you needed an appointment just to approach him. Then it was a question of getting up enough courage to speak. Remember, I had been reading about this guy for a long time. So I'd look at him and keep looking and I imagine he got tired of having my face always turned toward his whenever we were within ten feet of each other. The truth is, I'd be thinking, "Man, I wish I could play like him, but it's gonna be hard."

Finally my free ride is over. The Yankee hopeful returns home and here I am, listening to a lot of bragging going on. Especially Dad. Soon as our neighbors and friends walk into the house, he's telling them, "Would you believe, Mick wore a Yankee uniform—same as DiMaggio! And Joe knows him personally!"

What can you do? He was prouder than I had ever seen him. He knew I would make the team the next year. I saw it in his eyes, the way he'd strut down the street, as though the buttons would pop right off his shirt.

That winter of 1950–51 after the Joplin season I worked in the mines again, repairing motors for the pump crew. Here nobody cared if I was a future Yankee star or the King of Siam. To them I was a miner, no different than the rest. We would drill holes and install the motors to pull fresh air into the shaft. They required constant maintenance and I'd have to go down there, cleaning, fixing, and sometimes taking them out altogether for an overhaul. I'd slowly ride up in one of those cans, 300 or more feet to the surface, with a hoisterman controlling the hook, the speed and smoothness depending on his touch; his foot on the brake, a steel wire cable winding around a spool, the cable marked. He knew exactly when to start and stop that can. And this guy Lug Jones was on the hoist every day, having a party. One time he let go of the controls and I plunged halfway to the bottom before he jerked the lever and caught me. I went to my knees, cursing, and came out of the can ready to kill him. He laughed, said it was part of the game, the only part where there could be some fun. That's how it was, figuring you'd never go into the mines again, except the next day you'd be back doing the same thing.

We were down in the mine all day and we'd bring our lunch pails with us for the midday break. Five or six miners would eat together, all of us kind of tense because cave-ins were frequent. If you heard the sound of loose rocks or gravel, you'd sound the alarm and everybody would scramble. So the rule was: Don't throw rocks. Of course, there was always some comedian who'd throw a rock at somebody's steel helmet during lunchtime and the whole gang—let me tell you—we would run like hell!

The trouble was that after too many false alarms, we'd started to ignore the danger signs. But what are rules for?

The tension got so bad we literally beat up on each other to let off steam. The accepted weapon was a paddle. Everybody had to take it, initially as a fledgling, then every time you misbehaved. You couldn't fart when you ate lunch and you couldn't put a mouse in somebody's lunch pail—for anything! And if I told someone I hit a 780-foot home run, so long Mickey Charles! No kangaroo court necessary, just eyes making contact, a quick nod, and watch your ass 'cause it was a-comin'.

The idea wasn't to kill people. What happened was, a man would give five or six shots with the board, trying to get you to yell. If you didn't yell, you'd get a chance to hit him with the board until he yelled. So you can imagine that we'd hit each other pretty hard.

I also remember a slow period. They sent me out with Hardrock and Adolf, my pump crew pals. A truck drove us into the country somewhere. Adolf handed me a shovel, the idea being to shovel my way back to town, clearing a ten-foot spot around what seemed like a million telephone poles. You've got to understand that we have lots of prairie fires in Oklahoma. My job was to clear the brush and grass away from the poles so they wouldn't burn. I hated it, working all alone out in the cold. To me, it was worse than getting put on a chain gang. Well, I probably cleared fourteen or fifteen poles, then spent the rest of the day tossing rocks in the air and hitting them with the shovel, like I was playing baseball.

That winter my dad started hurting. I think he knew something. One evening, as we sat in our living room, he laid his head against the armchair, his smile fading. I said, "Hey, Dad, how's it going?" He said, "Well, except for this crick in my back . . ." wincing a bit, then brushing aside the problem when I asked him if anything was wrong. We talked some about the Yankees, just letting the time pass. Finally he said, "After you make the majors, I'd like to see you marry Merlyn and I'd like to have a little freckle-faced, redheaded grandson." He wanted me to settle down, have a family life, afraid that if I went to New York as a single man it might hinder my baseball career.

As I said, my teenage adventures with girls had not been very productive. Sure, I did my share of backseat groping. But most of it was kid stuff. The first time I actually had the opportunity— and my protection—I didn't even know how the thing worked. I thought you were supposed to unroll it and then put it on. The girl gave up before I figured out the mechanics. Boy, was I embarrassed.

But the real scare was caused by still another girl. Her parents showed up at the mine, asking for my dad, saying they needed to talk to him. First thing he thinks is "Ugh, the girl's pregnant," thinking it was me who did it because I had dated her for a month or two while she was also seeing some other kid. Came a stormy evening in tornado season and we were on the front porch doing some heavy petting when Dad came up slowly in front of the house in the old LaSalle with Mom and the kids. Out of the corner of my eye I saw them take off for another turn around the block. But I didn't move. I was busy.

At this point, the wind was howling so loud you couldn't hear much. I lost track of time. Because Dad came back and waited for quite a while with the motor idling. Finally he slammed the car door. "Are you going to set there until we all get blown away?" I tore myself free.

I thought I would really be in hot water when her parents came to the mine. But before long the other fellow that she had been seeing admitted to being the father of the child.

After that, I got much more serious about Merlyn. On a winter night I took her into Miami. We were walking toward the movie, passing Dawson's Jewelry Shop. A nice little place, the window lit, trays of rings and watches placed on tiers under a soft light. She stopped and gazed at the display. "Oh, aren't those rings pretty!" I stood alongside impatiently, wanting to catch the last show. "Can we go inside and take a look?" she asked.

Now we're at the counter. A ring is on her finger. She raises her eyes and says, "This is what I'd like for Christmas."

I think, "Geez, she's really serious." It was a diamond ring, about a quarter of a carat, and cost $250, as much as I made in a month playing ball for Joplin. Then my father's wish—and everything's fine. At that exact moment, I decided to get engaged. I grin. "Well, Merlyn, you might as well pick out the wedding ring too."

My half brother Theodore had just been discharged from the Army. He gave me most of his mustering-out pay. He said, "If you want the ring, get it." The next day I was back in the jewelry store. An hour later I walked into my house to show Mom the ring.

Her eyes got real shiny. She said, "Dad's in the bedroom. Why don't you show it to him?"

"Aw, Mom . . ."

We had a great Christmas.

Merlyn and I were indefinite about our plans. The only understanding was that we would be married someday. Meanwhile she had a job at the First State Bank in Picher, filing checks and things in the accounting department. I'd cash my checks from the mines and bring the money to her for deposit, leaving a few dollars aside so we could take in an occasional movie or football game. Sometimes Hardrock and Adolf would drop me off at her house after work. One time they fooled me. I was in the truck with them, ready to open the door and jump out. Adolf grabbed the handle, Hardrock pinned me down and punched on the horn. When Merlyn appeared at the window, they both started singing: "Dear Mick, I'll send your ball glove home . . ." I could see Merlyn's face, red as a beet, as the truck sped away. My wonderful pals.

In January 1951 a letter arrived from Yankee farm director Lee MacPhail, instructing me to report to spring training at Phoenix in the middle of February. I loved looking at that letter, but I didn't answer him, figuring a ticket would arrive any day for transportation, along with a check for expenses. So I kept busy on the motors, driving a truck, shoveling, all the other stuff. But there's no ticket and no check in my mailbox. Now we're into the middle of February, I'm getting worried, and the pump crew isn't helping the situation. They're yelping, "See, you can't trust them dadgummed carpetbaggers from Noo York."

Finally a sportswriter and photographer show up, representing the Miami *Daily News Record.* The sportswriter says: "Hey, Mantle, aren't you supposed to be playing for the Yankees?"

"They didn't send no ticket or nothing."

"Yeah? Well we got a call from Lee MacPhail, saying to get ahold of you because he doesn't have your home telephone number or any idea in the world where you work."

"Ain't no phone in the house. Besides, Harry Craft knows I'm a miner down here. They should've checked."

"That's a quote, right?"

"Guess so."

The photographer took a picture. I still have it; standing in front of the pump crew's truck, smudgy-faced grin, chesty pose in gray overalls, cap squared tight across the forehead. A nineteen-year-old kid looking to be a man. Click.

I dashed straight to the mine company's administration office and placed a collect call to Mr. MacPhail. Next thing you know it's on the AP wire, with a story saying: "Mickey Mantle, heading for Yankee stardom, has not yet reported to the team's spring training camp because 'I haven't gotten my ticket yet.'"

Tom Greenwade brought it down the following morning, along with some expense money. I packed away two pair of Levi's, a solid gray sport jacket, a tie with a painted peacock on it—wide enough to contain all the feathers—also my crepe-soled shoes and Marty Marion Playmaker glove.

A lonesome trip it was, riding through little Oklahoma towns toward the Vinita railway station. I sat beside Dad, watching the scenery. Mom's hand was resting on top of my straw-covered suitcase. She said, "There's nothing to worry about, Mickey. You'll do good if your mind's set on being a Yankee."

We were standing together on the station platform, staring out at the tracks as the train came rumbling in. I heard Dad's voice above the commotion, shouting, "No need to wait. You know what to do!" I climbed aboard the train, pausing to wave, panic-stricken at the thought that winning a trip to the Yankees' first school for farm prospects would end in disaster. An awful realization, despite the raves over my hitting performance at Joplin the previous season.

"Take care!" my mother cried. Their faces vanished. The towns fell away—and the old farmhouses, sagging barns, pastures, woodlands, groves and groves of hickory trees . . . The train sped across the state, heading for spring training and Phoenix, Arizona. I sank into the seat. Everything I ever knew disappeared outside that train window.

Chapter 7

Half a dozen or so of the Yankee players were in camp when I arrived. Guys like Hank Bauer, Billy Martin, Gene Woodling, Jackie Jensen, Cliff Mapes, and a bunch of rookies—Gil McDougald, Tom Morgan, Andy Carey, Moose Skowron, Bob Cerv, Gus Triandos, Tom Sturdivant—about forty of us getting an opportunity to show Casey Stengel and his coaches what we could do.

What I didn't know is that Harry Craft had already sent in a report to Lee MacPhail that more or less covered my problems as a shortstop. It said I would probably make a great major leaguer, providing they groomed me for center field.

However, those first few days I was put under the wing of infield instructor Frank Crosetti. In his time he was one of the best shortstops around, a tough, wiry guy who made all the defensive moves. I had first met him during my September trip with the Yankees. Needless to say, he had also read the report.

Comes a morning when he trots over and grabs my cherished Marty Marion Playmaker glove right out of my hand—a three-fingered job, the pocket pretty well soiled and scruffy from two action-filled seasons of professional ball. "Where the hell did you get this thing?" he demanded. I turned crimson. And he pauses. "Never mind, we'll try to find you a better glove." At the next infield practice he gave me a Bob Dillinger model, the same type he used to wear himself. I'm positive Crow bought it with his own money. But nice as the gesture was, it still didn't make me into a shortstop.

I remember him showing us rookies how to execute the double play. "Now listen carefully, fellas. When the ball is here, you touch the bag like this and get the runner out . . ." A squeaky-voiced infielder chimed in. "No no, that's not the way you do it, Crow." And I'm thinking, "Jesus Christ, get a load of this guy, trying to tell Mr. Crosetti his business. He's gotta be nuts."

Who else but Billy Martin? Well, the old master starts chewing his cud. Then he says, "You're right, Billy. You do tap the back foot on this particular play. Yeah, you give it a quick brush when the guy is charging down the basepath to hurt you."

That was my first memory of Billy Martin. Funny, the more he talked, the more Crosetti listened because even then Billy had a good grasp of the fundamentals. Yet, under those circumstances, it would've been the same as me telling Joe DiMaggio, "Hey, Joe, throw the ball like this instead of like that."

To me, it was a matter of knowing your place and I was an apprentice, being paid while learning a trade. Which worked out fine, as most of the players and coaches were willing to help. Unfortunately, DiMaggio had his own troubles, though you'd never suspect it while watching him take his cuts in the batting cage later in spring training. He still had the long stride, the swing full of rippling energy, smooth and natural. You couldn't tell there was anything wrong, that he had a bad heel. Of course, it made all the papers, actually dominating the other stuff coming out of camp. The big question was not about where the Yankees would finish in the standings, what rookie would stay, what rookie would leave; for all intents and purposes, that information wasn't important compared to DiMaggio and his aching heel.

The first day he showed up I was hitting pepper on the sidelines. Some other rookies who had been kept in camp were taking turns at fielding the ball. Just my luck, one got by an outstretched glove just as DiMaggio passed behind our game. It nicked his ankle and skidded away. He swiveled his head in my direction, staring bullets. I felt sure I'd be gone that night.

Joltin' Joe, the Yankee Clipper. He was really special. Nobody told him what to do. Not even Casey. Regardless of anything, DiMaggio went through the paces strictly on his own terms. He wanted the 1951 season to be his last hurrah, to save his strength for the opening bell in order to give his best shot before retiring the following spring.

The odd thing is, I hardly knew the man. He was a loner, always restrained, often secretive. If you weren't family or a very close friend, you didn't dare probe into his personal life. He'd shut you off in a minute. Shy as I was, I never went to him seeking advice. Too scared. It was a simple hello and goodbye. Press me further and I'll also admit that DiMaggio never said to me, "Come on, kid, let's have a beer and talk."

However, I made an impression where it really counted. Oh, everybody knew I had led the Western Association in four offensive categories the year before, but nobody knew about my speed. It brings a smile now, remembering when I used to run up that country road in Whitebird. And once, on a late summer afternoon, toward dusk, when me and Dad were loping along the same road, going home, having a serious discussion over who ran the fastest, one thing led to another until he finally said, "Do you think you could beat me?" I shrugged and he said, "Let's race." He pulled off those big old lead-toed mining shoes and we had a race. Seventy-five yards to the front porch, neck and neck. You could have separated us with a thin piece of paper, that's how close it was. At Commerce High they didn't have a track team, otherwise I might've been a world-class sprinter. To me, running came as natural as hitting the ball. They went together, one and the same.

So now, at the Yankee camp, I lined up against rookies Al Pilarcik and Tom Sturdivant, who were supposed to have blazing speed. They dug in, straining, ready to go. I stood with my hands and arms hanging loosely. Then the signal—*bang!* I jumped off in a headlong rush to the finish line and beat them both by ten yards. The coaches were shocked and Casey was hollering, "Look at that kid run! Let's find out some more about him."

Casey thought maybe the other two guys slip-started or something. So we raced again and I outran them. Well, I beat them a few times more and Casey said, "Let's see how fast he can run the bases."

I did it in just under thirteen seconds. It was unbelievably fast. Casey got so excited he made me run it again and again and again. He must have had me running those bases all afternoon. I nearly got sick from it.

A few days later they had me stationed in the outfield. Bill Renna, Bob Cerv, Hank Workman, Pilarcik, myself—all vying for a position. Casey got Tommy Henrich to start hitting me fly balls. It came easier than playing shortstop. In fact, if you can move fast and throw, you can play the outfield. As to the refinements, I picked up on some that needed to be learned, such as judging the distance to the walls, judging the flight of a ball by the sound it makes when the bat strikes it, judging the speed at which it approaches, and when to flip the glasses down as it comes out of the shadows. Tommy Henrich taught me that. Old Reliable worked with me a lot that spring.

Practice makes perfect, right? So now the exhibition season gets under way. Casey puts me in center field, my first game as a Yankee. And Cleveland shortstop Ray Boone hits a line drive straight at me. I ran in a few steps and flipped my sunglasses down. *Bam!* Nothing but blackness. The ball caught me square on the forehead.

Gene Woodling was playing left field. He picked up the ball, threw it back in, rushed over, grabbed me by the shoulder, looked me in the face, and said, "Did the glasses break?"

I shook my head to clear away the fog, then ran over to third base, where the bat boy had another pair of glasses waiting. I looked down at the dugout after I put them on. Everybody was laughing.

After that I had nowhere to go except up. This was the year the Yankees switched camps with the New York Giants. The team had previously trained at St. Petersburg, Florida. Here in Phoenix, the dry climate allowed you to hit the ball farther because the air was so thin. It seemed that everything I hit went off the bat for a home run, both lefty and righty. Skipping the details, let's say that in Phoenix I went on a hot streak and stayed hot. They couldn't get me out. Maybe if I had trained at St. Pete, where the ball has a tendency to hang, it would've been a different story. I don't know. It's these kind of "ifs" that can either make you a hero or send you to oblivion in a hurry.

Anyway, we broke camp and Casey kept me on the roster.

The other rookies were leaving in bunches. Finally, only Gil McDougald, Tom Morgan, and myself remained. Yet, in the actual scheme of things, I was still hoping to go to Beaumont to play for Harry Craft. At this point I didn't have a Yankee contract, nor did I expect one. Not in my wildest dreams. I just hoped they wouldn't send me to Binghamton. They had me ticketed there, along with Moose Skowron. I liked Moose, loved his company—but Binghamton? Without Harry and the guys I'd played with at Joplin, it wouldn't have been the same.

As it happened, the Yankees took me on a California junket. We faced a lot of Pacific Coast League clubs; at Hollywood, Los Angeles, Sacramento, San Francisco, Oakland—wherever. In one game, I caught a fly ball in medium right field and threw it to the plate on a line. Had the runner out by six feet. I heard later that Tommy Henrich thought it was the greatest throw he had ever seen. But even more, I kept tearing the hide off the ball. The reporters went ape. They didn't care about my outfielding or anything else except Mantle at the bat. Casey added to the excitement when the press swarmed around him after the games, saying I was great and all. To me, though, it was a crisp smile and a "Keep in there, kid." Then I wouldn't hear another word unless he felt I needed some more encouragement. And he'd say, "Keep in there, kid, you're doin' good." A real testy schoolmaster. He had me buffaloed a long time, until we sorta adopted each other.

While I'm on the subject of my so-called rise to prominence, I'll tell you what happened at an exhibition game against the University of Southern California. I lived up to the press notices by hitting two homers, a triple, and single. Half the student body must've been in the stands and it seemed as if every one of them came heading toward me as I walked out of the locker room. Absolute bedlam. They shoved scraps of paper into my hand for autographs, clawed at my shirt, pushed and screamed. It shook me. Yeah, I finally realized the price I might have to pay for being called the next DiMaggio.

I learned the hard way. When we got back to Phoenix, there was a letter from home. The draft board again. Another examination. My dad wrote, telling me that they wanted me to come in within ten days. As a capper, I was told that a lot of people were asking why I wasn't soldiering in Korea. To be candid, the war was the furthest thing from my mind. Certainly I knew about the mounting casualties, the talk going around that General MacArthur was planning an all-out fight against communism, even thinking of dropping an atomic bomb on China. Well, I could understand how some people felt, especially those who resented seeing young, apparently healthy guys hitting baseballs while their own sons and husbands were being killed in battle.

Meantime, despite the nagging reminders, I was caught up in trying to make the majors and giving my dad a little happiness.

The exhibition season was nearing its end. We had a final trip through Texas and Kansas City before coming east to play the Brooklyn Dodgers at Ebbets Field. Of course, I told Casey about the draft board notice. "No problem," he said. I would ride along with the team until we reached Kansas City. From there I'd go home, take my physical, and wait on the results. Okay. We headed out, played our games in Texas. At Kansas City I met Dad, who was bubbling over, all the while hiding his deeper concerns. He really looked sick, paler and thinner than I had seen him only two months ago. He shrugged it off—"It's nothing, I'm in good shape"—and grinned reassuringly.

I felt relieved, but still you gotta know how it was. Any outward display of affection between us would have been considered a sign of weakness. And God knows—I took him for granted. He'd always be there, no matter what. So I seldom called him that first year or wrote him to say, "I'm doing all right. How're you doing?"

We did have good times together, the two of us alone in the woods, shooting at quail, tracking rabbits around fence rows, enjoying everything whether we bagged anything or not. I had so many chances then to tell him he was the greatest guy in the world. But everything was left unspoken.

When we came into Miami, I was mentally prepared. If the country needed me, I'd be proud to serve. However, to be on the safe side, the draft board sent me on to the state induction center in Tulsa.

Millions of people didn't seem concerned one way or another about the fate of a kid ballplayer not yet old enough to vote. Still, I had gotten an incredible amount of publicity and the crank mail really poured into Washington.

I can't knock the system. It's democracy and I wouldn't have changed anything for a minute—even though my lifetime goal was on the line. I thought I had been treated fair and square when the Tulsa board ruled that anyone having osteomyelitis would be automatically disqualified for military service. But on a plane coming into New York for the pre-season Yankee–Dodger windup, I discovered that the controversy wasn't over. I opened the paper and read a sports column. The writer says, "So Mantle has osteomyelitis. What's the big deal? He doesn't have to *kick* anybody in Korea."

You learn to tolerate such things in life.

And the next thing I know, I'm in Brooklyn. In those days, the Dodgers produced their own special magic: Jackie Robinson, Pee Wee Reese, Duke Snider, Carl Furillo, Roy Campanella, Gil Hodges—a super team. And what a ballpark. Right after getting there, I learned that the right field wall had more angles than a crooked man with a crooked stick. Casey pointed them out during practice. We stood in front of the scoreboard and he's saying something like, "Played over here in 1912 and they liked me well enough until 1917 when I got fired. They brought me back in 1934 got rid of me again in 1936, but they were so wild about me they paid me for doing nothing in 1937—" I don't know what the hell he's talking about, so I say, "You mean you actually played here?"

And he says, "Son, what do you think—I was born at sixty?"

Well, I made the Old Man proud. Got four straight hits, including a homer over the scoreboard, and finished the spring exhibitions with a .402 average.

That day, as it also happened, I met Whitey Ford for the first time. He was in the Signal Corps then, stationed at Fort Monmouth, New Jersey, and had come in for his wedding. I tagged along with most of the team, kinda lost among the well-wishers. One drink, a handshake, and that was it.

Chapter 8

So Whitey got married and the next thing I knew I was on that train, going to Washington. Like I said earlier, it was an unbelievable experience: the anticipation of Opening Day, the doubts and the wondering, and then signing a contract that jumped me up from Class C ball to the *real* Yankees—"Geez, am I here already?"

And it was raining cats and dogs. The downpour had us trapped in the Shoreham Hotel. We didn't leave the building, just paced and paced, waiting for a break in the clouds while the tension of Opening Day kept growing. On the third day the word came. Forget Washington. We're going back to New York to play our opening series against the Red Sox. I felt tight as a drum, thinking of those fans, their expectations of me, how I'd handle myself at Yankee Stadium—

After all this, by the time we pulled into Grand Central Station and came up the stairway to grab a cab to the Bronx—could've been Mars, for all I knew—I was completely exhausted, drained dry. Now, in the late afternoon, I'm standing on 42nd Street with Joe Page and Charlie Silvera—traffic, car horns honking, people ducking under umbrellas, and cabs weaving and lurching past like giant yellow gnats. We flag a big old Checker. "To the Concourse Plaza Hotel," says Joe.

The hotel was only a couple of blocks from the stadium. As we go by, Joe pokes me in the ribs and chuckles, "There it is, phenom! Take a good look cause that's the house that Ruth built. And you're gonna tear it down with your hitting."

The next day I got up at seven to be at the ballpark at nine. The clubhouse guys were the only ones there. My name was on the lineup sheet: Jackie Jensen leading off, Rizzuto batting second, me third, then DiMaggio, Yogi Berra, Johnny Mize, Gil

McDougald, Jerry Coleman, and Vic Raschi in the pitcher's spot.

We come trotting up the dugout steps and in front of us is the biggest crowd I've ever seen in my life. About 50,000—twenty times the population of Commerce. It seemed the whole world was there. I stood frozen. Nothing moved. Then, Yogi walks up to me and says, "Hey kid, are you nervous?" I look at him. "No."

He says, "Well, how come you're wearing your jockstrap on the outside of your uniform?"

I took off for right field as if my ass had caught fire and didn't stop grinning until they finished playing the National Anthem.

When the last note died, it was panicsville again. I was about to play my first major league game and the only thing that registered was the awesome roar of the crowd, plus a realization that I was sharing the same field with Joe DiMaggio and Ted Williams. Ted was in a class by himself. The Splendid Splinter. An Einstein at the bat. Precise, mechanically perfect, every swing beautifully executed. I can still marvel at the way he used to stand up there, leaning in, shoulders held high, the bat cocked, ready to whip around as though guided by a computer. *Swish!* You had to see him to know he was the very best and I doubt there will be another one like him on the scene for a long long while.

So if I remember anything about that afternoon, it's Williams getting under a pitch and lofting it skyward. A real cloudbuster. I circled beneath, searching, searching, and finally jumped sideways, barely grabbing the damn thing. By then Williams had already kicked the second base bag in disgust on his way to the Boston bench.

My first official hit came in the sixth inning off Bill Wight, a tricky left-hander. A line drive single between short and third to score Jackie Jensen. I couldn't stop thinking of myself roaming the same ground where Babe Ruth once played and looking at his monument behind the center field fence—the sweep of the stands, the façade, the whole place sparkling—I'll never forget it.

Something else, though, about the Bronx. All those storefronts and fruit markets and apartment buildings—it seemed like a million of them! Inconceivable. I was a country boy, not in the least prepared for it. And here the Yankees had me in a little room at the Concourse Plaza. I remember walking back and forth from there to the stadium, wishing each day to have a sensational game so my dad wouldn't worry about me. At night, without a roommate and almost nobody to talk to, I'd usually sit around reading the sports pages or simply stare at the walls. And there were times when the world of baseball seemed so far off, no longer the game I knew and loved as a boy.

Bronx nights—hearing the El trains roaring overhead, wondering where all the people were going to and coming from. Then the diners, the cafeterias, the greasy spoon restaurants . . . leaning forlornly over a cup of coffee and listening to the strange New York accents, to guys in dungarees and leather jackets bunched together at the counter, arguing baseball. I'd walk back to the hotel, head down, lost in thought, thinking only of my family and Merlyn. Because you gotta know, it didn't come as easy as they wrote.

The New York fans were led to believe some kind of Superman had arrived on the scene. He was going to hit ball after ball over the center field bleachers, clear into the Harlem River. He was another Ruth, another DiMaggio, maybe better than both. But I was neither. I had enough trouble trying to be Mickey Mantle.

In those beginning weeks I hit the ball pretty good from the right side. Fastballs coming in high and tight to the left side had me flailing away at empty air. Funny, I'd hit them regularly during batting practice, but during the game, the cagey pitcher would take advantage of my glaring weakness: high and tight, up and in. "You're out!" Time and again I'd drag my ass to the bench, shaking with anger, muttering, "I can't wait to see you goddamned pitchers get old."

It was a case of too much too soon. Too many people expecting more than I could deliver. And the New York crowd can be very cruel if they think you've let them down. I'd hear their shouts coming from the right field stands, guys screaming at the top of their lungs—boos and catcalls, curses—"Go back to Oklahoma, you big bum!" Oh yeah, it was intimidating. I actually dreaded the idea of going to the ballpark, knowing a bunch of fans were already waiting at the players' entrance, anxious to get their licks in. Here it was, the end of April and they still hadn't seen a home run off my bat. So how could I blame them for being mad?

As for the press, well, where once adjectives like "sensational" and "extraordinary" preceded my name in print, now some of the very same writers were wondering if the words should have been changed to "questionable" or even "inept."

On May 1, 1951, at Chicago's Comiskey Park, I hit my first homer off Randy Gumpert. It was a long one, I remember that. They said it carried about 450 feet. But those shots were rare. Meanwhile the word got around to the opposition. Just feed the kid a chest-high fastball on the inside of the plate when he's batting lefty. They knew. Anything up on the letters with a little extra juice and it was "Goodbye, Mickey Charles." Especially in Cleveland, where I faced Bob Feller, Early Wynn, Bob Lemon, and Mike Garcia—four of the best. They worked me over like surgeons. And I went down swinging against Dizzy Trout and Virgil Trucks in Detroit. Then there was old Satchel Paige of the St. Louis Browns. What was he, forty-five or fifty at the time? Well, he still had more moves than a snake: the corkscrew windup, the submarine pitch, and that great rainbow curve of his, which tied me in knots.

One day I decided to bunt on him. We had a runner in scoring position, bottom of the ninth, and I took two straight cuts, missing them both by a wide margin.

Paige's next pitch was a fastball. I bunted and ran to first as fast as I could go. It was a foul ball, the last out of the game. Paige doffed his cap and flashed a big toothy smile. I was still running out the play, halfway up the foul line, as the Browns started back to their dugout.

Moments later Casey was in front of my locker, arms crossed, his eyes burning into mine. "Nice going, son. You sure fooled us. Next time I want you to bunt, I'll give you the sign."

He had every reason to ship me down to the minors.

But he stuck by me as long as he could. If an unfavorable article appeared, pointing a finger at my strikeouts, he would call me in and say, "Never mind that crap. All you need is a couple of hits. It's only a slump. Everybody has 'em." I'd sit there, barely absorbing his words, just waiting for the ax to fall.

In fact, this was going through everybody's mind in the front office and probably through the minds of the veteran ballplayers, consistently good hitters like Johnny Mize and Bobby Brown. Meanwhile here's this unproven rookie from Oklahoma stealing some of their thunder away. Because invariably you'd find a gang of reporters closing around me in the clubhouse after the games, firing questions, sticking microphones in my face, demanding, "What did you hit?" "What about the error?" "What about the bad throw?" "What about—" Hey, why didn't they talk to Johnny Mize or Bobby Brown? Maybe John belted a home run that day and, as for Bobby, he might've won the game for us. And their efforts would be glossed over by the press. So, as my teammates undressed, showered, changed into street clothes, and left the stadium, there you'd find me, literally pinned against my locker, trying to ward off a lot of reporters with stupid questions.

However, I kept going, even as the slump deepened and the anxieties built up to such a degree that I'd swing at anything thrown my way, including pitches in the dirt. I smashed bats, kicked over chairs, and one time actually pounded both fists on top of the dugout in front of a nasty crowd. Oh yes, Casey's patience began to wear thin.

There's more. One time Eddie Lopat was pitching a real squeaker for us. I lost my concentration and let an easy pop fly drop at my feet. Lopat grabbed me between innings. "You wanta play?" he snarled. "If not, don't screw around with our money. Just get the hell out of here because we want to win." I swallowed hard, then slumped down on the bench. I saw the end coming—and soon.

Finally the straw that broke the camel's back. A doubleheader against Boston. I struck out three times in the opener, started the second game, and fanned twice more—five in a row. Casey signaled to Cliff Mapes. "Get in there for Mantle. We need somebody who can hit the ball."

The weeks dragged. There was a Western trip, I guess Chicago or some such place, some hotel where I scribbled a few lines to Merlyn, telling her that I loved her and wished we could be together. I was too down to write my folks. Besides, they read the papers, so they knew what I was doing anyway.

I had been reduced to playing part-time, sharing the right field job with Jackie Jensen. Came July 12, a night game at Municipal Stadium, and my mind was taken off my troubles. We had Allie Reynolds on the mound. He was all business, quick as lightning, retiring the last seventeen Indian batters in order to wrap up a no-hitter. Our whole dugout emptied. We climbed over each other, trying to get at Allie. It felt great. I was excited about baseball again.

Next day, during a train ride into Detroit, I overheard Casev and the coaches whispering. Bits and pieces of conversation: "The kid's too young." "Too inexperienced." "Send him down to Binghamton." "Maybe Beaumont . . ."

Then going to Briggs Stadium on the team bus, jokes floating across the locker room, I'm putting on my uniform, and . . . the party's over.

The clubhouse guy says, "Casey wants to see you."

Casey's in his little room. He has tears in his eyes. He says, "This is gonna hurt me more than you, but—"

"No, skip. It was my own fault."

"Aww . . . it ain't nobody's fault. You're nineteen, that's all. I want you to get your confidence back, so I'm shipping you down to Kansas City."

I'm crushed.

"It's not the end of the world, Mickey. In a couple of weeks you'll start hitting and then we'll bring you right back up again."

"Uh-huh."

"I promise."

On my way out, he says, "Believe it. I'm counting on you."

I leave the clubhouse without talking to anyone. The guys are still practicing out on the field.

Traveling secretary Bill McCorry hands me a one-way plane ticket and escorts me to the airport. When he says, "Don't worry," I feel so sorry for myself that I can barely hear him.

I got off in Minneapolis, where the Kansas City Blues were playing a series. It was Triple A ball, one rung below the majors, which put me in a strong position for a fast comeback. So straight away I dragged a bunt down the first base line, legging it across the bag to beat the throw. When the inning ended, I jubilantly trotted to the bench and picked up my glove, only to hear manager George Selkirk bark, "What's the matter with you?"

"Nothing. Why?"

"I'll tell you why. They didn't send you here to bunt. You're here to get some hits and get your confidence back."

"Yes, sir."

What a start. Worse yet, I returned to my position in a state of shock. A moment later there's a long drive to center field. A blur. I flipped the sunglasses, turned and twisted. The ball took one bounce and disappeared over the fence. I threw the glasses after it.

I guess Selkirk wanted to throw me over the fence, too. As it was, he already had a bunch of malcontents to deal with. Really tough guys. Practically every night someone was at someone else's throat. It got so bad I hated to take a shower. All that yelling, the hot tempers—one night Rex Jones grabbed Clint Courtney's towel, which instantaneously led to a knock-down-drag-out brawl. And some of the guys who weren't fighting were either drunk or getting drunk. Pitchers carried pints of whiskey in their back pockets, right in the bullpen. It was like that. A comedy of errors.

I felt totally separated from the club. I didn't drink—not then —but I was pushing a full-sized slump that nearly drove me crazy. No rhythm, no timing, nothing but a whole string of outs and a bunt single to show for fifteen plate appearances.

Well, I got a telephone call from Harry Wells, saying that since things were kinda slow in the vault business and since his wife was now sufficiently recovered after a serious operation, he figured it would be nice if we spent a little time together. "Anyway," he said, "your mother thinks it may boost your morale." Good old Harry. I told him to meet me at the Aladdin Hotel in downtown Kansas City.

The following morning he showed up with a nervous grin on his face. "Slumps come, slumps go," he mumbled. I looked at him. "Harry, why don't we just go and eat?"

It was no better when we found a quiet little restaurant, sat down, ordered ham and eggs, and stared into our plates— breakfast unfinished. Harry called over the waiter and paid the check.

That weekend the Toledo Mudhens came to town for a two-game series under the lights. Harry attended, of course. He saw me run my hitless streak into the ground. Twenty-one outs in a row—swinging, or tapping an occasional bleeder to the infield or a weak fly to the outfield, or this or that. What difference did it make? I was beyond caring. I had lost my desire for the big leagues. I can count the reasons, but mainly you can say it was the lonesomeness—and also the pressures, never so relentless, knowing I had to accept the fact that I wasn't the best. And the salt in the wound came from a torrent of abusive language, which kept pouring down at me, game after game. Furthermore, a huge stack of mail sat in a corner of my room, mostly anonymous letters and postcards written by a lot of fans who called me a draft dodger and a creep, among other things.

At the Aladdin Hotel I showed a handful to Harry and he's going "Boy oh boy" and "What a world," his eyes blinking in utter disbelief because there are guys out there who want me dead. For real.

The night Harry went home I walked him to his car outside the ballpark. It was late, the light stanchions darkened, not a soul around, yet I'm saying, "Let's walk fast before somebody takes a shot at me." Suddenly a dried-up little old man tottered over, cigarette butt in mouth, looking like some kind of lunatic as he fumbled in his pants pocket for God knows what. I jumped a foot.

"Only want your autograph, Mickey. Wouldja?" he asked, removing a creased scorecard, his hand trembling.

"Get lost, fella."

Harry nudged my sleeve. "Aw, go on, Mick, give it to him. He helps pay your salary."

I signed the scorecard, even apologized, then watched the old guy shuffle away, staring at him curiously, almost laughing because the whole thing was so pathetic.

Harry dropped me off at the hotel and drove home. Afterward I trudged the streets of Kansas City. A few days passed. I finally called the Eagle-Picher mines, asking for Dad. He came to the phone with a tired-sounding "Hello."

"It's me. I'm in Kansas City."

"Yeah, I've been reading."

"Yeah, well, it looks like I can't play here either."

"What?"

"I'm not hitting, Dad. I just can't play anymore. I can't—"

"Hell you can't. Where are you staying?"

The way he said it I knew his body had tensed up and I could feel his disappointment.

"I'm at the Aladdin Hotel."

"Okay. I'll be there."

"When?"

He hung up. I paced the floor, waiting, rehearsing what I would tell him. After what seemed like years he was at the door; haggard after the five-hour drive from Commerce, but his eyes were blazing. The same look he used to give me when I was a little boy and did something to displease him. He didn't need a whip, only that stare.

He said, "All right, tell me again."

"Ah, Dad, listen, I tried hard as I could. And what for? Where am I headed? I'm telling you it's no use and that's all there is to it. I'm not—"

"Now you shut up! I don't want to hear that whining! I thought I raised a man, not a coward!" It was as though he had leveled a double-barreled shotgun at my head.

"Dad, please . . ."

"Sure, I'll please you. I'm gonna pack your stuff, that's what I'm gonna do. You can go back and work in the mines like me!"

The sight of him, his face as white as a sheet, his eyes full of sorrow and shame as he flung socks and shirts into my bag, all the time muttering, "I thought I raised a man . . ."

I groped for something to say that would stop him. It happened slowly, welling up from deep inside, those lost memories of us at the Baxter Springs ballpark, with him pushing his way through the crowds, grinning, looking everywhere and bragging to everybody about his kid. And days when he just sat slumped, the mines robbing him of his strength, dog-weary, probably thinking of all the dreams that had turned sour in his own life, what life had to be for him now, and I realized it was the thought of me making good that kept him going. Something he could cling to, no matter what.

"Okay, I understand . . . give me another chance. I'll try, honest I will."

He hesitated. A hint of a smile and he slapped the bag with his hand. "What the hell. Why not, huh?"

A few minutes later, downstairs in the coffee shop, he simply said, "So you've had your slump. You're not the first and you sure won't be the last. Everybody has them, even DiMaggio. Take my word. It'll come together. You'll see."

That's how it ended. We ate, he patted my back, I took a quick sip of coffee, then watched him walk up the street toward his car. I stood there, looking, and all I saw was the strong youthful father I had always known.

The next day I went back to playing ball, really bearing down, telling myself over and over, "I'm gonna do it for him."

We played our next series in Toledo. I hit a double, a triple, and two homers over the light tower. My last time up they told me I needed a single to go for the cycle, so I bunted. By then we were way ahead and as I went into the dugout George Selkirk looked at me and winked as if to say, "I'm not going to get on you this time." During the next forty games, I went berserk: 11 home runs, 50 RBIs, a .361 batting average.

We did it, me and my dad. I was on my way back.

Chapter 9

The Yankees brought me up from Kansas City around the end of August.

Back in New York, I was sharing an apartment over the Stage Delicatessen on Seventh Avenue in the Midtown area with Johnny Hopp and Hank Bauer. Our place had a small, narrow kitchen, a living room, a bedroom in the rear big enough for two beds, and a small bedroom containing an army cot, where I slept.

In those days they treated rookies like gofers. When either Hopp or Bauer wanted anything from the delicatessen, I'd run downstairs and get it. Hopp, a longtime veteran who had spent most of his career in the National League, had come over to the Yankees in 1950. And Bauer: if you leveled with him, he was a pussycat; if you struck a nerve, you had a tiger on your hands. He grew up poor in East St. Louis, Illinois, and could spin stories that would knock your head off. Like his wartime experiences as a Marine, landing on Guadalcanal, Guam, and Okinawa. Who needed newsreels? I saw it all through Hank. So I did what I was told, even if it meant running down to the deli every ten minutes. That's how much admiration I had for the man.

We were playing a doubleheader against the White Sox in Comiskey Park. It was between games and some guy was leaning over the side of our dugout, trying to look in. He had this huge bucket of beer with him—it was spilling on Whitey—and he was hollering, "Where's Hank Bauer? I served in the Marines with Hank Bauer."

Well, this guy looked like the same type of Marine as Hank: tough, with a neat crew cut and his nose mashed all over his face, you know, like it had been beaten on forever.

So the beer is still pouring down and Whitey said, "Hank's

over there." Then he glanced up at the guy and added, "God-damn, what did those Japs fight you with over there, shovels?"

The Stage is still operating at the same location but under a different management nowadays. Back then it was owned by Max and Hymie Asnas. The older brother, Max, introduced me to matzoh ball soup. "Taste, taste, you'll hit homers with this." And Hymie stuffed me with whopping portions of cheesecake. Between the two of them, I gained a lot of weight that year, ballooning from 165 to 190 pounds on their delicious food. It was so good I ate just about every meal there.

Then I'd find myself outside sometimes, right next door in front of the Stage barbershop, gawking at the Broadway comics who'd congregate between shows, guys like Joey Bishop, Fat Jack Leonard, Jerry Lester, Larry Storch, and Buddy Hackett.

One day before a night game I was getting a haircut and sitting right next to me was bandleader Harry James. He was a big baseball fan, especially a Cardinals fan, and we got to talking. He said that if I was ever in Vegas to be sure to stop in and see him. He and his wife, Betty Grable, lived in a house facing the Desert Inn golf course. Sometime later Merlyn and I, along with Whitey Ford and his wife, were on vacation in Vegas and we went over and had dinner with Harry and Betty. They were very nice to us.

I went to the movies nearly every day back then. If we played a day game I'd catch the evening show; night games I went around noon, usually sitting in a last row balcony seat, alone, checking my watch because the rules were that you had to be suited up and ready for batting practice three hours ahead of time.

But those Broadway lights, the neon glowing, hamburgers sizzling behind plate-glass windows, a carnival atmosphere, with Dixieland sounds floating up basement steps on 52nd Street and strange characters in wide-brimmed hats padding along, maybe to sell drugs or take you for a ride—who knows? I couldn't avoid the newsstand dailies. Big black headlines, grisly photos, a murder a day. This is how it looked to a nineteen-year-old kid from Oklahoma. But I was starting to like the excitement of the big city.

I had never been on a subway. The first time I took one I got off at the wrong stop. Somebody told me, "You wanta go to the ballpark? No problem. Take the Lexington Avenue express and get off at 161st Street." So how the hell did I wind up at the Polo Grounds? Easy. I took another train and got off at 155th Street. The rest was hard. Trudged across the Macombs Dam Bridge in a nervous sweat till I reached Yankee Stadium. After that experience, I got around by cab.

I was beginning to feel safe and comfortable in New York. Then here comes a phone call, waking me up early one morning: a smooth talker, saying my golden opportunity had arrived. "I can get you endorsements, personal appearances, motion picture deals—they're here, for your immediate consideration. The sky's the limit. Trust me. You'll be a millionaire within five years. Tell you what. I'll be over to explain the whole package."

I didn't even have a chance to brush my teeth. He was at the door in a flash, a short, chubby guy with a razor-thin mustache, horn-rimmed glasses, flashy cufflinks, and pinky ring. He points me to a chair. Talk about action. Before the seat is warm, he whips out a contract which states that as of *now* he is my exclusive agent, which also gives him the right to 50 percent of my income for ten years. Fine. But before he leaves, a little voice inside my head is telling me, "Hold it, Mickey. Something stinks around here."

He told me, "You don't have to sign this till you see a lawyer. I've got one."

Meanwhile he waved papers and explained things—while I thought about all that money. He got my signature and I walked out happy.

Around that time, a very pretty showgirl named Holly came into my life. Once in a while when the team was in New York and I had the evening free after a day game, we'd go out for dinner or Holly would hang out with me at the apartment on Seventh Avenue. I guess I developed my first taste for the high life then—meeting Holly's friends, getting stuck with the check at too many fancy restaurants, discovering scotch at too many dull cocktail parties. It was a lot of fun—while it lasted. One way or another Holly got acquainted with my new agent. And one day he came to me and said, "Mick, I just sold Holly 25 percent of my 50 percent interest in your earnings."

I was in a hell of a mess and I started feeling really bad about Merlyn.

Years later, after I was married, Merlyn and I were flying down to Cuba with Harold Youngman and his wife Stella on their private plane. We stopped at the airport in Montgomery, Alabama, to refuel and in the terminal Harold grabbed my sleeve.

"Hey, Mickey, is that your picture?"

And there I was, big as life, on the cover of *Confidential* magazine over a story about Holly, the girl who claimed that she "owned 25 percent of Mickey Mantle—and sometimes 100 percent."

Well, I reached into my pocket, bought all of those magazines, and dumped them in the trash. At every airport on that trip, Harold and I would sprint out of the plane to buy up the magazines before Merlyn could see the incriminating evidence.

But when we got home from that trip, there was a stack of *Confidential* magazines waiting for us in the front yard.

Anyway, back to that agent.

As I said, I palled around with Hank Bauer quite a bit during that summer. I had one sport coat and one pair of slacks until Hank took me down to the garment section of Manhattan, a place called Eisenberg & Eisenberg, where they fitted me with two business suits. Thirty-five dollars apiece. Also some shirts and ties. At another store I got a pair of dress shoes.

Later, while in the clubhouse, I finally decided to tell Hank about my deal with the agent—the bare bones of the arrangement, that is.

He said, "I dunno, Mick, it sounds kind of strange. You should definitely talk with Frank Scott. He's my agent now and he also represents some of the other guys."

Frank had been the Yankee traveling secretary through the late forties. A real advocate for the players and a nice guy. I knew him from the season before, when he gave Moose and me some expense money for our Western swing with the Yankees.

"Well, uh, Hank, what's your split with Scotty?"

"The usual 10 percent. Why? What are you paying that guy?"

I felt like I'd been hit by a truck. Hank understood my problem and immediately put me in touch with Scotty. He promised to look into the situation and there it sat for a while. Hank also said, "You better tell the Yankees about this. They'll handle it."

And they did.

I might have made my share of mistakes that summer. But by the end of the season, I was playing pretty good baseball and so were the Yankees.

In the middle of September, we were in second place, trailing Cleveland by only a game. Casey matched Allie Reynolds against Bob Feller, with something like 65,000 fans watching. The Chief delivered, holding Cleveland to five hits, taking the win. Next day we moved out front, beating them in a thriller. It was tied 1–1 in the bottom of the ninth. Bob Lemon on the mound, Joe DiMaggio inching off third as Phil Rizzuto laid his bat on a shoulder-high fastball thrown inside, the toughest pitch in the world to bunt. I was on deck, hoping I wouldn't have to drive Joe in and already counting my World Series money. Phil pulled it off. DiMaggio scored and Lemon disgustedly hurled his glove into the stands.

With five games left in the season, needing two more wins to clinch the pennant, we played a doubleheader at the stadium. If you don't remember, it was September 28, the day Reynolds pitched his second no-hitter of 1951. I sat it out, as Casey decided he'd go with his more experienced players against the Red Sox. No reason to have a still-shaky nineteen-year-old in there. The stakes were too high. Perfectly understandable. But even more perfect was the ringside seat I had at the far end of the bench. A terrific view as I saw Reynolds breeze through eight hitless innings while we built an 8–0 lead.

Top of the ninth, two out, and up steps Ted Williams. He popped up foul between the plate and our dugout. Yogi fell backward trying to catch the ball. It glanced off his glove; Williams was still alive. The very next pitch he hits another one a mile high, an exact replica of the previous foul pop, and drifting down in the same direction. This time Yogi held on for the final out.

In the clubhouse everybody went nuts—even Del Webb, in his own fashion. He hugged Yogi and said, "When I die, I hope the good Lord gives me a second chance the way He gave you one."

The next game we had Vic Raschi pitching. They called him the Springfield Rifle. He led the league in strikeouts that year. He was a battler, always pushing himself to the limit of his abilities and probably beyond, playing the bulk of his career on damaged knees. Well, he nailed the pennant for us, getting his twenty-first win. We made it a lot easier for him when we scored seven runs in the second inning. Another landmark event was when DiMaggio hit a three-run homer in the sixth. Turned out to be his last in regular season competition—No. 361.

I finished the series protecting center field while the regulars coasted, enjoying the leisure of a hard-won victory. And across the river the Giants were getting ready for the shot heard around the world. It seemed like the older Yankees had their hopes pinned on the Giants. Economics again. The Polo Grounds seated twice as many fans as Ebbets Field. I didn't understand the simplicity of it all until Gene Woodling spelled it out. "The more those turnstiles click at World Series games, the more money you make. That's why we're here."

Sick as he was, Dad drove up from Commerce and arrived in time for the Miracle on Coogan's Bluff, where he eyewitnessed Bobby Thomson's last-of-the-ninth homer off Ralph Branca. So the Giants won the pennant. Fine and dandy. And as far as it goes, I was knocked off my feet when Casey announced that I'd be his starting right fielder in the World Series opener against Dave Koslo.

Actually, Dad had two friends from back home with him on that trip and they had a few experiences of their own. One day the three of them went out and spent some time in a tavern. It seems they wound up in a subway during rush hour—everybody jammed together and the heat was awful—and my dad's friend Trucky Compton began to feel sick. There was no room to move or bend over or get out, so Trucky just grabbed some poor man's hat and puked in it.

As I recall, Dad and his friends also thought that the statue of Atlas in Rockefeller Center was actually the Statue of Liberty. They were so excited about it and I was sorry to disappoint them with the truth.

Certainly my father felt tremendously happy about my success, something he had dreamed about from the moment I was born. Little Mickey . . . his son, his best hope in a world that had all but beaten him down.

Now he was out at the stadium, picking up tickets for himself and some friends one day, when I introduced him to Holly.

"Dad, this is Holly. She's a very good friend."

Maybe she winked at me. I don't know. But Dad knew that something was up—and he didn't like it a bit. Later he took me aside.

"Mickey, you do the right thing and marry your own kind."

"It's not what you think, Dad."

"Maybe not, but Merlyn is a sweet gal and you know she loves you."

"Yeah, I know."

"The point is, she's good. Just what you need to keep your head straight."

"I know."

"Well, then, after the Series you better get on home and marry her."

I half turned from him, nodding silently. There was nothing more to discuss.

Chapter *10*

I played the first game of the 1951 World Series, feeling like I didn't belong. Dave Koslo held me to two walks and the Giants beat us, 5–1. I was afraid to look at the lineup card for the next game, but finally gave it a passing glance. Right field—Mantle. Leading off again.

I remember what Casey said as clear as a bell: "Take everything you can get over in center. The Dago's heel is hurting pretty bad."

I trotted out to right field and looked over at DiMaggio in center. Injured or not, he was so smooth and sure of himself: if he had to, he still could've skimmed across the grass from foul line to foul line, with what he knew about the hitters. I relaxed.

The third inning. Larry Jansen was pitching. I dragged a bunt single. Rizzuto pushed me to second with another bunt. Then Gil McDougald pumped a dying swan over second base that no one could reach. I scooted home for my first World Series run, knowing my father was in the stands.

The sixth inning. Willie Mays led off for the Giants. It was his rookie year too. I had heard a lot about him during my short stint in the American Association, how he did in Minneapolis, hitting a ton before I arrived at Kansas City. Now he stood at the plate, batting right-handed. I moved a couple of steps toward center field, thinking about what Casey had said. And Willie connected. A high pop fly carrying between me and DiMaggio in short right center. I went for it and heard DiMaggio yell, "I got it!" That's when I slammed on the brakes. My spikes caught on the rubber cover of a drain hole buried in the outfield grass. *Pop.* The pain squeezed like a vise around my right knee. I lay there, absolutely motionless. It's been said that I went down so quickly it appeared that I had suffered a heart attack. My own recollection is at best a blurred picture of DiMaggio kneeling at my side, asking, "Are you all right?" I tried to say, "What happened?" I even thought I'd been shot. He leaned forward, his voice full of concern. "Don't move. They're bringing a stretcher."

Everything closed in. The Yankee trainer, Gus Mauch, was there—Crosetti placed a towel under my head—players milled about—the crowd grew noisy. Dad was in the dugout, looking worried.

That evening Gus Mauch wrapped my knee and put splints on both sides of my leg. When I went home, I had to take the bandages off because the injury had swelled up so much. The next morning I wrapped the knee again and hobbled out on crutches with my dad. We took a cab down to Lenox Hill Hospital.

As we pulled up to the entrance on 77th Street, Dad got out of the cab. I followed, leaning on him as I stepped onto the curb. But when I put my full weight on him, he just crumpled over on the sidewalk.

They put us in the same room. There we stayed, viewing the World Series on television. Meanwhile they ran some tests to determine the nature of his illness. I was worried about Dad. He'd been a big strong miner all his life, around 200 pounds, but when he had shown up in New York to watch the Series I had noticed his khaki pants were almost falling off him. He had lost a lot of weight, maybe 30 pounds or so.

My knee was operated on. I had torn some ligaments and could forget about baseball for a while. Dr. Gaynor of the Yankees made a special cast, fitting steel weights at the bottom. I was supposed to sit around all winter, lifting those weights, adding more and more weight till I could lift twenty or thirty pounds. I never used them.

There was a soft knock at the already opened door: one of the doctors who'd been attending my father, his face grim as he approached my bed. I stared back into his eyes, daring him to tell me what I had already known for a long time. At length he said in a low, almost inaudible voice, "It's bad news. Your father has cancer."

"Where?"

"It's—well, it's Hodgkin's disease. I'm afraid there's not much we can do."

"Is there a chance?"

The doctor gave a slight twist to the corner of his mouth, then shrugged. "You can take him home. Let him go back to work or whatever he wants. I'm sorry, Mick . . ."

He was dying.

That fall I bought a home for Mom and Dad. There was a World Series check to go with my salary, so I had enough for a sizable down payment. A neat, comfortable seven-room house in Commerce, at 317 South River Street. Plenty of space for the family. We also had our own phone. Two rings meant us.

But after we'd moved and unpacked some brand-new furniture and I finally had my own bed and lay there trying to sort things out, it seemed that nothing made any sense. Nights I'd be in front of the TV, my bum leg propped on a stool, a can of beer in my hand. Mindless. Toward mid-November the cast was removed. I lazed around, feeling sorry for myself instead of doing the exercises prescribed by Dr. Gaynor. I thought the muscles would automatically come back, good as ever. I was twenty years old and I thought I was a superman.

If you add it all up, that winter and the first few months of 1952 were the end of boyhood days. For me, the crunch came two days before Christmas.

Merlyn and I got married. We had a small ceremony at her parents' house in Picher—just the preacher, the immediate families, and Turk Miller, Dad's closest friend. He served as best man. Merlyn came out of the bedroom. I came from the bathroom. We cut the cake and took off shortly after that. Then, in a dumpy little motel not far from there, we spent our first night together.

Bill Mosely and his girlfriend joined us on our honeymoon. It was supposed to be my big surprise to Merlyn: a plush hotel, breakfast in bed, the whole works. The story was, a guy representing the Chamber of Commerce in Hot Springs, Arkansas, had made the arrangements. How I came to hear about this promise of a glorious weekend, free of charge, no strings attached, well, that escapes me now. What I can still see, though, is a picture of us driving up to the Chamber of Commerce and being met by a lot of blank stares. "Who?" "What guy?"

Between us, Bill and I had barely enough to pay for one night, let alone a weekend. So we slept there and went back home the next day.

Back in Commerce, we rented a garage apartment in an alley. Nearby there were some bowling lanes where my dad used to play with his friends from the mines.

I clearly remember a Christmas parade. Merlyn was marching in it . . . I had promised to watch her. That morning I was in the bowling alley with my dad and his pals and when the parade started all of the pin boys ran out to see it. Of course, I wanted to go too. I wanted to see Merlyn. But my dad made me stay behind and set pins for his group.

One morning, out of desperation, Merlyn and I put Dad in the back of our car, and drove to the Mayo Clinic, hoping against hope they'd be able to help him. It was an endless ride, creeping along ice-slicked roads at no more than fifteen miles an hour, peering through a frosted windshield, the snow flying all around. At dusk we came into Rochester, Minnesota, and here on a dry shoveled walk we led him slowly to the entrance of the Kahler Hotel, where we stayed. There is a network of underground corridors in Rochester, connecting the hospitals, clinics, and hotels. For the three days that they were checking out Dad, I remember that we never went outside, just went to and from the hotel along one of those corridors.

He underwent exploratory surgery. Merlyn and I waited and waited until finally the doctor appeared. He didn't have to say anything. My father was too far gone. They just sewed him up and a few days later he went back to Commerce with us, his life flickering away quietly. And when I saw the despair settle deeply in his eyes, I began to doubt God.

And what of Merlyn, baseball, everything else? Could I hold

on to that? All I knew was a bottomless sorrow and I couldn't express it to anyone.

Maybe some nights I'd slip off in my Chevy and try the local bars, have a few beers with the guys, tell jokes and laugh. Innocent byplay. Time went fast. What difference did it make? It was tough getting a good night's sleep anyway.

At this point I was also working for Harold Youngman. He owned a construction company in Baxter Springs. Started the business on a shoestring shortly after World War II, building roads and adding equipment as his state highway contracts grew by leaps and bounds. When I first heard about him, I pictured a coarse, hard-nosed guy of questionable character, but the man I met was the exact opposite. The more I got to know him, the more I realized he was a wonderful human being. He hated phonies, stayed clear of bores. If he liked you, you had a friend forever. Well, whatever he saw in me, all I know is that I was paid $300 a month to hang around and look official. And when we talked, he always had that understanding smile, was always ready to offer a word of encouragement or stern advice if warranted. He didn't have a son. I guess he accepted me as his own. And it made what I was going through a hell of a lot easier.

That spring I went down to St. Petersburg, where the big question was DiMaggio's replacement in center field. I had no idea who it would be, not with me still hobbling around. The other contender was Jackie Jensen. Casey kinda nursed me along. A week or two later I began running some, of course at nowhere near the speed I had before the accident. After a while, Casey alternated me with Jackie.

One good thing. Merlyn had come down with me. It was her first trip to Florida and she arrived all dressed for winter: corduroy dress, woolen scarf, and boots. We stayed at a place on the beach with a fantastic view from the window. Except I didn't look out very much.

By mid-March I'm believing in myself again. There's a particular game at St. Pete—we're playing the Braves when I get called over. Casey asks, "How's your knee?" I give it a pat. He says, "Okay, I'm putting you in right field." It's the fifth inning and I go nine more in a 1–0 overtime loss, which nonetheless has me feeling as if I've crossed the Great Divide.

Throughout the exhibition season the question regarding center field was still up in the air. Casey handled himself with the composure of a chess master, each move deliberate, studied, measured against the standards set by DiMaggio. He played me for a week, then switched back to Jensen, figuring I wasn't ready for the job.

We broke camp and headed north to New York, Merlyn driving all the way by herself, bag and baggage. I made the arrangements. We'd spend the season there, living at the Concourse Plaza Hotel. I'll admit it wasn't the Ritz. Here we were in a dreary room: no stove, no refrigerator, one closet, a tiny bathroom, a bed, a chair, and bare walls. Furthermore, we couldn't afford to rent a TV set. It cost ten dollars a month—heavy cash, after sending money home to help my family. My poor father was somewhere in Denver, getting treated in a clinic that claimed it could cure cancer by massage or something. I don't know the details; never called to find out. Didn't want to know, I guess.

The worst moments were spent during our first road swing. I not only worried about Dad but also about Merlyn, now left on her own to be a baseball widow in New York. Suddenly she was caught up in it all. I gave her twenty dollars or so for food and told her, "If you run short, order in and charge it to the room." She didn't. She would have a light meal out, then go around visiting other players' wives, preferably those who had TVs and children who loved cookies.

Much later, she finally talked of her loneliness: the boredom, the petty gossip and jealousies, and wives looking to compete against other wives, as if they had their own kind of ball club, with the same insecurities as their husbands. "At first I didn't mind it," she said. "You get used to the silly jokes, even the cutting remarks. It's only when I found myself waiting around, just like the rest, unsure of what you were doing—"

But she learned to roll with the punches.

On May 3, the Yankees traded Jackie Jensen to Washington for Irv Noren, another center fielder. I was surprised and somewhat amused when Casey declared that if we weren't going anywhere he would have given Jackie a full shot and let him learn while he was playing. Well, he sure learned his stuff after the Red Sox acquired him from Washington. He won three RBI titles overall and MVP honors in 1958. As for Noren, he came into New York immediately after the trade and played center field against the White Sox.

I was the lame duck in right field.

On May 6, with the Cleveland Indians in town, I was getting dressed to go to the ballpark. I remember standing by the window, looking down at a stream of traffic along the Grand Concourse. And the phone rang.

"Mick, this is Casey."

"Hi, skip. What's up?"

"Your mother called. She thought you were here at the stadium."

I waited, holding my breath, and when the words finally came I just stared blindly across the room.

My father was dead. Why? What had happened to him in the thirty-nine years of his life, with all the scrambling and disappointments and frustrations? Where did it get him? He needed me and I wasn't there. I couldn't make it up to him. He died alone. I cried, "What kind of God is there anyway, to let him die like that!"

No excuse—I lashed out and smashed my fist against the wall, then looked at Merlyn, helpless, choked with grief.

She came over and hugged me.

"Merlyn, please . . . I'm going down to the ballpark."

A pause. "Will you be all right?"

"Yes."

At the door, she said, "When are we going home?"

"I don't know. I guess I'll leave tomorrow."

Another pause. "I want to be there for the services."

"No, you don't need to."

The corners of her mouth softened. I saw her tears and heard the door close behind her.

When I got out to the ballpark, Casey called me into his office.

"I'm really sorry, Mick. We all hate it. You can sit out the game tonight if you like, but I really think you should try to play."

I did play. I'm sure Dad would have wanted me to.

I went to the funeral alone. Dad was buried in the GAR cemetery, on a flat plain of the road between Commerce and Miami, in Oklahoma soil. Many of his friends are buried there—miners who lived, worked, and died without really being known—and his father and two brothers are buried there, too. And my mother has a plot next to him where she will be buried when she dies.

I stood before my father's grave, remembering a thousand things from the past . . . So many chances then to let him know how much I loved him—and I never said it, not once.

My mother, gently: "Come, Mickey, the car is waiting."

"In a minute. You go ahead. I'll catch up . . ."

This is me and my dad.
He's about twenty-two years old,
I guess. I'm about
three. He was some kinda guy.
[Mickey Mantle Collection]

Me and Uncle Luke,
my mom's brother.
I don't remember
this picture, but
I guess he was a
ballplayer, too.
[National Baseball Library,
Cooperstown, N.Y.]

1951. I was working in the mines, waiting for the Yankees to send me money to pay my way to spring training. When I got banned from baseball, I had some cups made with this picture and the captions on the cups were: "Don't worry about me. I can get a job doing anything." [Mickey Mantle Collection]

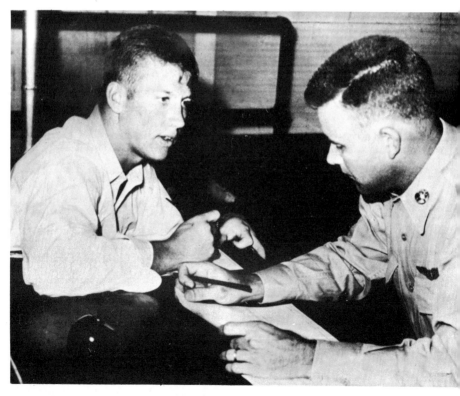

One of my trips to a draft board in Oklahoma in 1951. [UPI/Bettmann News Photos]

Me and Casey. This is when I came back to the Yankees after being sent down. Both of us were very happy. [UPI/Bettmann News Photos]

My second season with the Yanks.
Look, Billy's got on argyle socks.
I'm saying, "Billy, I can't wait till we
start making good money so we don't
have to carry our own bags."
Look at those baggy pants!
[New York *Times*]

These were happy days. I had just come back to the Yankees from the Kansas City Blues.
I roomed with Johnny Hopp and Hank Bauer. [Ernest Sisto, New York *Times*]

Our wedding. Merlyn and I got married in Merlyn's parents' house. She came out of the bedroom and I came out of the bathroom. Turk Miller, one of my dad's friends, was the best man and the bridesmaid was Merlyn's sister Pat. [Orrick Sparlin Studio/Mickey Mantle Collection]

The city of Commerce had a Mickey Mantle Day in 1952: a parade through the town and they gave me this set of silverware. Years later, our house got burglarized and somebody stole it. [Miami *News Record*]

Ty Cobb was in the Yankee dugout one day and Casey had him talk to me about not striking out so much. [AP/Wide World Photos]

The World Series is just over in 1952, Merlyn's pregnant with little Mickey, and that's me with Merlyn and my mom getting ready to head for Oklahoma. I loved that shirt. [AP/Wide World Photos]

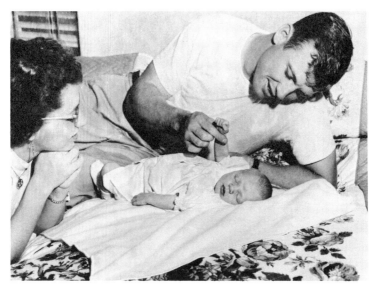

This is the first time I saw Mickey Jr. He'd just bawl all the time. I thought he was the greatest thing in the world. [Orrick Sparlin Studio/Mickey Mantle Collection]

I had a skin rash and couldn't get rid of it, so Casey told me, "Go on home and see the baby and maybe you'll get rid of the rash." Sure enough, on the way home I lost my rash. But I decided to stay there a couple of days. When this picture appeared in the paper, I got a telegram from Casey. He said I'd better rejoin the team right away. [Orrick Sparlin Studio/Mickey Mantle Collection]

Me and Harold Youngman.
I've kidded him a lot, but
he was the best friend I ever had.
[Mickey Mantle Collection]

Me and Billy Martin in a card game. I caught him cheating. [The Harwyn Club/
Mickey Mantle Collection]

Chapter *11*

I returned to New York with a tight smile painted on my face.

Casey was also wearing one. Straight off the top, during spring training Billy Martin cracked his ankle in two places; Yogi Berra stretched ligaments in his right foot; Vic Raschi's knee had deteriorated badly; Ed Lopat developed a sore arm; and once again, the continuing dilemma over me. Not the least of it, Bobby Brown and Jerry Coleman were targeted for military service, which put an additional strain on the whole situation. In a nutshell, there was little room for humor when I reported to Yankee Stadium.

We played the Red Sox, then went to Cleveland, where I stewed on the bench except for one brief appearance at third base. Casey put me in for defensive purposes. As it turned out, I fielded .500—two errors in four chances.

At the time, Bobby Brown was our backup at third, but I guess he was thinking of retiring. After my terrible performance, Bobby said, "This is the last straw. No question, I'm really going to retire." I guess he was only half joking.

Meanwhile I was still an irregular. Then, on May 20, Casey started me as the center fielder, batting third against Chicago pitching. I hammered out four straight singles, two lefty and two righty, jumping my average up over the .300 mark. After that I rolled. And so did Billy Martin. He was back at second base, his ankle mended, when all of a sudden his big nose attracted the attention of Jimmy Piersall. It happened before a game in Fenway Park. Piersall, a rookie shortstop then, waltzed up and started agitating Billy. "Hey, Pinocchio, what's with the schnozz?" That did it. They squared off under the grandstand. According to Billy, he whipped two short rights to Piersall's face and knocked him flat—and if Bill Dickey hadn't jumped in as a peacemaker, he would've beaten the living daylights out of Piersall. "Nobody screws with my nose," he said. And weird, shortly after the fight, Piersall ended up in a mental institution. When we got the news, Billy said, "You think I can't punch. Hell, I knocked that guy crazy."

At the time we had no idea Piersall was anything other than a highly competitive, hot-headed kid. Billy certainly was. He'd lose his temper faster than anybody if he thought he was right and somebody challenged him. Because, okay, he's a fighter, always looking for a way to stay on top, to get the advantage and never back down. He hasn't changed. With all the accomplishments, he still has a burning need to prove himself.

Casey loved this kind of combative spirit. At a clubhouse meeting after the fight, he said in plain English, "If we're gonna win this thing, you better move your asses like Billy here. Of course, I want your enthusiasm directed to the finer points of baseball, which is a wonderful sport for young gentlemen, I would say."

We caught fire in June, going into first place and holding the lead through the late summer. My turning point was a day in Cleveland. Joe Collins hit a ball that reached the upper seats of right center field. He came back to the dugout, passed me on the on deck circle, and said, "Go chase that, kid." There was a Chesterfield cigarette sign a little farther out from where he tagged his homer. I hit one up over there, rounded the bases, took a sip of water, then sat down next to him. Without looking up, I said, "What did you say, Joe?"

During our last Western trip we played a pair at Chicago, winning them both. The following day it was a single game with the Indians. Manager Al Lopez had Mike Garcia waiting for us. The Big Bear. He was *all* business and our lead was razor-thin; a game and a half, as I recall. On the train everybody felt terrific, knowing we were *really* going to take care of Garcia. Well, alongside me sat Phil Rizzuto, who grew up in Brooklyn. So naturally he was fairly ignorant of country life. Besides, Phil had this fearful aversion to anything that crawled, especially snakes.

"Did you ever see one?" I asked.

"*S-n-a-k-e-s!!!* Holy Cow, I can't *stand* those things. Don't bother me with such idiotic questions, willya?"

I said, "Did you ever see a rattler?"

He covered his head.

"But, Phil, it's not what you think. I owned one. Pulled out his fangs with my fingers and trained him as a house pet. A cute little bugger—"

"Please, Mickey, what are you trying to do, make me blow the pennant?"

That's Phil. A beautiful guy, not a bad bone in his body. Always trusting and so gullible it made him a pushover for all the pranks we used to play on him. One time Charlie Keller put Phil in his footlocker and locked him up. And Phil laughed it off. No one could get him mad enough to lose his temper.

One year Phil won an Austin-Healey sports car for being the most popular Yankee. It was real small and Phil drove it down to St. Pete. A couple of veterans grabbed ahold of the car with their bare hands and wedged it sideways between two palm trees. Phil couldn't drive it out. Still, I think he sorta appreciated the joke.

Now back to that crucial game in Cleveland, September 14, a packed house. We scored four runs in the third inning, the key hit a bases-loaded single by Yogi. We went on to win, 7–1. I helped, doubling off Garcia and hitting a homer off Lou Brissie. The decisive performances belonged to Lopat and Reynolds. Eddie pitched his heart out before Allie took over in the late innings, saving his second straight game. We left town riding a cloud of joy.

At Yankee Stadium a few days later, our lead was cut to a game and a half again. Bobby Shantz of the Athletics shut us out. Next day Lopat returned the favor, blanking the A's on a four-hitter. Then Reynolds finished them off with a shutout. Incidentally, it was during this game that Harry Byrd struck me out swinging. No. 106. I wound up with 111 to lead the league that year, setting a New York Yankee record for futility.

Well, when you keep aiming for the fences, you're bound to strike out a lot. Check it out. You'll see that all the power hitters from Babe Ruth to Reggie Jackson fell into the habit. But who remembers them for their strikeouts? For example, fans are still coming up to me, saying, "I was there at Griffith Stadium when you hit that shot 565 feet" or "I'll never forget sitting in Yankee Stadium and watching you hit one into the bleachers" and so on. To tell the truth, I've long forgotten how far most of those home runs went. In fact, I've forgotten half the stuff they've written about me—that is, the home runs and the distances. I mean, Stan Musial and Ted Williams were both every bit as strong as I am. The difference is that they were always trying to meet the ball while I always wanted to kill it. If you swing for distance, you almost have to have the bat in motion before the pitch is even released. You can't chop at it and expect it to go 500 feet. You take a full cut and generate a little extra power, praying you don't miss.

So, with all due respect, I never figured myself to be a Pete Rose. Charlie Hustle, right? The world's greatest singles hitter. He chokes the bat, protects the plate, and concentrates on getting a piece of the ball. It's his thing. And I have a world of admiration for him. However, if I had played my career hitting singles like Pete, I'd wear a dress.

Now, Ted Williams is a man after my own heart. He hit for distance. He had 521 lifetime home runs. He had the best bat control of anyone I ever saw. Only once in my entire career did I talk to him about the science of hitting. Actually, I was talking to him one day in the clubhouse before an All-Star game and I said, "Hey, Ted, maybe you can tell me the secret of your success."

He said, "Sure. Come here, let me show you something. You're a switch-hitter, Mantle, so which hand do you grip the bat with and which hand do you guide it with?"

I said, "How the hell do I know?"

He said, "Pay attention. You gotta grip the bat with one hand and guide it with the other, see?" He grabbed a bat. "This is tight, you understand? Here, let me see you do this—no, not that—this!" I thought, "I gotta do this? Shit, I won't get a hit for two weeks." He said, "Let's see your stance. Hmm. Take a deep breath, plant your back foot against the front foot, grip the bat with this hand, arch your elbow, and don't lock your hips . . ."

By now I didn't know which end was up. He got me crazy just thinking about it.

Billy and I were roommates that year. In fact, we roomed together from then until he was traded in 1957. And let me tell you, we had some fun. The team put us up in swanky hotels around the league, places like the Shoreham, the Kenmore, the Book Sheraton, the Chase, the Del Padro on Lake Michigan in Chicago, the Wade Park Manor in Cleveland.

Between road trips Billy and I and our wives would sit around in our New York apartment, taking strolls, sitting in air-conditioned movies, but mostly sitting around at home in our bathing suits—no cross ventilation and all that heat—just watching to see if the cord hanging from the window shade would move. Sometimes a whole day would pass with no breeze, the cord straight and still.

We had some funny nights in the apartment. I remember once, it must have been one in the morning. Billy came creeping on his hands and knees down the hallway to peek into our bedroom. I was creeping along to peek into his and we bumped heads in the dark. *"Shhhhh!"* he whispered, then we both cracked up.

Terrific times. If I tasted the high life in 1951, I got a bellyful starting in 1952—especially on the road. Parties, flashy people, hard liquor, staying out really late. Billy and I were often the life of the party. We wouldn't go upstairs to our old room until we were just about ready to drop. And I remember the night that we clinched the pennant. There was a celebration at the Hotel Warwick in Philadelphia. We stayed to the bitter end, telling jokes and drinking scotch.

Later, in the elevator, I asked, "How's Lois?"

"She's fine," said Billy. "She's going out west soon to have the baby."

Merlyn was pregnant, too. And I knew our days in the apartment up on Grand Concourse were numbered. I guess I was a bit sorry to see those good times end. But I was pretty excited about having a kid of my own. A boy, I hoped.

In the National League the Brooklyn Dodgers came back, beating out the Giants by four games to clinch the pennant. Now they went gunning for us. It took us seven games to beat them. I'd say Allie Reynolds, Vic Raschi, Johnny Mize, Gene Woodling, and Bob Kuzava were important contributors. And Billy saved the victory with his breathtaking running catch of Jackie Robinson's bases loaded, two-out wind-blown pop fly that nearly landed on the mound. My personal highlights were: homering off Joe Black in the deciding game and Robinson hitting a line drive to me in right center, three skips into my glove. He rounded first base, acting like he would stop. I used to pick guys off first on that play pretty often. This time Casey had told me that Robinson would be watching for my throw. So after I caught the ball on the bounce, I faked a throw behind him. And sure enough, Robinson took off for second. I threw to Billy and we had him out by ten or fifteen feet.

I'll never forget the sight: Jackie getting up, dusting himself off, and giving me a little tip of the hat, his eyes saying, "I'll get you next time."

After the Series he came into our clubhouse and shook my hand. "You're a helluva ballplayer," he said. I thought, "Man, what a class guy. I never could have done that, not in a million years." I'm really a bad loser.

Later, back in Commerce, the main drag was glistening under bright skies as district bands and drum corps from all over Ottawa County marched along. Merlyn and I were in the backseat of an open convertible, waving at the crowds. Literally hundreds lining the sidewalks to give me a hero's welcome.

That night they staged a banquet at the old Spartan Cafeteria. My family and friends were pretty excited. I made a brief speech—three words of thanks. Then I sat on the dais, with Barney Barnett alongside, plus Tom Greenwade, Allie Reynolds, my mom, Roy and Ray, Barbara, little Butch, and Merlyn. I felt more than grateful. I was so damn proud of them all. If only my father could've been there.

Like he once said, "It all comes down to winning." It's what you work for all your life. And now the thrill of knowing I was a

Yankee starter, that we were the champs. Well, no thrill ever seemed bigger or more rewarding than that one. Somehow the wins seemed to get less and less exciting as the years went by. This was special. I was young and somehow it meant the world. How many times can you feel the same intensity as the first time?

Chapter *12*

After all that notoriety in New York, though, things hadn't changed much in Oklahoma, aside from the Spartan Cafeteria banquet. Total strangers in Commerce, who had never given me a second glance, were behaving like old buddies. And I suddenly discovered some "close" relatives I'd never even heard of before.

But for the most part, life returned to normal. I remember running into a distant relative from Spavinaw one day.

"Hey, you're Mickey, one of Mutt's boys, right?"

"Yeah . . ."

"Well, what you been doing these days?"

"I've been with the Yankees for two years."

"You don't say." Just like I'd been working in the mines all along!

Merlyn and I built a new house across town from my mother's. Altogether we put $16,000 into it. Merlyn's father ordered the lumber and got us a real bargain, as he owned a lumberyard in Picher. I wasn't busted, mind you, but in those days when you won the World Series you didn't get $50,000, you got $7,000.

One afternoon I got a phone call. It was from Billy Martin, who was in Oakland, talking about his off-season. I detected something in his voice. No, the baby was doing fine. They named her Kelly Ann and he had been attending a lot of banquets, always on the go . . . And finally his voice dropped. "Lois wants a divorce."

"What? I can't believe it."

"It's true, Mick. But I love her. I didn't want this to happen."

He said he would call me soon and let me know if anything

had changed. "I'll probably spend the winter in Kansas City," he said. "Maybe I can get myself together there."

I didn't see him again until spring training.

In March 1953 the lineup was set. Casey had Joe Collins at first, Billy at second, Rizzuto at short, McDougald at third, and Yogi—unfailingly—the catcher, with Ralph Houk and Charlie Silvera backing him up. Yogi hardly ever missed a game, so Ralph and Charlie languished in the bullpen. It's unfortunate; they played behind Yogi, otherwise they surely would have been starters. Bauer, Woodling, Noren, and myself were the outfielders, and Whitey Ford returned from the service to join our starting pitchers: Raschi, Reynolds, and Lopat. And we had Johnny Mize. He provided the bench power. Strong as a bull. He led the National League in many offensive categories over his career: doubles once, triples once, home runs four times, and RBIs three times. The Big Cat also won a batting title over there and was among the league leaders several times. This would be his fifth and last season as a Yankee. After that he retired, carrying home a .312 lifetime batting average, and later made it to the Hall of Fame.

As for the man, I can tell you that he came from Demorest, Georgia: slow-talking, shrewd, suspicious, quick to criticize.

We were playing the Dodgers in the 1953 World Series. Carl Erskine pitched the third game. He had a great overhand curveball; it started out eye high and it would drop in front of the plate, making a lot of hitters look foolish. That game he struck out fourteen batters. I was foolish four times and Joe Collins was foolish four times—eight right there—and meanwhile Mize is on the bench, grumbling, "How the hell can you guys swing at those lousy pitches?" Casey inserts him as a pinch hitter. A dramatic moment because Don Bollweg had just struck out to tie the record. So here comes Mize, swaggering up to the plate. He takes three swings at Erskine's specialty and misses completely. The fourteenth strikeout, setting a new World Series record.

Another thing about Mize, he loved to save money. We always used to look for deals on clothes downtown, but Mize always knew where to get a better buy. A real expert on what was selling where and for how much. Well, I had bought a suit. It cost $150, a small fortune in those days. Now Mize sees me wearing it. He says, "Hey, that's nice. Where did you get it?" I said, "Oh, I got it at Kolmer-Marcus." His eyes widened. "Kolmer-Marcus? Oh my, why did you go there?" Now his eyes narrowed. "How much did you pay for it?" "A hundred and fifty dollars, John." He says, "Oh God, you were robbed!" Then confidentially, "Listen, Mickey, anytime you want, see me. I can get you a better suit than that for a helluva lot less."

Once when we were playing the Browns, we were staying at the Chase Hotel. The bus was due to leave at 5 P.M. for the ballpark.

A sweltering day, no air-conditioning on the bus, and Whitey is in the hotel lobby playing the pinball machine. We're waiting, with Mize complaining loudly about the heat. Finally he says, "Who are we waiting for?" And somebody said, "Ford."

"Get him on here. What the hell's going on?"

At last, Whitey climbs aboard and Mize says, "Goddamn, Ford, don't you know this bus is supposed to leave at five o'clock?" Naturally everybody's looking but not saying anything because it's Mize. Whitey plops right down next to him, crosses his arms, yawns, and speaks to the ceiling. "What's on sale today, John?"

Whitey was funny and sharp. A casual talker, good-natured, always with a slick approach. He and Billy were friends before I came to the Yankees in 1951, but the three of us became as close as brothers. Close as I ever got with my own.

Whitey was a streetwise kid from Astoria, Queens, and Billy got his street smarts in Berkeley, California. We were young and determined. We had the feeling that nothing could stop us. We were going to be the best damned ballplayers in the world.

As it turned out, Whitey entered the Hall of Fame in 1974. No pitcher deserved it more. Just look at his lifetime winning percentage: .690. Then look at Nolan Ryan's record. Even though he's a great strikeout pitcher, he wins one, loses one. Always around .500. Yet Nolan gets a million dollars for breaking even. Whitey and Nolan—no contest. I don't care what the situation was, how high the stakes were—the bases could be loaded and the pennant riding on every pitch, it never bothered Whitey. He pitched his game. Cool. Crafty. Nerves of steel. Only thing is, while Casey managed us he would never use Whitey in rotation. He saved him for the stronger clubs and held him out against the weaker ones. If Casey had pitched him in rotation, he would have had more 20-game seasons than he did. When Ralph Houk took over, Whitey really came on, racking up 25 wins in 1961, then winning 24 in 1963 to lead the league in wins *and* percentage both years. No telling how many more games he would've won if given the opportunity to pitch every fourth day. For me, he was the greatest pitcher who ever lived.

And Billy was special, too. During our Yankee years he wasn't the most graceful infielder you ever saw. Certainly Jerry Coleman was a lot smoother at second base. No, Billy wasn't pretty to watch, but he would always find a way to beat you. Which is why he became a great manager.

There was a guy named Harry Byrd. He pitched for a while for the Philadelphia Athletics. A tall right-hander from South Carolina. Great big guy. Threw real hard. Sometimes he'd run our right-handed hitters right out of the box with sidearm fastballs inside, shaving them closer than the family barber. So one time before starting a series against the A's, Casey calls a clubhouse meeting and says, "Listen, we gotta do something about this guy Byrd. I'll give anybody a hundred dollars for getting hit tonight."

Sure enough, Billy got hit three times. He stood a hair away from the plate, practically over it, taking three shots in the ribs. After the game he walked over to Casey and said, "Skip, you owe me three hundred bucks."

Whitey and Billy were a lot alike. And I'm not so sure they would have been as close if I hadn't been there. They were both leaders, strong-willed and stubborn. I was more of the follower; I went along with their ideas. Who knows what might have happened if I hadn't provided a softer edge. The point is, we always enjoyed each other's company. Usually we were all together. There were cartoons that came out in the New York papers in those days that showed the three of us as the Dead

End Kids. Casey would be the principal up on the platform and we would be like three truant schoolboys awaiting our punishment—but we'd be hiding slingshots and BB guns behind our backs, ready to cut loose again.

Billy and Whitey have heard me joke often enough that if it weren't for them, I could've played ball till I was forty years old.

On April 10, 1953, I hit a home run over the 100-foot-high grandstand at Forbes Field. Until then only Babe Ruth and Ted Beard had done it. Of course I'm proud of that. But let's be honest. The greater accomplishment was getting to Forbes Field in the first place.

On April 9, we were winding our way back from Florida to open the season, living on the train and playing exhibition games along the way. It's bitter cold when we arrive in Cincinnati. So we play the game, and then Whitey, Billy and I make a beeline across the river, to Covington, Kentucky, a live-wire place, to have some fun before catching the train to Pittsburgh. We had to be back at the station at ten o'clock for the all-night ride, which would get us in the next morning in plenty of time for batting practice.

Okay.

At nine-thirty I started looking for the others. We finally found each other at eleven, too late for the train. We said, "The hell with it. We'll catch a plane in the morning and get to Forbes Field with time to spare." We said, "Yeah, Casey will never know. We'll act like we were on the train." Billy: "That sounds okay."

I get up at dawn, unglue my eyes, and stare through the window. A frigging blizzard. An hour later we're at the airport. It's socked in, snow up to your ass and all of the flights are canceled. Holy shit, what do we do now? Whitey says, "No problem. Follow me." So we grab a cab. I slide into the front seat and tell the driver, "Take us to Pittsburgh." He goes, "C'mon, buddy, I hear that crap all the time." He thinks we're either off our rockers, wise guys, or eccentric millionaires out on a lark. Finally I convince him that we're serious. He gets on the horn and calls his router. "Listen, I got three monkeys here who say they want to go to Pittsburgh. What's the charge?" It comes to $500. And somehow we get there. But the team is already taking batting practice. All Whitey has to do is run with the pitchers. Who'd ever notice? The batting cage is another story altogether. You show up or else. Well, me and Billy are in the locker room, pulling our socks on as fast as we can, praying Casey hasn't missed us yet. We're hunched over, tying our shoes. I'm whispering to Billy, at the same time concentrating on getting dressed. Finally I give him a sidelong glance and see that I'm actually talking to myself. Billy's gone. He's in the toilet. And there's a hand on my shoulder. Casey's voice: "I don't know where you assholes have been. I don't know what you've done, but I wanta know . . . Where's the other little bastard?"

He storms out, saying me and Billy are going to play the whole ball game, every inning. Believe me, after that long drive from Cincinnati, slugging through the snow while dozing in fits and starts along the way, besides being nearly $200 short because of the cab fare, I'm not looking forward to playing tiddledywinks, let alone baseball.

And here's Billy, sneaking out of the toilet, laughing like hell. We go out, no batting practice, just a couple of minutes left to play catch and limber up. My first time at bat I hit that long home run over the grandstand.

Casey has a pasty smile waiting. "Nice hit, Mickey. Take the rest of the day off."

I walk right past Billy, who's sitting at the far end of the dugout, his eyes upturned, and he's whining, "Teacher's pet . . . teacher's pet . . ."

We were boys then.

April. At an exhibition game in Brooklyn—roars, jeers, excitement—I'm about ready to step into the batter's box, idly chatting with Roy Campanella and the plate umpire . . . and hear the public address announcement booming: "Ladies and gentlemen . . . now hitting . . . number seven . . . Mickey Mantle." I stride up and the voice booms even louder: "Mickey doesn't know it yet, but he just became the father of an eight-pound-twelve-ounce baby boy."

A month later the season was in full swing. I still hadn't seen my son, Mickey Elvin, named after me and my dad. I guess the tension was getting to me because I had broken out in a rash. Every day I had to cover myself with calamine lotion.

Well, the rash kept getting worse—especially whenever I would sweat. And you can imagine how much I was sweating.

So the doctor told me not to play for a few days to give the rash a chance to heal. Casey told me to go home, see the baby, see the wife, and recover. But he wanted me to come back as soon as I could.

On the flight home, the rash cleared up like magic. I saw the baby—a cute little redhead, just like my dad had predicted—and while there I decided to get in some fishing.

A photographer from the Miami paper caught me with the fishing pole and the picture ended up in the paper. The next day Casey was on the phone, ordering me to get back to the team on the next plane.

Because of baseball we had to move all the time. From our home in Oklahoma to spring training, to New Jersey, where we rented a different house each year. It was really tough on Merlyn after all the kids were born.

I generally traveled those long hops by plane with the team and she had to follow in the car with the children.

I rented our first house in New Jersey that summer of 1953. Sometime in July or August I went out to the airport and picked up Merlyn and little Mickey.

I was really happy to have them with me and we were relieved to be out of our apartment in the Concourse Plaza. At the same time, the responsibilities began to weigh me down. There I was, barely twenty-two, with a wife and a child to support. I also had my family back home. My father was dead and I was the major breadwinner. My position with the Yankees, certainly until that great year in 1956, was hardly secure—I had to prove myself every day. To top it off, poor little Mickey was sick with asthma and he was also allergic to milk.

I was busy in 1953 between March and mid-October. Mostly

on the field. Early in the season at Washington, I hit a towering fly off Chuck Stobbs. The ball just carried and carried. They say it left the field at the 391-foot mark, struck a beer sign on the football scoreboard, cleared Griffith Stadium, and landed in somebody's backyard. Our publicity director, Red Patterson, was up in the press box. He says he went searching for the ball, found it, took measurements, and said it was a 565-footer. The next morning the papers were full of accounts of Mickey Mantle's tape-measure home run.

The thing I remember best—Billy was on third when I hit it. As usual, I rounded the bases with my head down.

The Yankees always wanted me to tip my hat after I hit a homer and run the bases with my head up. But I didn't want to show up the pitcher any more than I already had, so I would keep my head down. You can see it in the photographs taken after most of my home runs. It almost looks like I'm embarrassed.

Anyway, as I came around the bases, there was Billy, tagged up at third, laughing. I reached the bag and almost ran into him. But he got away just before I fell over him. I followed him home.

Then the big fat headlines, maps, diagrams, arrows pointing to the scoreboard where the ball went over, photos, feature stories, interviews, and full accounts of what was supposed to be the longest home run in major league history. Yet people forget that Billy hit the home run that won the game.

I guess I should mention a brawl at Sportsman's Park, one of those baseball fights that started when Browns catcher Clint Courtney singled and deliberately spiked Phil Rizzuto, who was covering second base. He cut Phil's leg in two places. The Yankees immediately reacted. Billy led the charge. I also saw Whitey, Gil McDougald, Allie Reynolds, Joe Collins, Hank Bauer, and a few other guys jump in to pound the shit out of Courtney. If Casey weren't so old, I think he would've joined the fight. Me? I'm not a fighter. Most of the time I used to run in to be a peacemaker. Billy Martin and Clint Courtney liked to fight. When this one was over, one of the umpires had a dislocated collarbone. Gene Woodling narrowly missed getting skulled by a bottle thrown from the stands and Courtney's glasses were ground into smithereens. Whitey claims that particular contribution.

"Look at all the money Rocky Marciano gets for knocking guys out," said Billy. "I didn't make nothing and put on a better fight. On top of which, I got fined!"

Then a day against the A's, playing hurt with a swollen right knee, I pinch hit a grand-slam homer over the left center field roof. The following night in Philadelphia we had a near-disaster. It happened on the team bus while racing from Shibe Park to the train station. I sat in the back between two seats. The driver tried to enter a lane marked TAXIS ONLY. There was a low overhead sign. No way to get through and we crashed. The top of the bus was sliced open as if by a giant can opener. Baggage came tumbling down off the racks and we went sailing in all directions. It was chaotic. Gene Woodling sprawled forward all the way from the backseat, winding up on his hands and knees near the driver's seat. The driver went through the windshield. The two guys who got hurt the worst were Johnny Sain and Allie Reynolds. In a few minutes everybody was off the bus, except our trainer, Gus Mauch, who made believe he had a broken neck or something. I guess he figured it was his chance to sue the bus line and collect a fortune. As he sat there, all twisted up like a pretzel, somebody outside yelled, "Don't light a match! There's gasoline all around!" Gus catapulted from his seat, grabbed his medicine kit in midair, and *zoom*—he was off the bus in a split second. Fortunately, the driver recovered.

Shortly after that Allie retired. I understand he collected a small sum from the bus company in an arbitrated settlement. Me and Billy demanded all kinds of compensation. We asked for over $500 apiece, but got nothing for our troubles. What the hell. Give us credit for trying.

In August, during a series with the White Sox, I reinjured my right knee on a pivot throw to second base. The ligaments were torn and for the rest of the season I wore a brace. Besides, I was being hounded by letters from people who still didn't like me— injured *or* healthy.

I received hundreds of letters, but one in particular sounded kinda serious. It was from a guy who said that he'd gotten a brand-new .32 rifle. He threatened to shoot me with it if I showed up for the Red Sox series starting on September 7.

I gave the letter to Casey. He said we'd better inform the FBI. This brought in a pair of agents. Typical J. Edgar Hoover guys: conservatively dressed, very polite, and something cold and steely in their voices. They pulled me off at the Hartford station, one stop before Boston.

We went to a restaurant. One of the agents leaned across the table and said, "I think you ought to be prudent and miss this series, Mickey." The other agent agreed, then told me there was always the distinct possibility of a deranged person showing up at Fenway Park to shoot me. "He could hit you from a thousand different locations and never be seen."

"Thank you for the warning, but I'm going to Boston anyway."

"Okay, it's your ass," they said.

All I remember is, I hit a home run in one of the games and it was the fastest time I ever circled the bases. Now, while packing to get out of Boston (the FBI had warned me not to stand near any hotel windows), I didn't realize I was walking past mine when suddenly Billy hollered, "Look out!" I dove under the bed and he doubled up *laughing!* From there it was a running gag, with Billy hollering "Look out! Get down!" everywhere we went.

Another pennant for the Yankees. Five in a row. When we finished thirteen games ahead of the second-place Indians, there was a victory dinner held at the Stadium Club. It fizzled and died before the evening really got started, so Johnny Kucks, Andy Carey, Gus Triandos, Whitey, Billy, me, and several others—about fourteen of us—decided we'd have a much better time elsewhere. We slipped out and went to the Latin Quarter. We saw a great show. A high-kicking chorus line, brassy music, plenty of drinks on our table. Everything was mellow. Then the check came. Billy said he wanted to take care of it. I said, "Naw, let's all chip in. We can handle it."

Whitey had a different approach. "Why don't we sign the tab and have them send it to the stadium. We'll settle up later."

"Well, in that case—" And Whitey signed the tab for me, Billy, and himself, with Dan Topping's name also affixed as the responsible party.

Walking east toward our hotel on Lexington Avenue, I noticed something fidgety about Billy's movements. He was bent forward like Groucho, hurrying along, muttering, "We shoulda paid the bill" and "We'll get in trouble" and looking back and forth anxiously as I tried to keep up with him.

Early next morning the phone rang. Billy answered, which he hardly ever did. I heard him say, "Yes, sir, yes, sir, we'll be right there." He jumped into his clothes. I asked him what was going on. He said, "We're in for it, pal. That was George Weiss."

Now I'm talking to him through the bathroom door. "Well, what the hell did he want?"

Between the gurgling and spitting, he says, "We've got fifteen minutes to be in his office or he's gonna fine us five thousand apiece."

I jumped into my clothes.

We rushed to the Squibb Building on Fifth Avenue—Yankee headquarters—sat down in the outer office, and waited an hour. We sat there like two truants from grade school, waiting to be sent in to see the principal—the guy with the paddle. The secretary said we could go in.

Weiss was glaring at us. He said, "I have a full report here." He jabbed his finger at a thick manila folder. "What do you think? We're stupid? We don't know what you two have been doing?" He tilted his chair back and with slitted eyes added, "We know everything. So I'm fining you a thousand each for what's been going on all year. That's for openers. And now—" He buzzed the secretary. "Tell Mr. Topping the boys are ready to see him."

We waited another hour for Topping. Then we walked in. And he threw the Latin Quarter bill at us. "What is this?" I looked at it. Billy looked at it and handed it to me.

"Well?"

I confessed. "Yes, we signed the tab. We wanted to have a

good time. The party at the Stadium Club ended too soon. We were only . . ." He said, "I can have you all sent to jail for forgery."

Billy turned white as a sheet. "Mr. Topping, it's a mistake. Please, I'll take the blame."

It didn't matter. We were all fined $500 each, except for Andy and Gus because Topping didn't know they were there.

We took the Dodgers in six games. Billy had twelve hits and eight RBIs, including a single that scored Bauer with the Series winning run. I guess you could call it a special occasion for Casey, maybe his finest hour. He had brought five consecutive world championships to New York. And this time we celebrated in royal style. Players and wives, whole families, executive groups, media people, honored guests—they were all at the victory party. Food, drinks, and music came from all sides. In the middle of everything, Del Webb walked over to our table. "Don't worry about the fine, boys."

"Thanks."

He pointed to Whitey, who sat at a nearby table. "Tell Ford to come on over and talk to me and I'll do the same for him."

A moment later I tapped Whitey's arm. "Webb wants to see you."

"What about?"

"He's going to forget the fine."

"To hell with him," he said, cutting into his steak. And I figured we were in trouble again.

Chapter 13

Willie Miranda was with us for part of the 1953 season. He occasionally filled in at shortstop. A crackerjack fielder, but weak at the bat. I liked him, actually. Miranda came from Cuba. He had a cheery personality and spoke pretty good English. One day he started telling me about his country. He said it would make a wonderful vacation spot for me and Merlyn. "You must go," he insisted. "You'll have lots of fun."

So shortly after the World Series we flew down to Cuba with Harold Youngman and his wife Stella. To say the least, the island was everything Willie had described. Magnificent beaches. Easygoing Latin surroundings. Wonderful climate. A real paradise. Except—at the time Batista was in power, a law unto himself. Nothing moved unless he put his stamp of approval on it. Willie didn't tell me this and in those days I don't think it would have made much of an impression anyway. My thing was baseball, not politics. Of course, Willie did air some facts about the conditions there. When I met him at our hotel in Havana, he talked of the revolution and a guy named Fidel Castro who was holed up in the mountains with rebel forces. Just then Harold Youngman came over, shook Willie's hand warmly, and said something like *"¡Viva la revolución!"*—which got Willie a little nervous. In a low whisper: "Harold, we don't kid around about that kind of thing here. Batista is a devil. Please keep it down."

The Hotel Nacional had a plush gambling casino and even the most naïve tourist could pick out young prostitutes at the bars. Same problem on the street. One morning Merlyn and I were strolling along when a little kid about twelve sidled over. "Meester, Meester, would you like to have my sister?"

I laughed. "How much?" Merlyn glared at me. Still in good humor, I told the kid, "Stay here. I'll get rid of the old lady." She was shocked. So I sent the kid away and we walked back to the hotel, very slowly—until I convinced her it was only a joke.

The Cubans played an exciting brand of baseball. Within the next dozen years a number of them were starring in the big leagues. Camilo Pascual, Bert Campaneris, Tony Oliva, Tony Perez, Pedro Ramos, Luis Tiant, and Orlando Pena, to name just a few. I may even have watched one or two during our stay. At the invitation of the government, I attended a game with Merlyn. We had special box seats and I received a standing ovation. Meanwhile a bunch of Batista militia were stationed in the dugouts with machine guns, expecting the guerrillas to attack at any moment. Above the roar of the crowd we could hear sporadic firing. Weird. All that cheering with the war so close. We cut the vacation short. Couldn't wait to leave.

By late October I was back working for Harold Youngman. I helped him out as best I could. Not that he needed anything, materially speaking. He was already a wealthy man. He had built this fine home in Baxter Springs. His road construction business was booming and he was adding more and more equipment to handle asphalt paving jobs that kept him hopping in three states.

Meanwhile I still wanted to have some fun, so I set up a basketball team: the Mickey Mantle–Southwest Chat All-Stars, after Harold's company. Roy and Ray and some other exceptional athletes from the area were on the roster. We played now and then at high school gymnasiums. I was the coach and got into a couple of games. Once or twice we even took on the Harlem Globetrotters, who happened to be touring in our area.

I felt good. What could go wrong?

I soon found out. While switching directions on a fast break to the basket, I twisted my bad knee painfully and landed in a Springfield, Missouri, hospital, where Dr. Yancey removed a piece of torn cartilege. Three days later I went home. When spring training came around, I had a slight limp. As a result, I began favoring that leg, which eventually weakened the other knee and led to pulls and strains elsewhere. The arms, the shoulders, the back—they dogged me season after season. Nobody to blame but myself.

Well, part of me can't sit still. Something I can't explain. Starting in my teens, I was as restless and hungry as any kid you can conceive of, always wanting to win, hating to lose. To me, it's like a death each time it happens.

And that winter I was on the *go*. Kinda made it tough for Merlyn, though it sure was good for me and Billy Martin. He had come down from Berkeley to visit us and he will tell you it was one of the best times he ever had, especially when we went out hunting quail.

There's an old saying in Oklahoma: "You can't eat a quail a day seven days in a row." But Billy could eat four of them every morning for breakfast. Gained twenty pounds over the winter. When he wasn't eating at our house, he would be at my mother's. She'd fix him biscuits and gravy, a half dozen eggs, pork chops. Once his plate was loaded, he'd wolf it all down and come up for more. We were like family to him.

Billy more or less accepted the world as he saw it. You are what you are and don't bother me beyond that point. His nature overrode everything else. Still, there were moments when he'd start thinking about Lois and he'd get down. He couldn't accept the reality of a divorce. During the 1953 season I'd see him on the phone, begging her to take him back. Nothing worked. She'd hang up and he'd get so distraught. One particular day, when he realized there was no longer any hope for a reconciliation, he wrecked our hotel room. I mean, he literally tore it apart.

After the season Billy went on a Far East tour with the Eddie Lopat All-Stars. Before he left, we agreed that he would winter with us in Commerce. We'd do some hunting and fishing. He didn't have to ask. I knew he had nothing left in Berkeley.

So there he was, in front of our house, squeezing out of a brand-new Cadillac convertible, all weighed down with a bunch of Japanese cameras, field binoculars, silk dressing robes, little statues, a samurai sword, jewelry cases, probably $5,000 worth of stuff. He stood there, wrapped in a sheepskin coat, grinning from ear to ear. "Hi, pard, let's have a drink."

Merlyn was wondering what the hell we were getting into next. We took off in his car. The state was dry, no liquor served at bars or restaurants. I said, "We can get served at a place called the Stables. It's a private club over in Miami." Before going in, he removed his coat, placed it lovingly on the front seat, and went around to lock the doors. I said, "Don't bother." He said, "Are you nuts? I've got valuable merchandise with me." I said, "Billy, this is Oklahoma. You don't have to lock your doors." So we went in and had a couple of drinks apiece, rushing it because Merlyn was waiting on us to have dinner. Then we came out and found his car totally emptied. No cameras, nothing. He said, "You idiot, if we stayed in there for another drink, I wouldn't have had any wheels left either." Fortunately, he had locked the trunk, or they might have stolen his clothes too. As we drove and drove around Commerce, he was half out the window, gawking at passing cars. He kept saying, "Man oh man, if I see a guy wearing my sheepskin coat, I'll kill him." It was his introduction to Oklahoma. We never did find the coat.

Truth is, the people at home already knew how tough Billy was supposed to be. Their attitude, at first, was sort of guarded. There were snide remarks, references to his so-called virility, things like that.

One night Merlyn and I were doing something and Billy went over to the 400 Club in Commerce by himself. I planned to join him there. Well, I got to the club just in time to see Billy inviting a couple of guys to step outside with him. Seems they'd been teasing him, testing his bravery, and I guess he'd about had enough. They could tell that he wouldn't back down. He was ready to go.

From then on, everybody knew that Billy was for real. Nobody bothered him again. In fact, they got to love him and he loved everybody in Commerce. Even one of my best friend's wife.

I owned a Lincoln and we'd go road hunting for quail. The method was pretty simple. We'd pile into the car with a bottle of Jack Daniel's, then listen to country music on the radio—I'd taught Billy to love country music by then. In the cold weather, the quail would bunch together out of the wind in a ditch. Usually we'd find the coveys in a hedgerow.

Now, if you stopped the car as soon as you saw a covey, the quail would fly away before you could get off a shot. So instead we'd drive along real slow. As soon as a covey would come in sight, the man on the side nearest the birds would grab the wheel and keep driving. The man on the other side would get out and, when the car had cleared from his line of fire, he'd let go with the shotgun.

One day we were cruising along, looking for quail, when we saw a bunch of pickup trucks parked at a farmhouse. It was a public auction.

We stopped in, took our seats in the bleachers, and all of a sudden I saw the auctioneer pointing at us.

"Fifty. I have fifty. Do I have sixty?" And he pointed at us again. I started looking around, wondering who was bidding on this calf up on the block.

"Sixty, sixty-five, seventy. Do I have seventy? Seventy. Do I hear seventy-five? Sold to the man back in the top row for seventy."

Suddenly I realized that there wasn't anyone behind us. Billy had bought his first calf!

After he paid for it, I said, "What are you gonna do with that calf?" He had it on a halter, leading it with a long rope to my car. I said, "Billy, there's no way to fit that animal in here." He called over a boy. "Son, you want a calf?" The boy grinned from ear to ear. "Sure." Billy was happy. All he wanted was to see how it felt to buy something at an auction. I bet that boy never did know that he'd gotten a free calf from Billy Martin.

During this period Harold Youngman gave him a job. The same deal as mine. Part of Harold's business was to build highways. The other part was to bid on projects. He had to find out when new projects were in the planning stages, where they would be, how high the bidding might go. It was in this second stage where Billy and I came in—we were the public relations men. We'd fly in Harold's plane, a twin-engined Beechcraft, to various towns in the area and meet with the planning commissioners. We'd always bring Yankee caps and souvenirs, create goodwill, and pick up leads for Harold when we could.

I remember one time Harold was busy, so he sent me and Billy up to a place near St. Louis in the Beechcraft. It was snowing heavily and instead of landing on the runway we crash-landed in a cornfield. I still remember how scared we were and how the dry stalks beat against the underside of the plane.

Other than that, the work was easy. And Harold was pleased with us. He would sit in the cockpit, smiling, every so often turning around and saying, "Good work, boys. I couldn't have done it without you."

You couldn't help but love the man.

In the dead of winter, it gets colder than hell around Commerce, Oklahoma—just perfect weather for duck hunting. So we put on all the clothes we could find—long johns, galoshes over our shoes, sweaters, coats—you name it. Billy weighed about 165 pounds, but by the time we got him dressed, he probably weighed closer to 200.

We'd get into the car, Billy and me, along with my twin brothers Roy and Ray, and drive around the countryside. Some of the farmers welcomed hunters, others didn't, but sitting real close to about every farm there would be a tank (our term for a pond to water animals) and the tank would be dammed up at one end. Now, the trick in duck hunting is to sneak up on the dam side of the tank, then check to see if there were any wild ducks on the surface of the water. Technically, you couldn't shoot at tame ducks, but that rule—like many others—wouldn't stop us. The best way around the problem was to get the ducks to fly and then shoot because the tame ducks won't fly and the wild ducks will. Anyway, it's all poaching if you don't get the farmer's permission, which we never did. You've got to know what you're doing and this was Billy's first time.

That morning we found two or three tanks and got a few birds. Our third stop was at a pond located 50 to 100 yards from the road. We parked, inched up to the dam, and opened fire.

Then I looked over my shoulder and saw a white pickup truck

parking next to our car. On the side was a painted sign: OKLA-
HOMA GAME COMMISSION.

The first thing you do, of course, is run, even though what you
really have to do is get back to your car, which in this case was
parked on the other side of the game warden's truck.

We started running and those heavy clothes really weighed us
down—especially Billy, who began to fall behind. Next thing I
knew, Billy stopped.

"You guys go ahead. I'm going to shoot it out with him."

The game warden must have heard him because he turned
tail and started back for his truck. He must have thought we
were just plain crazy 'cause nobody had probably ever threatened to shoot at him before. The moment he was safely in the
truck, he took off. We jumped in our car and went off in the
other direction.

That's the last we heard of it.

Once in a while Billy and I would drive the Commerce High
basketball team to their games. Late one afternoon we went to
Vinita, about twenty miles away. He took the Commerce "A"
team, which included Roy and Ray, and I took the "B" team—
racing off in my Lincoln and his Cadillac, the seniors sitting in
both cars. It was almost dark and here we were, traveling
around eighty miles an hour, Billy on my tail, when suddenly he
opened her up full blast, getting ahead of me and roaring to the
top of a hill. I figured he would slow down, but he went even
faster, practically flying to the bottom where the road crossed.
A second later he swerved left to avoid a roll of barbed wire
(dropped by a truck?) and went into a spin. I slammed on the
brakes. At the bottom of the hill, I came upon his car. It was
turned sideways, the tires flat. He stumbled out of the wreck,
along with the kids, their eyeballs wide as dinner plates. And
Billy—the sheer gall! No sign of worry, just a wan smile. "What's
the matter? You give up?"

My twin brothers Ray and Roy were pretty fine athletes and
they certainly got a lot of practice chasing after balls when we
were kids. After they graduated from high school, they played

semi-pro ball for a team in the tri-state area and I felt they could make the big leagues. So I told Casey Stengel and he said, "Okay, I'll have Tom Greenwade take a look." But since they were coming to visit me in New York anyway, he decided to see them while they were in the city.

The twins drove my Cadillac up to New York. Three days later they arrived at the Concourse Plaza Hotel, where we had a great reunion. Only I didn't say a word about my conversation with Casey. I just brought them to Yankee Stadium. A half hour later Roy and Ray were in pinstripes, hitting batting practice pitchers with ease—long drives and sharp hits through the infield. Casey scratched his chin and said to me, "What do they feed you boys in Oklahoma?"

That June, 1954, Greenwade signed my brothers to a Yankee farm club contract. Class D, at McAllister in the Sooner State League. Both hit over .300, showing good power. The following year they went to our instructional camp in St. Petersburg. Roy was tremendous, batting .400 against the high minor league teams. Ray also excelled and they outran everyone except me, which lit some fires under people, namely the press guys who began speculating about an all-Mantle outfield. As it happened, the twins were assigned to Class C ball. Then Ray was drafted into the Army. Roy hurt his leg while running out a base hit and that finished his career. Two years later Ray got his Army discharge, but by then his enthusiasm for the game was gone.

I can't help thinking that when we were kids they had to go to all of my games and we played at home all the time. Maybe that's what eventually burned the twins out of baseball. Maybe they just got sick of it. Who knows, if our dad had been around a little longer, the all-Mantle outfield might have become a reality.

In those days, I lived it up and paid the price. I had to have another knee operation, once again at the Springfield hospital. In this instance, they removed a large fluid-filled cyst from behind my knee. When I got to Florida, Casey was livid. "If you had listened, you'd be playing now. But no—why listen?"

The irony is, I had a productive year anyway, batting an even

.300 and leading the league in runs scored with 129, besides making 20 assists, tops for all outfielders. I also knocked in over 100 runs for the first time (102) and hit more homers than ever before (27), but I also led the league in strikeouts again (107). The last month was soured because we lost a critical doubleheader to the Indians and fell eight and a half games off the pace. They took the pennant, deservedly so, with 111 wins, breaking the major league record. Keep in mind that we won 103 games, no small achievement, for a second-place finish— and this without the likes of Johnny Mize, who had retired before the season. Then there was the callous dumping of Vic Raschi the previous winter. George Weiss sold him to the Cardinals because of a contract dispute. To make an example of him so other veterans wouldn't hold out. And the Army snatched Billy Martin away in early April.

Jerry Coleman was my roommate while Billy was in the Army. A dedicated, serious guy, his temperament was the exact opposite of Billy's. He was in every night at nine or ten and made sure he kept in good shape. He took vitamins. I'd watch him stand before the bathroom mirror. He'd stand there forever, chewing his vitamins, brushing his teeth, massaging his hair. He had a receding hairline. Remarkable how he would rub and rub his scalp, a regular ceremony. Of course nothing grew. But what hope, what energy he packed into those powerful fingers of his.

Jerry was a helluva ballplayer, a real fancy Dan at second base. He could turn beautiful double plays. The peculiar thing was his grip at the plate—bat handle close to the stomach, hands midway up the bat, as if he were about to punch himself. Worst grip I ever saw, but he got the job done.

Gil McDougald held his bat funny, too; the fat part almost touching the catcher's mask, while his left foot and chest faced the pitcher. Casey once said of him, "Shit, if he can hit .300 that way, he oughta be able to hit .400 holding the bat properly." The old man finally moved Gil around and I think it was a mistake because his average didn't go up. In fact, it tailed off a bit toward the end of his career. Which suggests something. You shouldn't mess with a batter's natural stance when he's either in a slump or looks silly at the plate. A good hitter will eventually correct himself without you trying to improve the way he swings the bat. But Gil did just about everything else right. A class ballplayer. Rookie of the Year in 1951. He could field most any infield position: second, third, or shortstop. Wherever he played he looked great. Then he hit the shot that bounced off Herb Score's skull, above the right eye. Sickening. I can still hear the *crack*, see Gil freeze halfway out of the batter's box, and Herb laying there on the mound, knocked cold, bleeding. One pitch and all that promise down the drain. It was tragic. It scarred Gil nearly as much as Herb. He was never quite the same after that.

When Bobby Brown left the game, he left with no regrets; *he* retired in 1954, still a young man, his future bright and promising. Of those I've played with, I think his situation came closest to mine, in the sense that his father always wanted him to play baseball, was always on him to do better, working tirelessly to prepare him for the majors. The same devotion as my dad's— "Goddamn, how could you have swung at that pitch?" Once Bobby had a lousy night at the stadium. His father drove him home. They were driving across the George Washington Bridge and Bobby's moaning, "Oh, I feel awful. I was terrible." When they came to the middle of the bridge, his father pulled over and stopped. He said, "Why don't you jump?"

It shows what can happen when you get totally wrapped up in dreams about somebody else's future. They become your own. And that's the kind of background Bobby had, same as mine, insofar as father-son relationships go.

Bobby and I had another thing in common. When he played for the Yankees, his uniform was No. 6. He spent most of the 1952 and all of the 1953 seasons in the military. When he returned in 1954, they gave me No. 7, and I wore it until the day I retired.

Bobby handled a bat pretty good and only a few others could match him as a pinch hitter. I won't mention his abilities at third base. I'd rather quote Casey again. "Bobby reminds me of a fella who's been hitting twelve years and fielding one." Maybe true. However, there's no question that his hands worked wonders in another profession. After retiring from the game, he took a hospital internship, then went on to Fort Worth, where he gained national recognition as a cardiologist, and completed the circle by coming back to baseball as president of the American League. Yes—an exceptional human being.

Chapter *14*

As a professional baseball player, I lived in two worlds and I had two families. In the summer, the team was my family—Billy and Hank and Whitey and all the other guys. The spotlight was always on, the pressure to win and achieve was always there. Our life was a constant round of parties, meetings with celebrities, public attention. And the team pretty much banded together as we traveled around the country or settled in for a home stand at the stadium.

But on the day of that last game—on the road or in New York —I was always ready to get back with my other family. After that final out in the World Series—win or lose—I couldn't wait to get in the car and go home. It was as if a big boulder had been lifted off my shoulders. I would know that for the next three or four months there would be nothing to do but relax, play with the kids, whatever.

That past winter of 1953–54, when Billy was with me, I fell into the routine of getting out of the house by saying we were going fishing. Instead, we would go into Joplin, have a few drinks, and before I knew it I was drunk. I wouldn't even think about going home.

So the next winter I had pretty much settled into that pattern. After the season, my work was done. So I started hanging around with guys who didn't have jobs and by noon most days you could find me in a bar with them, drinking.

There's no question that it became a bad problem. I know it took a toll on Merlyn and the kids. And I'm sure it took a few years off my baseball career.

One night in Commerce I left the house and Merlyn stood on the porch, asking how long I'd be gone.

"Just a couple of hours, honey."

She smiled, satisfied. And I went off to see my buddies at the 400 Club, my usual watering hole, where I started around nine in the evening, killing a few beers at a table along the bar, and meanwhile all the guys were bullshitting and ordering the same, then graduating to boilermakers, adding scotch and soda, vodka, wine. By now I was plastered on bourbon straight up and knew I was gonna be hung over in the morning.

It was practically five in the morning and I was on my way home. Going past my neighbor's house, I saw some activity. The guys were packing the car, so I stopped to say hello. They were going fishing and I said I'd join them. They were happy to have me along.

I said, "Lemme go home first. I gotta pick up my gear." One of the guys said, "I've got all the stuff in my trunk." So we took off. And for all Merlyn knew, somebody had kidnapped me because I didn't come home for two days.

Before falling into a drunken sleep, I figured we were going fishing at Grand Lakes or somewhere else close by. I didn't wake up till we reached Lead Hill, Arkansas. No phones or anything, and I couldn't call Merlyn to explain. So I stopped worrying about it and let the time roll by. Forty-eight hours later I was home with a nice catch of fresh bass. I thought Merlyn would be happy.

She opened the door. I brushed past her and deposited the fish on the kitchen table, as though nothing had happened. She said, "Your car was just sitting there, locked. Nobody knew where you were." She cried. "How can you do this to me?" I felt terrible, but I shrugged and went straight to bed without a word spoken about the whys and wherefores of my trip to Lead Hill.

Merlyn took a terrible mental beating that winter of 1954. She hardly ever knew where I was or what I was doing. One night, after spending an evening at a bar with my friends, I came home and found the front door locked. No sound inside, the place dark. I knocked and knocked, then walked to the garage. It was shut tight. I punched out some little paneled windows, stuck my hand through the splintered glass, unlocked the inside latch, and reached down to raise the door. A moment later I switched on the kitchen light. There was no food in the refrigerator. I stumbled into our bedroom. Her closet had been cleaned out. Damn! She had taken Mickey Jr., loaded the car, and left me.

Drunk as I was, I knew that she must have gone to her folks' place, so off I ran.

Fortunately, the guys who'd dropped me off had known something was wrong. They saw me break into the house and I guess they saw me cut my hand. They let me be for a bit, then followed me as I ran all the way to Cardin. Then they picked me up and drove me to the hospital. The cuts took about thirty stitches and after I was bandaged they took me over to Merlyn's family's house.

Mr. Johnson came to the door and I was still pretty hot.

"I know that Merlyn's here. But I just want the keys to my car."

"Mickey," he said, "you're too drunk to drive . . ."

"Like hell—"

"Now, settle down, Mickey."

"No. Throw me the keys and I'll leave."

"Well, Merlyn's clothes and stuff . . ."

"I don't care about that. Just do as I say or I'm going in after them."

He saw the bandages on my hand and shook his head. Five minutes later he brought out the keys. I strode to the Lincoln, clicked open the door, then threw Merlyn's clothes and groceries all over the yard. Her father looked at me as though I had gone crazy—and maybe I had. He said, "Come on, Mickey. You're in no condition . . ."

"My hand is okay. It's only a scratch." The car was in reverse, so I shifted, coming forward, the headlights glaring. But I didn't see the telephone pole. The car door flew open and hit the pole, which ripped the door off its hinges, smashing it against the front fender. That scared me. But the car didn't stop until it got stuck in a ditch near the road.

So I jumped from the car and started running down the highway toward Commerce in the dead of night like a wild man. Suddenly Mr. Johnson pulled alongside and yelled, "Get in. I'll drive you home."

The next day, after I sobered up, Merlyn came back home. And everything was all right again.

She deserves a lot of credit. She stood by me through the rowdy times, the drinking and carousing. I wouldn't admit it was getting out of hand.

Chapter 15

We won the pennant in 1955, but Brooklyn captured the World Series and made Johnny Podres an instant legend. The big talk in camp that spring, though, was the seventeen-player swap between us and the Baltimore Orioles and our acquisition of Elston Howard, the first black player in Yankee history.

Baltimore sent over five minor leaguers, shortstop Billy Hunter, and two right-handed pitchers: Don Larsen and Bob Turley. They were the keys to the whole deal. In return, we gave up Gene Woodling, Willie Miranda, pitchers Harry Byrd, Jim McDonald, Bill Miller, catchers Gus Triandos and Hal Smith, and two of our farm prospects.

I loved the way Bob Turley could pick up pitches from the opposing pitcher. He'd study them from the dugout and accurately pick out the little telltale signs indicating when a fastball was on its way. Bob would signal me with a piercing whistle if he saw one coming. More than once I'd hear it and unload a home run. Now, there were some giveaways that I spotted myself. For instance, one Boston pitcher would clomp down real hard on his front foot while releasing the fastball. That was as good as a whistle.

Turley could throw hard. When he was right, nobody threw harder. Besides his tips on pitchers, he was also very smart businesswise. Wherever we went, sooner or later I'd find him unfolding *The Wall Street Journal* and reading it from front to back. So we'd talk and he'd say, "Such-and-such stock should have a radiating effect on the market" or "Such-and-such stock should continue its bearish trend into the next quarter" and so forth. "Oh really?" Most of his tips were Greek to me.

Don Larsen is naturally remembered for his perfect game in the 1956 World Series. What most people forget is that he was

3–21 with the Orioles the year before the trade. As a Yankee, he won 45 games in five years.

Not that impressive until you see just 24 losses during the same period. Don introduced the "no windup" pitch. He'd just settle the ball in his glove, grab it with his pitching hand, and throw. Ted Williams said Don was the hardest pitcher to hit because of that delivery. In addition, Don had a good fastball and a slider and he swung a wicked bat. Larsen and Tommy Byrne—they were our best-hitting pitchers. Casey used to bat them eighth, in front of Billy, which made Billy so mad that he'd turn the lineup card upside down to show himself batting lead-off.

I remember the time when I was out drinking with Larsen and got the hiccups. You know how everybody has a magic remedy to get rid of hiccups, right? Larsen gave me a shot of vinegar. I drank it straight down and it damn near killed me. I couldn't breathe. Anyway, Don could drink more than any two guys I ever met. He loved the nightlife. Sleep was his mortal enemy. Once in spring training he had a car accident. Nothing fatal, except that it happened at 5 A.M. George Weiss blew his cork. He went to Casey and demanded an explanation as to why Don had broken curfew. And Casey said Don was mailing a letter.

Where was Don the night before he pitched his perfect game? I haven't the slightest idea, but you could smell liquor on his breath that day. I'll tell you this, he came to the ballpark feeling pretty good. In fact, to Don the whole game was a joke. After each inning the guys left him alone, not because of the smell but because they didn't want to jinx him, and he'd say with a smile and a laugh, "You think I'm gonna do it?"

Two things I did provided some help. I homered off Dodger pitcher Sal Maglie to give us a 1–0 lead and I snared a 430-foot drive to left center by Gil Hodges over my shoulder, one of the best catches I ever made in my life. And Andy Carey deflected a ball toward Gil McDougald, whose throw to first barely nipped Jackie Robinson. And then Dale Mitchell, batting for Maglie. Ball one. Strike called. Strike swinging. Foul into the left field stands. *Strike three called!*

Plate umpire Babe Pinelli made a lot of money working the chicken circuit and demonstrating how his arm stabbed the air on that last pitch. But from where I stood in center field it looked like a bad call. Whatever it was, Mitchell took it and Larsen had his perfect game. Yogi caught him in a bear hug, kicked him in the nuts, and then whirled him around. Pandemonium. In the midst of it all, Don couldn't wait to get to the clubhouse. He had a beer waiting in front of his locker.

A year later—the 1956 Series. In our last-game victory over the Dodgers, Johnny Kucks pitched a three-hit shutout and Elston Howard hit a home run to help win the game.

We'd come a long way. Only a few years earlier, there were lines blocking the stadium ticket booths, people carrying signs and chanting, *"Don't go past the gate! Don't go past the gate! The Yanks dis-crim-i-nate!"*

Back then several other clubs had black players: Jackie Robinson, Roy Campanella, and Don Newcombe of the Dodgers; Willie Mays, Hank Thompson, and Monte Irvin of the Giants; and in our league there were guys like Luke Easter and Larry Doby of the Indians; Sad Sam Jones, who pitched for Detroit; and Minnie Minoso of the White Sox. A black Pete Rose. He played hard. Today it's about evenly divided between white and blacks everywhere in organized baseball. It's a whole new ball game.

In those days, the only black player in the Yankee organization was Vic Power, a good ballplayer but not a superstar. George Weiss resisted all attempts to bring Vic up to our club. George was waiting for a truly outstanding black player for the Yankees.

Then along came Elston. He had a tremendous minor league season in 1954. Everyone could see that he would be a great major leaguer—and he was. We finally had our black star. And he was one of the best teammates I ever had.

No matter what I've said about Weiss being cheap, insensitive, and dictatorial, you have to give him his due. He spent thirty-five years working for the Yankees, built the best farm system around, judged talent with the cunning of a riverboat gambler, and was a shrewd, totally dedicated man. As a businessman, I guess you can say he was a success.

Certainly Weiss's investment in Elston paid off handsomely. One of the first things Elston did was hit a triple that won a ball game. Joe Collins and I rolled out towels from the clubhouse door to his locker. The red carpet treatment. We would have done it for any rookie. This I'll say too. The team had its share of Southern ballplayers, me included. Of course, there were old habits, some of us forgetting ourselves in the heat of battle, using regional profanities and expressions that wouldn't find much favor elsewhere. I can remember a day in Cleveland when Lary Doby was playing. He was a great hitter, always a threat. And Casey's yelling from the bench, "Get that eight ball out of there!" Elston happened to be sitting right beside him at the time. Casey turned his head and patted Elston on the knee. "It's all right, son. You know I don't mean anything by that."

Casey loved Elston. What's more, there wasn't a prejudiced bone in his body. So when certain blacks accuse this one white player or that white manager of racism, maybe, just maybe, they don't have it right.

Still, this was way before Martin Luther King started the civil rights movement. Black guys had to put up with a lot of garbage, especially down South. The Yankees stayed at the Soreno, one of the big old ritzy hotels in St. Pete. Elston had to live in the black section of town, I think with a doctor. If we went on a trip by bus and stopped off at a restaurant, Elston wasn't allowed in. Lord, what must've gone through his mind. Once or twice the team secretary would bring food out for me as well and I would eat with Elston. He never complained and I don't remember anyone on the team treating him bad.

Casey played him in the outfield for a while because Yogi was catching every day and he wanted Elston in the lineup. He could hit and hit with power and he was good at several positions, whether catching, playing first base, or the outfield. It was only after Yogi began to slow up that Elston got the recognition he deserved as a catcher. He was one of the best.

Elston's only problem was speed—he didn't have any. I remember Casey used to say, "Goddamn, we've finally got one and he has to be slow." We called him "base clogger" because if you hit a double you had to stop at first and wait up for him.

As it happened, each year we kept bringing new guys to the club, always improving, always having something going to get us into the Series. So now, 1955, the Dodgers finally beat us, but we didn't have much time to think about it. Two weeks later we took off on a goodwill trip to the Far East. Different clubs had been going there since the days of Ruth and Gehrig. After the war it became a regular event. I know the Lefty O'Doul All-Stars went in 1951, the Giants in 1953, and Eddie Lopat took another team over that year (when Billy collected his little statues and such). This time the Yankees had us scheduled to play twenty-four exhibition games, a rough grind, considering we just came off a full season of intense competition. If I had had my choice, I certainly would've chucked the whole tour. Merlyn was pregnant again and I wanted to be home with her. However, George Weiss made it clear that he expected every Yankee to do his duty, choosing his words carefully, a veiled threat. So I took off with the team, pissed.

The team allowed one traveling companion per player. And since Merlyn was pregnant, Harold Youngman came along in lieu of her. Our first stop was Hawaii. It turned out to be an experience I'll never forget.

Harold and Billy and I were on Waikiki beach: Harold with a coat and tie and straw hat under an umbrella, Billy and me in trunks sprawled on a mat. Billy must have been watching the surfers because he suddenly tapped my arm.

"Let's rent a couple of surfboards." He knows I can't swim, yet a few minutes later I'm stroking away on a board in crystal clear water. I look back and the beach seems to be shrinking. Billy's close by and I yell, "Hey, we're getting too far out! Let's turn around!" He says, "You're only twenty feet from the beach. You can still see the bottom. Don't worry. Nothin's gonna happen."

So I keep stroking and look back again. The beach is gone, the waves are getting higher and higher, and the surfboard and me are riding up and down like mad. "Hey, Billy, these waves are scaring the shit out of me!" He laughs. "What are you talking about? You can still see the bottom."

The hell with that. I see a ten-story wave coming directly at me. As I start turning back, it flips me off the board. I go straight down, hit bottom, and shoot up like a Polaris missile.

Billy tries to grab the board, misses it, and swims over. I'm losing my strength: I think I'm a goner. I imagine the headlines: YANKEE STAR DROWNS! And Billy is yelling, "I got you, pard! Take it easy! Relax!"

As he tries to pull me up, I put a headlock on him and pull him under. And suddenly we rise to the surface again. Billy flops me over his board and a gentle wave carries us in. I'm flat on my back on the sand, limp as a rag.

"You okay, Mick?"

"Yeah . . ."

"Good. I shoulda hit you. You almost ended my career."

He had saved my life.

Before we left Hawaii, they told us to get shots. "Don't drink the water if you don't take 'em," we were told. Well, Billy said he knew all about those shots; made your arms swollen and sore for days, so he and I didn't get them.

When we got to Japan, there were millions of cheering fans at the airport, acting like they had forgotten the war. We rode through the streets in open jeeps and those Japanese fans wanted to touch us. Well, the other guys had taken their shots (I remember Don Larsen's arm had swelled as big as a baseball) and when a fan would reach out to them, they would flinch. After a few minutes of this, the whole team was miserable—the whole team, that is, except for Billy and me. We had a fine time.

The Yankees gave us each about $500 in Japanese yen to spend. Me and Billy blew most of ours in a poker game. And there were parties that lasted and lasted.

One night practically the whole team got looped. It happened at our hotel, about three o'clock in the morning, some of the guys running through the halls with nothing on but their jockstraps, yelling and singing and making so much noise that Casey came storming out of his room to shut us up. He was wearing flaming red pajamas. Charlie Silvera took one look and said, "Hello, Santa. Where's your reindeer?"

One night at a Tokyo nightclub just Billy, myself, and a bunch of geisha girls were sitting ringside, enjoying this big floor show and a couple of Japanese men were sitting at the next table, popping a bunch of firecrackers, the ones you pull the strings out of that shoot confetti.

So I call over a waiter and order a lot of firecrackers. Now the confetti is going both ways and the place is in an uproar. All of a sudden there's an announcement: "Ladies and Gentlemen, would you stand up please and welcome the New York Yankees." Spotlight. And here they come, the entire Yankee team and their wives.

Me and Billy hit the floor and start crawling under the tables on our hands and knees while the band's playing "Take Me Out to the Ball Game."

After making it halfway across the room, Billy whispers, "What the hell am I crawling for? I'm not even married."

I didn't stay the whole trip. A week in Japan was enough. I told Harold, "Help me figure a way to get home without upsetting Casey."

We put our heads together. What we did was, Harold called his office and instructed the secretary to fake a telegram saying I had to rush right home because Merlyn was going to have a baby any minute.

The telegram arrived. I showed it to Casey, who informed George Weiss, and he said okay, I could go home.

Two months later, on December 26, our second son, David, was born.

Merlyn and I were outside the Freeman hospital in Joplin, just pulling into the parking lot, when I saw her sister Pat and her husband, John LaFalier, getting out of their car. We said to each other, "Good God, you too?" and laughed our way up the front steps because none of us had any idea that Merlyn and her sister would deliver on the same day.

That was when George Weiss learned about the phony telegram. He called Commissioner Ford Frick and Frick slapped me with a fine—against whatever I was supposed to get on the trip. The only thing that made me sore was that Weiss didn't even have the courtesy to congratulate Merlyn.

Chapter 16

Before 1956 I was doing pretty well, but I sure wasn't Babe Ruth, Joe DiMaggio, and Lou Gehrig all rolled into one. That season I started to do the things they thought I would do.

I won the Triple Crown, leading the American League (and the majors) in batting average (.353); home runs (52); and RBIs (130). The only previous players to lead both leagues in these categories were Rogers Hornsby in 1925, Lou Gehrig in 1934, and Ted Williams in 1942. In addition, my major league-leading 376 total bases, 132 runs scored, and a .705 slugging percentage made me the American League's Most Valuable Player and the recipient of the Hickock Belt as Professional Athlete of the Year. I was also selected the Player of the Year by *The Sporting News*. I'm proud. They're fantastic honors, yet I don't mind saying the biggest kick was beating out Ted Williams for the batting championship. We had a horse race down to the last few days of the season, both of us hitting .348 when I went into Boston for our last regular season series. And there I passed him with six hits in nine at bats. Somebody asked Ted what he thought about it. He said, "If I could run like that son of a bitch, I'd hit .400 every year."

I believe him. He's my number-one idol, the greatest hitter that ever lived—or at least the greatest that I ever saw. He made it mostly on line drives, very few bloopers, and no leg hits at all. Besides, in the Fenway series he had to face Whitey Ford, Johnny Kucks, Tom Sturdivant, and Don Larsen—tough, even for Ted. So I'm grateful to our pitchers.

The pennant was wrapped up by mid-September. Around this time I got home run No. 50 against Chicago's Billy Pierce and Whitey coasted to win No. 19. Then at Baltimore he lost a 1–0 heartbreaker to a kid named Charlie Beamon. It was his final chance for a 20–game season. I remember because I dropped a pop fly that let the run score and then I popped out, deep to the second baseman in the ninth, leaving Whitey stranded on third base. I always thought Whitey could have made it if he had tagged up and raced home.

Everybody enjoyed playing behind Whitey. He had so much confidence in himself that he lifted the whole team. I know he lifted me. I felt we would never get beat when he pitched. Stick a baseball in his hand and he became the most arrogant guy in the world. Off the field he was as smooth as butter. If you tried to rile him, he'd give you one of those rosy-cheeked smiles and walk away. He hated arguments. To him, they were a total waste of his time.

What I *really* liked about Whitey—what we liked about each other—was that we didn't bring our good and bad days back from the ballpark. Once the game ended, it wasn't one of those things where he'd say to me, "Geez, you should've moved over a few steps to right center for that pull hitter." By the same token, I wouldn't question him about his pitching. Of course, if I had a particularly bad day in the field or at the plate, it would bother the hell out of me. But if Whitey was shelled off the mound—and it did happen a few times—so what? He knew he'd win the next one. And he had discipline. On any night before they scheduled him to pitch, he'd leave the ballpark a little early and go home. You know, like Rod Carew and Steve Garvey, guys who lead Spartan lives for the most part. The thing to do: go out, have dinner and a couple of sociable drinks, then get to bed on time. Whitey invariably followed that routine whenever he had a game coming up and you can bet I was always ready to celebrate a victory with him. Lucky for us both because he won 236 games pitching for the Yankees. And that's not counting his record of 10 World Series victories.

The same year, 1956, Johnny Kucks and Tom Sturdivant emerged as important contributors. Kucks was a shy, introverted type. He stood about six-foot-three; lean, loose-jointed, a right-hander whose best pitches were a slider and a sinker. As a result, many a bat splintered off Johnny's serves. He won 18 games and looked great. It was his year, too.

Tom Sturdivant—another big winner. He posted a 16–8 record. Tom started out as an infielder, switched over to pitching, and came up in 1955, mostly to sit and observe. He was from Gordon, Kansas. A hometown neighbor of mine, so to speak. His wife Ryba and Merlyn were the best of friends. Tom had a nauseating giggle. When he grinned, his two front teeth would stick out. That's why we called him Bucky Beaver.

I was doing really good that year. Opening the season in Washington, I hit a pair of home runs that cleared the center field fence and went up into the trees. I hit those off Camilo Pascual, one hell of a pitcher.

At Yankee Stadium, May 30, I hit another one, this time off Pedro Ramos, also of the Senators. The ball struck the façade high above the third deck in right field, only eighteen inches away from going out of the park completely. Another one came in Kansas City, striking the upper right field deck and ricocheting back to the infield. Then there's a home run I hit at Tiger Stadium, this one traveling more than 500 feet out of the stadium and into the streets.

Then Chicago, when I put a ball twenty rows deep in the left field upper deck, another memorable tape-measure job. And at Fenway Park, September 21, I hit one so hard that it reached the center field back wall in a second. Tom Sturdivant said he never saw a ball move so fast.

Ted Williams has said that I would have been a much better all-around hitter—indeed, would have lifted my lifetime average twenty points—by just trying to meet the ball and not going for the homers.

We both played in the 1956 All-Star game, my second one with Ted. Looking back on it, if I had to do it over again I'd have taken more of an interest in those games. Ted was enthusiastic and tried very hard every time he went up against the National Leaguers. But the majority of guys from our league treated the event as a three-day party. Actually, I had the same feeling myself. Now I can't stand it when someone tells me that the National League beat us nineteen out of twenty-one times and that they were superior. Bullshit. We beat them more times in World Series play, where it counts. I think what it is, during All-

Star competition, the National League comes together as a uni-fied group, pulling for the victory, cheering, encouraging, showing great spirit, whereas we didn't even bother with team meetings. We'd come to the game and say hi to each other in the clubhouse and "Let's get it over with."

Yes, I certainly looked forward to the All-Star extravaganzas, but only because they gave me three days off in the middle of the season, which was my big chance to run around with some players from the other league for a change. One time they held the game in Washington. Ralph Houk was our manager and I stayed out till the wee hours with Don Drysdale and Harvey Kuenn, then showed up at Griffith Stadium, went immediately into the whirlpool, took a shower, then another whirlpool—trying to get sober.

Ralph came in. "Are you okay?"

My eyes were like two piss holes in a snowbank. "Yeah, I guess . . ."

"Well, you don't look too good. If you can't shake it off, we'll take you out after three innings."

He took me out after three innings. I was not your most alert ballplayer that day. I'll also state without fear of contradiction that most of the other guys were like me. It was swell being together, as long as we weren't serious. Ted Williams—a de-mon. Me and Whitey—two kids at a picnic. We got three days off, so let's hoist a few.

Right after the 1956 All-Star game at Yankee Stadium, George Weiss canned Phil Rizzuto. Phil had slowed consider-ably going to his left and right and he could no longer make the long throw from short.

Toward the summer he began thinking of retirement. As I recall, he was pretty well fixed, having a part-ownership in a clothing store and a few other investments. Yet he was still a vital cog in the Yankee machine, a cheerful, happy little guy who had sparked the Yankees to nine pennants and seven world championships. So the way he was handled by George Weiss is a crying shame.

Weiss had sent for him on a pretense, using his old cat-and-mouse tactics, saying, "Now, Phil, be a good fellow and tell me what you think. We have to release one of our players to get an outfielder we want." Phil didn't know that Weiss had already claimed Enos Slaughter on waivers. "So here's a list of names. Who can we let go?" And there's Phil going down the list, very carefully, very seriously, suggesting this name and that name and each time Weiss says, "No, not him" until Phil looks at him and shrugs. Weiss points a finger at Phil and the trap is sprung.

I didn't see Phil leave the stadium. However, the news hit everybody like a bombshell. Jerry Coleman had come off the field and spotted him in civilian clothes, walking toward the parking lot. Jerry told me that Phil was devastated and didn't want to talk to anybody.

Weiss covered himself through a public announcement, which basically defended the move, and to appease the thousands of irate fans, he added his best wishes for Phil's continued health, happiness, and success.

So Phil was gone. We had Gil McDougald full-time at shortstop and that year he and Billy formed the strongest keystone combination anywhere in baseball. Altogether, our lineup hit 190 home runs to break a season record set by the 1936 Yankees. We swept into the series, beat the Dodgers in seven games, and I went home.

Chapter 17

That winter, since I had won so many awards and had had such a good season, I started to get a whole slew of enticing offers. Frank Scott was my agent then. He had created Mickey Mantle Enterprises, taking 10 percent of my outside earnings. I kept the rest. Scotty did a helluva job. I made after-dinner speeches, signed autographs and shook hands at shopping malls, attended banquets in New York, Los Angeles, Chicago, Cleveland, Kansas City, St. Louis . . . Yeah, I also did radio and television commercials, endorsing just about everything, including a pancake mix called Batter Up. I even did a record date with Theresa Brewer, "I Love Mickey."

Frank kept me busy, but I had absolutely no business sense back then. I'm not sharp, can't concentrate on money matters, never liked the wheeling and dealing. Fact is, it's hard for me to sit and listen to anything concerning money finance. Today when my lawyer, Roy True, starts talking about a $100,000 contract, he'd better get it told in twenty minutes—thirty, tops —or I'm out of his office on my way to the golf course. I know Roy is going to do the right thing whether I'm with him or not.

Roy and Harold: two of a kind. Both have been great friends of mine.

In early 1957, Harold formed a corporation, sold stock to some of his wealthy friends, and gave me 25 percent of a motel he was building in Joplin at the end of the Oklahoma Turnpike. We called it the Mickey Mantle Holiday Inn. I paid five cents a share for my stock.

When we had the Grand Opening, a large crowd was on hand, people driving from miles around just to see me and maybe stay over in one of the rooms, preferably the Mickey

Mantle Suite. I guess it was an attractive reason. They could go home and say "I slept in Mickey's bed." Another reason.

We had the legitimacy of being an official Holiday Inn, number 200 in the system. Harold got them to okay my name in front of theirs on their sign. To my knowledge, it was the only one they ever approved and several thousand Holiday Inns have gone up since then.

Ours originally contained thirty-five units, which more than doubled after a short while, and we featured an intimate lounge called the Dugout Club, soft lighting, little round tables, the walls lined with action photos, gloves, bats, all kinds of memorabilia. Nice. We ran the motel eight years, then turned it over to a group of investors from New York, making a substantial profit. I collected $100,000 down, in addition to a payment plan of $1,000 a month over the next twenty years. Harold saw to that, too.

The hell of it is, when I won the Triple Crown, people with big ideas came out of the woodwork and despite Harold's warnings I listened to most of their cockeyed schemes.

Around that time, Merlyn and I were at home one evening, just getting ready to eat. Through the window, I saw a Cadillac pull into the driveway. It had seen better days. The exhaust pipe was trailing black smoke. Now this guy climbs out, wearing a glittering cowboy suit and hat. He knocks on the front door. I open it, and he introduces himself. "C. Roy Williams is the name. May I come in?"

The next minute I'm looking at a policy that he's printed up. The Will Rogers Insurance Company. On the front of it there are caricatures of me and Merlyn flanking old Will. Very flattering. So he says, "Now's the time, Mickey. You can get in on the ground floor. Ten years from today the company should be right up there with New York Life and Prudential and you know *they're* doing well."

Merlyn coughed. My signal to excuse myself. We go off in the other room. "Look," she says. "Get rid of that man. He's a phony."

"Don't worry. I'm not going to sign anything."

We walk back and he says he's going to have pictures taken of us standing together, holding hands. An All-American family. "It's for our advertising campaign. We'll be scheduling *The Saturday Evening Post, Cosmopolitan, Ladies' Home Journal, House Beautiful . . .*"

He says that he can get me into this thing for $5,000 and that I would own half the company.

Merlyn offers him a beer and we go off in the other room again. She says, "You better go and talk to Harold."

So I went to talk to Harold and told him the story. He asked for some background information on Williams, like who his lawyers were, who he was connected with, and such things.

Later I talked to Harold again. "Hate to tell you this," he said, "but your insurance man's lawyer is a shyster from Pryor, Oklahoma. And no doubt Williams is a shyster himself."

So I told the guy that I couldn't invest in his company. It didn't faze him a bit. He already had enough capital to launch the business and, besides, it would be easy to find another name player willing to put $5,000 into a sure thing. "However, Mick, if you change your mind, I'm staying at a motel two miles from here. I'll be there till tomorrow morning. Call me before then and I'll probably have an opening for you in the Will Rogers Insurance Company. If you don't, it's your loss."

That night I'm tossing and turning, can't sleep a wink, thinking about C. Roy Williams. I'm agonizing. "Is it possible that Merlyn and Harold have the guy wrong? What if he's legit? What if I let the deal go by and the Will Rogers Insurance Company grows into a multimillion-dollar empire and I lose out because I didn't give him a measly five thousand dollars?"

Next morning I went down to the Bank of Commerce and had the teller make out a certified check. Then I drove over to see Williams, all fired up and hoping he was still at the motel.

He was in the room, packing his suitcase.

I eagerly gave him the check and that made me half-owner of the Will Rogers Insurance Company.

A week later there's a knock on my door. A man from the FBI flashes his credentials, looking like he's about to spring a big surprise on me. He says, "I have a picture here . . ." It's neatly tucked in a cellophane slipcase. "Did you ever see this man before? We've been trying to find him since he got out of prison."

None other than C. Roy Williams. Left and right profile shots, no cowboy suit, only stripes and numbers.

When they finally caught him, he had sold his Cadillac and didn't have a cent to his name.

As a result of that business decision, I thought I had blown my whole relationship with Harold. Thank god Harold was understanding. I was only twenty-five years old, getting a little cocky —also grossing up to about $75,000 in outside income and figuring there was no telling how much I would make by the time I was thirty.

I guess it showed because a lot of relatives and friends came to my door, saying, "Listen, can you lend me a thousand or so?" They assumed I had it, could afford it, and wouldn't turn them away. Consequently, there were many borrowers and I knew they'd never pay me back.

So I started to worry about that—and besides, I was tired of the constant traveling. I would drive from Commerce to Tulsa to catch a plane. In those days we didn't have the turnpike. It was still being built. And old Highway 66 led east and west, passing through many little towns, each with its various obstacles, such as traffic signs, speed zones, railroad crossings, signal lights, etc. Almost a three-hour drive to the airport. That's six hours both ways, plus however long it took riding the planes to wherever I had to go.

One day a fellow named W. O. Bankston called me, long distance, wanting to know if I'd be interested in taking over a bowling alley in Dallas. He said bowling was the new rage, the fastest-growing indoor sport of all time, and this was a good chance to get in on the money—"The thing is, Mick, Dallas is ripe for the picking."

"Dallas, huh? Well, what's the deal?"

"Simple. You move down here and I'll put your name up on this place. It's in a nice shopping center. There isn't another alley within five miles. Everything points to you making a lot of money."

I thought about it and decided to talk things over with Harold.

Harold and I were sitting on his terrace atop a bluff, looking out at the Spring River and the distant Arkansas hills. A few miles from his home he had a tremendous cattle ranch with beautiful horses, the best grazing land you'll ever find. The ranch was just one of his vast holdings across the length and breadth of the tri-state area.

He turned to me and said, "I'd like to see you stay around here, Mickey. You already own a piece of the motel in Joplin and I can take care of you in other things. There's no limit to what we can develop together."

He meant every word. He would've done anything for me if he could.

"I appreciate it, Harold. Still, there's the problem of traveling and Dallas has an airport right in the city. A real convenience. I'll save all kinds of time getting to personal appearances. And the bowling alley proposition seems real promising. I believe I'll do okay there . . ."

"For your sake, I sure hope so. But if you ask me, I think it's a mistake. I've always thought it's a helluva lot better to be a big fish in a small pond than a small fish in a big pond." He looked out at the hills again. There was a long silence. Finally a rueful smile. "Well . . . it's your decision, Mickey. Do what you think is best. I won't interfere."

The truest friend I had and I hurt him.

Yet maybe after everything I simply wanted to prove I could do pretty well on my own. Which I couldn't. I should've stayed put in Commerce. Because from the vantage point of twenty-seven years later, I'm positive that with his great business head and know-how in general, Harold would have made me a millionaire.

Water under the bridge. All the same, I've done most of the things I set out to do in life anyway.

One afternoon before we sold the house and moved to Dallas, Merlyn went shopping and left me at home with Mickey Jr. At this point in my life, I was still adjusting to my winter role as a father and I welcomed the opportunity to be with my boy. However, to give your undivided attention to a spunky three-year-old is a mighty tough job, no matter how you slice it, and my kid had me going.

Less than an hour later I had him up on a chair at the 400 Club. This way I could keep a close eye on him and at the same time relax over a few beers. As things happened, some guy who worked there started a ruckus. He was picking on one of the customers. Whatever the beef, I sided with the customer, thinking the other guy was completely out of line. Right there, I jumped in and we started wrestling on the floor.

About this time Merlyn's father walked in. I'd been gone from home for about four hours. Merlyn must have been worried. She sent him out to look for me.

The first thing he sees when he walks in is Mickey Jr. sitting at the bar by my beer and me fighting like a cowboy.

He said, "I'm taking your boy." And he left.

About six months later, Merlyn went down to Dallas to look for a house. W. O. Bankston drove her around. Frank Scott's wife came along, too. Finally, a real estate agent showed them a house in North Dallas in a secluded and wealthy residential section. It was beige-colored, ranch-styled, set on an acre of land. She didn't have to look any further. The whole setup was perfect.

By the time I got to Dallas, we were all moved in. It was the first time I had seen our new house and I loved it.

So I went ahead and signed a lease for the bowling alley at a rental of $2,300 a month. A breeze. I thought the alley would be a gold mine. As Bankston had stated, there was no real competition. Our lanes were filled day and night. A big assist came from the Brunswick people. They provided us with leads that helped to bring in the local leagues, social clubs, and individual enthusiasts. An ideal situation, less a couple of disturbing factors that were overlooked while the alley was being redecorated and refurbished.

For one thing, it lacked outside visibility, as it happened to be located under a bank. You had to walk down two flights of stairs to get there. Inside the place was drab and dimly lit. Still—the cash register kept ringing, everything ran smoothly, and those minor concerns were soon forgotten.

Meanwhile my mother, my brothers Roy and Butch, and Roy's first wife Patty had come to Dallas. We got them settled in the vicinity and everybody but Patty took a job at the bowling alley. Things were going good; everybody was working.

Chapter *18*

In January 1957 I went to New York to negotiate a new contract. I had proved myself by winning the Triple Crown and hoped that George Weiss would double my salary. There's no question that my contracts had been a problem for Weiss right from the start, when Casey had talked him into signing me for $7,500 instead of $5,000 in my rookie year. Apparently that irritated him. The next year I got $10,000 after hitting .311. From there I went to $12,500, then up to $17,000; a little bit more each year, paid reluctantly. And always through his assistant, Lee Mac-Phail, who I got along with just fine.

Earlier, in 1956, I was at Lenox Hill Hospital, having my tonsils removed. Lee came to see me about money. The stitches were in and I couldn't talk. There was a lot of nodding and shaking of heads and me grunting and after a few minutes of this we still hadn't arrived at a satisfactory figure. Not anywhere near what I expected. I was looking for $35,000. I thought the time was ripe to make the big quantum leap.

So Lee takes note of my request and says he'll tell Weiss and then leaves. The next day there's a bevy of beautiful nurses standing on either side of my bed, all excited, in a tight-fitting pose with me in the middle and up front a press photographer is going, "C'mon Mick, smile for the little birdie there . . ."

The phone rings. It's Lee MacPhail. He says, "Listen, I'm trying my darndest to resolve our problems, but with the way things are you'll have to see Weiss himself."

I croak out an okay.

"Fine, fine. He expects you to be in his office tomorrow morning at nine o'clock sharp."

I go. And on the way to his office I'm getting so mad my stomach is tied up in knots. There's a water fountain across the hall. I stop off to take a drink and almost choke. I start hemorrhaging in the throat. They have to take me back to the hospital.

George Weiss. A tough old bird. I settled for $32,500, just to get away from him.

Now, here I was a year later, at his door again, determined to raise the ante another $32,500 while my name still had value. What made things even more urgent was the pressing thought that my father and his brothers had died young. So if my family was to be left secure, I had to stand firm.

Weiss's secretary ushers me in at nine o'clock on the dot. He leads me to a chair, steps behind his desk, and asks if I'm ready for spring training.

"Yeah, I'm feeling good."

He smoothes his tie, smiles benevolently. I swear he looks like a sphinx, sitting there with his crossed hands, impassive face, and beady eyes. He says, "Well, Mickey, what kind of money are we talking about?"

I look at the wall and say, "$65,000."

"What's that, again?"

I repeat the figure, this time looking straight at him. He comes back, hissing through his teeth. "That's what I thought you said. All right. I believe you're serious. Therefore, I'll be serious. You are making impossible demands on us."

"Mr. Weiss, I'm not out of line. I mean, Ted Williams is making $100,000 and I understand Stan Musial and Willie Mays are getting around the same amount. I've had a better year than all of them."

It was true. I also hit more home runs than Yogi and he made more than me. I ask Weiss how come. He argues, "For one thing, he's older than you."

I get up. He says, "Sit down." Then Weiss takes a manila folder from his desk drawer. It's the same one he flashed in front of me and Billy after the Latin Quarter escapade.

His face darkens. He says, "Mickey, you're twenty-five years old—a baby. How much will you want ten years from now if I keep doubling your salary?"

"I can't help my age. All I know is, I show up at the ballpark every day and give 100 percent. I think I'm entitled to get what I'm asking."

He pats the folder, leans back in his chair, and twiddles his thumbs. "Nicely spoken. I admire your honesty. However . . ." With slow deliberation he checks through a batch of papers and suddenly slaps them down on his desk. "Here, take a look," he says, the venom returning to his voice. "I wouldn't want this to get into Merlyn's hands."

I'm looking at detective reports. I'm reading: "Mickey Mantle and Billy Martin left the St. Moritz Hotel at 6:00 P.M. Came in at 3:47 A.M." and so forth. Reams of typed pages, covering every move I've made off the playing field.

Our eyes meet. His shift away. "It can hurt your image, Mickey."

I figure, The hell with it. I don't have to take his shit. I can walk away from him and baseball. I don't need the Yankees. I have the bowling alley going in Dallas and the motel in Joplin. So I turn to him.

"Okay, if that's the case, then I'm gonna chuck the whole deal, stay home and run my businesses."

For a moment he says nothing. There's a slight flush showing on his cheeks. Then his voice lowers a couple of octaves. "Go ahead. Stay there in Dallas."

I shrug, walk over to the door, about to vomit. As I'm walking I hear him say, "While you're down there, I might just trade you for Rocky Colavito and Herb Score."

Heading toward the bathroom, I feel that it may happen, but I was as mad as I've ever been in my life.

The next two days dragged. I hadn't even unpacked my bags. I sat around the house, tense, depressed, buried in despair, having second thoughts about my demands, and finally realizing that George Weiss was simply doing his job, saving as much of the bosses' money as he could.

Of course I didn't want to leave the Yankees and go to Cleveland. To me, New York was the pinnacle, the end-all of the professional sporting world. I felt it would be a personal disaster to finish my career wearing any other major league uniform.

I remembered a conversation with Claire Ruth during an Old-Timers' game. I was standing by the rail of her box seat telling her I wished I could've seen the Babe play. Mrs. Ruth set me straight. "Get what you can while you're on top." And after a long pause, "Babe was pushing to take over as Yankee manager, knowing he'd only have another year or two left as a player. When it came down to dollars, Mickey, they handed him the pink slip. Two lousy lines notifying him that he was unconditionally released."

I never understood it. He was the greatest drawing card in the history of baseball and owner Jake Ruppert tossed him aside like an old shoe.

"Mick, are you awake? It's Del Webb on the line."

"Yeah . . . okay, Merlyn. I'll get it."

I turned over in bed and reached for the phone. Webb's voice came through loud and clear. There was absolutely no reason why we couldn't come to an amicable agreement. Of course the Yankees were willing to bend over backward to keep me in the fold. And yes, after that great year I had, I certainly deserved a pay hike. "After all, Mick, you're our main man. We'll do whatever we can to make you happy."

"Well, I've already discussed it with George Weiss. I gave him the figure and he threatened to ship me to Cleveland."

"Absurd. We wouldn't consider doing such a thing. I'm sure George had no intention . . . Look, Mickey, I'm personally inviting you down to spring training. We'll talk this over, friend to friend, and I promise you it won't be a wasted trip."

I said okay, I'd take his word for it. I would go to spring training.

In February Tom Greenwade was sent out to get me. He brought along my flight ticket and Del Webb's best regards. Then we drove to Love Field, boarded a plane, and went down to St. Petersburg together.

This time there were no tricks. I was resting on a bench at Al Lang Field, the stands empty, early morning, Del Webb sitting beside me—for the most part very quiet as I presented my case.

At last he shook my hand in a good warm grip and said, "It's a deal. I'll have a contract drawn up and you can sign it today."

So I got my $65,000 through him.

He had stripped George Weiss of his power, at least in this instance, and there's no question it hurt his pride.

Weiss never forgot.

This was my seventh year as a Yankee, and once again I was playing on a winning ball club. That year we acquired Kansas City pitchers Art Ditmar and Bobby Shantz and minor league infielder Clete Boyer, in exchange for Irv Noren, Billy Hunter, Tom Morgan, Mickey McDermott, Rip Coleman, and Jack Urban, a minor league prospect.

In Art Ditmar we gained a quality reliever. The Old Man also used him as a spot starter. I know Art got into an awful lot of games that year, including a scorcher at Comiskey Park. We'll get to that one later on.

Bobby Shantz came up with the Philadelphia A's. He had two spectacular seasons there before developing arm trouble. When the team was transferred to Kansas City, most people wrote him off. Well, Bobby did a helluva job for us. A pint-sized left-hander, I remember one time when he pitched to me in Yankee Stadium. I hit a ball that Elmer Valo caught against the 402-foot sign. It would've been my first major league home run. Now Bobby was real small, about five-foot-six, but he sure impressed me. There were a few other outstanding shorties in our league: Nellie Fox, the Chicago White Sox second baseman, and outfielder Albie Pearson of the Senators, who stood a mere five-foot-five. And of course we had Phil Rizzuto. He topped Albie by only an inch or two.

What's interesting about Bobby, he reminded me of Whitey. The same kind of pitcher. Crafty. He threw a sneaky fastball, two or three different curves, and could back a guy off the plate in a hurry. Another plus was his great fielding ability. He won four Gold Glove Awards during his four-year stint in Yankee pinstripes. And like Whitey, he was a lot of fun between games.

A big contingent of rookies were in camp, among them Bobby Richardson, Tony Kubek, Woodie Held, Norm Siebern,

Bob Martyn, Jerry Lumpe, Marv Throneberry, Ralph Terry, and Al Cicotte.

So slowly the old Yankee look was changing. A whole new bunch had stepped in and those days of me sitting and staring at Joe DiMaggio were gone. Hell yes. I had turned the corner from greenie to veteran, never clearer than when Casey would hold one of those rousing clubhouse meetings and pick on me in front of the younger players. He was a born psychologist, I thought, because he'd only bark at the guys who'd been around the track a few times. The kids still sweating through the learning process he handled gently. But he felt that once you reached maturity, you should know better, obey the rules, be responsible. He never had a curfew. But I remember a few times when I was in a slump he'd take me aside and say, "Mick, you're not doing so good. Let's get to bed tonight. Get a little rest, come out before regular batting practice, take a few swings."

One time in Boston Casey did impose a curfew after we blew a couple of games. He got hotter than a pistol. The veins in his neck bulged like Dizzy Gillespie's as he went on about how lousy we were going. "Yes siree, until I see some improvement I'm placing you all on a twelve o'clock midnight curfew!"

So that very evening Billy Martin and I get dressed in our best suits and go out to a classy chop house across town. We're sitting there talking and joking and the hours slip by. Billy glances at his watch. "Christ! It's half past eleven!"

We rushed into the street and hailed a cab. Ten minutes later we fly up the front steps of our hotel, swing through the door, and there's Casey standing in the lobby, giving a long-winded oration before a group of writers.

We made a U-turn and got the hell out of there. No way in the world to reach the elevator without walking past him. However, they had a back door to the Kenmore that you could use by going through an alley. It was a shortcut. The team often went in and out of there when we wanted to avoid the fans. This time Billy and I came from the other end and grabbed ahold of the back door. The damn thing was locked.

But he sees a little window above the door. Now he's perched on my back and I'm boosting him up to the window. Finally he clutches the ledge, pulls himself off my shoulders and head, and squeezes through. I'm waiting in the alley and I'm saying to myself, "What luck. He'll open the door and we'll be safe and sound in our room."

I hear Billy calling me. I look up. His eyes are sticking out the window. He says, "I can't open the door from the inside. It's locked. I'll see you tomorrow." It dawns on me that the only chance I have to get into the hotel undetected is to follow the same route he took. Well, there's a stack of trash cans piled in the alley. Must've been sitting there a week because they were spilling over with garbage. I push a few against the door, lift two more on top, and climb up on them. My shoes sink into the goop. I smell worse than a toilet from all the rotten vegetables. But the greasy stains on my suit help me to slide right through the window. I finally get in and there I am, sneaking up the stairs to my room.

I throw open the door. Billy is acting like he's snoring in his bed.

"Wake up!"

"Wha . . . Wha . . ."

"Look at all this crap over me! You coulda reached down and got me, you son of a bitch!"

Billy only laughed, turned over, and went to sleep.

That's the way we lived, but our time as teammates was running out.

The season started with me limping a bit and Billy suffering from a variety of minor ailments, which gave Casey an opportunity to try Bobby Richardson at second base.

Me and Whitey planned a birthday party for Billy in 1957, May 16, an open date on our schedule. We invited Yogi, Hank Bauer, Johnny Kucks, and their wives and made all the arrangements. Everything was set, right down to the baby-sitters.

Then the commissioner's office rescheduled a rain-out game for the sixteenth. However, the fifteenth was still open, so we did some last-minute phoning and the party was booked for that night.

We met at Danny's Hideaway, had dinner, and then some-body suggested that it would be a swell idea to catch Sammy Davis, Jr., at the Copacabana. We arrived a few minutes before he went on. The maître d' set up a special table. We ordered a round of drinks and the show began. Sammy came out singing and dancing. He was fabulous. Meanwhile, sitting at a table next to us was a group of guys who were members of a bowling team. Most of them were three sheets to the wind.

Before long the bowlers got kinda crude. They started to heckle the singer. We were embarrassed—in fact, they were ruining the show for us.

There was some unfriendly banter back and forth. We told them to shut up and they told us to shut up. It got worse and worse. We were recognized—loudly—when one of the bowlers stood up and said, "Well, the Yankees are here. Big deal!"

Some birthday party. People from all sides were straining their necks and buzzing about the *real* show going on in the back. Finally Billy says to one of the bowlers, "Listen, we're trying to have a nice time. Why don't you give us a break and be quiet, huh?" The guy staggers to his feet, leans against his chair with one hand, holds a shot glass in the other, and stares at Billy. "Why don't we talk about it outside?" Billy says, "Sure, pal, let's go."

Bauer came off his seat. "Where are you going, Billy?" "I'm gonna talk to him, that's all." I looked at Merlyn. "I think I better see what Billy's doing." At that moment I heard a loud crash. The next moment one of the drunks was lying in a heap over by the cloakroom, knocked cold. I thought it was Billy. I turned around and saw a couple of other bowlers near the kitchen, spitting curses at Hank. Whitey had a lock on his arms.

I know this. Bauer never laid a hand on anybody. Neither did Billy. And the only thing I touched during the entire uproar was a scotch and soda. The way I saw it, in the midst of everything, several Copa bouncers with saps probably grabbed the ring-leader and clobbered him. Whatever, we were hustled through the kitchen, down a narrow passageway, out a side exit which led to the lobby of the Hotel Fourteen, and into the street for a quick disappearing act.

While we waited for cabs to whisk us away, Billy's saying to me, "Please, from now on don't throw me any more birthday parties." And Yogi's going "Ho ho ho" through clenched teeth. Then a cab arrived. Hank opened the rear door, bowed his wife Charlene in, and jumped in after her as if he had just been airlifted off Guadalcanal.

The next morning I read it in the papers: YANKEES BRAWL AT THE COPA.

Whitey called me from his Long Island home. "The shit has really hit the fan. George Weiss is going to fine the whole bunch of us. Not only that, we have to appear before the Manhattan Grand Jury."

"Why? We didn't do anything."

"Exactly what I told Weiss, but he says one of us hit the guy and we're all in trouble."

We testified at the Criminal Court Building. Johnny Kucks was so nervous his legs quaked. After they finished with him, Billy took the stand and told his story. Then Whitey, Yogi, and Hank told theirs. By midafternoon I was getting tired of waiting to be called and worked up a real bitch of a headache. Finally an attendant motioned me into the chamber.

I sat in the witness chair. About fifty grand jurors were solemnly peering down. Remember the Nuremberg trials? Same atmosphere.

The judge's first question:

"Mr. Mantle, are you chewing gum?"

"Yes, sir."

"Well, get rid of it."

Then the district attorney started in:

"Now, Mickey, were you at the Copa the night of May fifteenth?"

"Yes, sir."

"Did you see a fight take place while you were there?"

"No, sir, I didn't."

"Well, did you see a gentleman lying unconscious on the floor near the Copa entrance?"

"Yes, I did."

"All right. Do you have an opinion as to how this could have happened?"

I thought about it and said, "I think Roy Rogers rode through the Copa on his horse and Trigger kicked that man in the head."

The grand jury was still laughing when the judge dismissed the case for insufficient evidence.

The same day I came to the ballpark and found Billy packing his stuff. I said, "What the hell are you doing?" He said, "I'm gone, Mick. Guaranteed, I'm out of here . . ." I said, "You're not going anywhere." I felt he was just too valuable to the team, that there was no way he would be traded in spite of Weiss's animosity. I honestly felt that Weiss was too shrewd, too much of a perfectionist when it came to winning with good players. He would overlook whatever reason he had to suspect Billy of doing crazy things, as long as it didn't affect his skills on the field. No matter what either of us did privately, when it got down to playing, we knew it was our bread and butter. We played sober, full blast every game.

He gazed around the clubhouse and spoke quietly. "This is just the excuse Weiss needs to ship my ass to another club. I'm telling you, it's gonna happen any moment now."

There was a pause. Trying to get him off the hook, I joked, "Well, I better check with Yogi and see if he's interested in having me as a new roomie."

He shrugged. "Come on. Let's get dressed for the game."

Chapter 19

In the late 1950s there were three kinds of fans in New York: Dodger fans, Giant fans, and Yankee fans. Their favorite question was: Who is the best center fielder in town? They debated it endlessly. Mays, Snider, or Mantle. Take your pick.

Now Willie, he was the best fly shagger I ever saw and he could kill you a million different ways. He'd steal third, steal home, hit the long ball, run, and field—Willie had everything.

When I was playing at my best, I was certainly as good as Willie. But he played at 100 percent all the time.

As for Duke, there's no question he was a superstar and a wonderful guy. I loved the Duke. In fact, I would have loved to have been the Duke. Listen, you could practically fit Ebbets Field right inside Yankee Stadium. It was only 297 feet down the right field line and 389 feet out to straightaway center. Duke was the only left-hander in the regular Dodger lineup, so of course he mostly saw right-handed pitching. Whitey and I figured out once that each year I hit about fifteen long outs at Yankee Stadium that would have been home runs at Ebbets Field. In my eighteen years I would have gotten 270 additional home runs if I'd been a Dodger.

Like Willie and myself, Duke had power at the plate, the same inner drive. He couldn't run or throw with us, though.

And I did a few things they couldn't do. I hit from both sides. I hit the ball farther. I ran faster. At full strength I thought I was as good as Mays or Snider or anyone.

In the early years Merlyn and I rented a number of houses in northern New Jersey. One year it would be a house in Ridgewood. Then we'd find another in River Edge. Then Leonia. Each summer there was a little spot to park ourselves with the kids. We stayed home most of the time. Once in a while we had visitors. Tom Sturdivant and his wife Ryba would often drop in when they lived nearby. When the team came back to New York from a road trip, Merlyn knew that I would be pretty tired of restaurant food. So she would usually prepare some of my favorites from Oklahoma: chicken-fried steak with cream gravy or fried chicken with beans. On game nights we'd get up a car pool, maybe four or five different players riding together over the George Washington Bridge into New York. We'd ride back home after the game. I'd usually unwind with a cold beer and then go to bed. That was my schedule.

Still, there are some who will say, "What a racket. Baseball's a snap." They see us playing a two-hour game and figure that's it. But behind the scenes we arrived at the park three hours before the game. If it didn't go into extra innings, we'd finish at about six in the evening. For a night game, we were suited up by five and home around midnight.

I welcomed the change; away from the ball field, being with my family. Out of sight out of mind, so to speak. And it worked fine until the neighborhood kids discovered where I lived. In each of those houses, it wouldn't take the kids long to find me.

Then there was no privacy. If they weren't out on the lawn, yelling and wanting autographs, they'd be waiting for my car, hoping to get me to sign their scrapbooks or pictures or toy bats as I walked into the house. Merlyn felt we were living in a zoo. So every summer we'd move to a different neighborhood where nobody knew us.

The last place we rented, was right over the bridge in Fort Lee. The people next door had a swimming pool. They were always staring at me in their bathing suits. One morning I was getting ready to do a television commercial in our backyard. As the director went over the lines with me, the crew began setting up cameras, stringing cable wire, the whole bit. All of a sudden our next-door neighbor raised a loud cry. "Hey, Mantle, we're not living in a public park, y'know! Get these guys off my lawn!"

Before we had moved in, the man who owned our house had lived there with five or six cats. Before the season started we gave him a big deposit, agreeing to leave the place the way we found it. Meanwhile the cats had gouged all the furniture and left pee stains on the carpet. Everything smelled horrible. Merlyn boiled the dishes, scrubbed, and cleaned. We even stayed in a motel at our own expense while the place aired out. We didn't hear from the owner the entire summer. When we were ready to leave, he came to say goodbye. I showed him every room, proud of the marvelous job Merlyn had done. After the inspection, he shook his head. "Sorry, I'll have to keep your deposit. The place needs a lot of fixing."

A Dodger fan, no doubt.

Living in New York had other problems. I was a walking billboard. I make no bones of the fact that I've always had a private corner, an innate shyness that prevents me from feeling comfortable when talking to strangers. As for my kids, I didn't want them subjected to the kind of attention I was getting. So they were shielded. The common ground usually led us to some other player's house. I know that Yogi's wife Carmen would invite Merlyn and our kids over to go swimming in their pool. And once—yes, like most families, we took them to the circus. We were living in River Edge at the time . . . Saw the big Madison Square Garden ad and showed it to Merlyn. She asked Mickey Jr. and David if they'd like to go. Their faces lit up. So we picked a day.

Somebody in the Yankee office got us front row tickets for one evening after a day game. It was the Barnum & Bailey Circus—I was really enjoying it and the kids were also having a great time. We got to see almost the whole show, the clowns, the lions and tigers, and the ringmaster cracking his whip. But finally the fans spotted us. First thing you know, there was a line of autograph seekers, so we left.

Mickey Jr. and David couldn't understand why. They cried all the way home. They wanted to see the elephants.

Fact is, the autograph problem is still with me. Ever since the mid-fifties, I haven't been able to take my family to attend the circus or ballgames or any other big public events.

By early June in 1957, the White Sox were in first place, about six games ahead of us. It ticked Casey off. The team was flat, lacking punch in the batting order, and our pitchers, with the exception of Bobby Shantz, weren't helping things to get any better.

Along about this time, Bobby Richardson began to look like a serious contender at second. Casey was starting to play him more and more and I thought that Billy might really get traded. Both me and Billy were miserable about it.

One night in Detroit, after we had dinner and hit a few bars, we got up to our room drunk, looking for something to do, just to be ornery. I think we were staying on the twenty-second floor.

I can't remember whether it was Billy or me who had the bright idea, "Hey, let's climb out on the ledge and see what we can see in the other rooms."

He went first and I climbed right out after him. Don't ask me now why I did it. But it seemed like a great idea: Follow the Leader. We started crawling along this ledge, me right behind Billy's rear end.

After about ten yards, we got kind of disgusted because there were no lights in the windows, so I said, "Let's turn around."

Well, at this point I realized that the ledge was only about three feet wide and I'm afraid of heights, scared to even look out of a skyscraper window. I can't turn around, I can't look down, and I sure as hell can't go backward. We have to crawl around the entire building, corner to corner, a bit at a time, our hands and knees covered with pigeon shit. We sobered up pretty fast. And we never did look in anybody's window.

When we finally got back into our room, Billy flopped down on his bed. He says, "You know, Mick, I think we oughta move to a higher floor. May be more action up there."

Then we were in Chicago for a three-game series. In the third game Art Ditmar was matched against Billy Pierce, the White Sox left-hander. Ditmar got into an immediate jam, allowing a walk and scratch single. Larry Doby was up next. Ditmar threw one right past his head, straight to the backstop. Elston Howard

About 1956.
One of our rented houses in New Jersey.
That's Merlyn pouring some
milk for little Mickey and me taking care
of David. [Bob Olen Studios/Mickey
Mantle Collection]

These are two of my best friends:
Moose Skowron and Phil Rizzuto.
I met them both
the year I came up from Joplin. You
can see for yourself that Moose's toes are
rotting off. [UPI/Bettmann News Photos]

This is me catching and Danny hitting, with David on deck. Mickey's probably pitching
and Billy's in the outfield. I'd probably just caught a foul ball in the nuts. [John Dominis,
Life magazine © Time Inc.]

Tom Greenwade (*middle*), the Yankee scout who signed me up, and Ralph Terry. Tom sent several guys to the Yankees besides Ralph and me: Hank Bauer, Jerry Lumpe, Tom Sturdivant, and Bobby Murcer. [AP/Wide World Photos]

Me and Maris at spring training. Roger came over to the Yankees from the Kansas City A's and became one of my best friends. We had a lot of good times together and never did have an argument. [AP/Wide World Photos]

This is one of me striking out
in the 1962 World Series
against the San Francisco Giants.
We won the Series, though.
[UPI/Bettmann News Photos]

This looks like an upper deck shot. Maybe. [AP/Wide World Photos]

A home run in the last inning and the fans are running out on the field. [AP/Wide World Photos]

Whitey's retirement day. He'd just got through making his speech and was walking back into the dugout. I was thinking, "It'll be me before long." [National Baseball Library, Cooperstown, N.Y.]

There's me and old Bowser. [National Baseball Library, Cooperstown, N.Y.]

March 1, 1969,
the day I announced my retirement.
The saddest day of my life,
except when my dad died.
[AP/Wide World Photos]

Mickey Mantle Day, June 8, 1969
Danny and I looked pretty seriou
until we got out to center field.
I looked up in the stands and said
"I feel like Dolly Parton's baby
when it's nursing.
Is this all for me?"
[Ernest Sisto, New York *Times*]

The same day and Joe is giving a speech. Lee MacPhail is standing right behind
DiMaggio. George Weiss is standing at the far right. [New York *Times*]

Me with Casey and Whitey at the Hall of Fame. One of the proudest days of my life.
[AP/Wide World Photos]

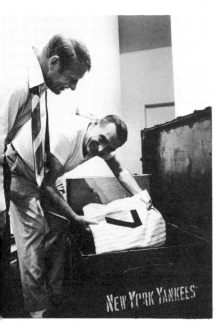

This is one of my all-time favorite people in the world—big Pete Sheehy. He'd been the clubhouse man since Babe Ruth's days.
Pete, Billy, and I would stay out way after everybody else left, drinking beer, and big Pete would tell us stories about Babe Ruth.
[Mickey Mantle Collection]

ABOVE, here's the greatest center fielder
who ever lived—with three other guys.
Take your choice
on which one's the best.
[Mickey Mantle Collection]

LEFT, me and Merlyn
in the dining room
of the Claridge Hotel.
[Mickey Mantle Collection]

chased the ball down as Ditmar scrambled to cover home plate. A knockdown pitch, they say. Certainly. It's baseball. The pitchers will tell you it's used to let the hitters know who's boss. Ditmar followed in the time-honored tradition. He was out to win—he didn't care how.

You could see it was going to be that kind of day. In the previous game we had a near riot when Al Cicotte, our somewhat wild righty pitcher, uncorked a fastball that whistled past Minnie Minoso's ear. It sent him sprawling. After the next pitch, Minnie flung his bat at Cicotte to show *he* was boss. Tit for tat. And that's great. It separates the men from the boys. If you can't take it, you better look for something else to do with your life.

All right. Doby was mad. One look and I would've bet that he was going to take a whack at Ditmar. Sure enough, he threw a bolo punch that grazed Ditmar's chin and knocked off his cap. If Doby had caught him flush, Ditmar would've been the first man in space. As they locked horns, both benches emptied. Seconds later I found myself jumping headlong into a pile of bodies. Moose Skowron was in there, his boilermaker arms wrapped around Doby, and Walt Dropo, the lumbering White Sox first baseman, was in there trying to pull Skowron off Doby, and Skowron had Doby by the pants and wouldn't let go. Now Enos Slaughter jumps on top of Dropo, then somebody jumps on Slaughter, and Whitey gets into the act to prevent Slaughter from being punished by Dropo. Finally the umpires restored a semblance of order. They ruled that Ditmar could stay in the game, but ejected Dropo, Doby, and Slaughter. Half the players from both teams were still jawing at each other when suddenly Billy threw a punch at Doby, missed, then landed three or four more in rapid succession before they were wrestled apart.

I walked Billy to the dugout. "How come you put the slug on Doby?"

"Wouldn't you? The guy said he was gonna stick a shiv in Ditmar."

The good news was, we won the game and we were in first place by the end of June.

The bad news: Billy was gone.

He was traded in Kansas City. True, we had missed a couple

of trains, stayed out after curfew, sometimes caroused and even came to the stadium in not too good shape, and there was the Latin Quarter and the Copa. But innocent as we were, in the long haul, it was always Billy who churned George Weiss's gut. Now, on June 15, as players chatted and speculated in the clubhouse about the trade deadline which ended at midnight, Billy kept to himself. He had already added things up. His gear was packed. He knew the ax would fall that night.

I checked the lineup card. Bobby Richardson was slated to start at second. The next moment I saw Billy run up the dugout steps and take off for the bullpen. I guess in desperation, thinking that if he could hide and Casey couldn't find him, the deadline would pass and he'd still be a Yankee.

After the game he came in crying. Whitey and I tried to console him, then broke down ourselves.

The three of us went out, headed for the nearest downtown bar. It seemed inconceivable that the next day he would be wearing another uniform. Weiss had masterminded the transaction, sending him and Ralph Terry over to the Athletics for Harry Simpson and Ryne Duren. They didn't matter just then. Only Billy did. We were like brothers. When they traded him, it was the same as if one of my own brothers had been sent away. Hell, except the time he spent in the Army, I had roomed with him since 1951. Together we helped the Yankees win five pennants and four World Series. We had shared the exciting victories as well as the bitter defeats and so many of them flashed through my mind.

I recall sitting in front of the St. Moritz on Central Park South, glancing at limousines as they stopped to pick up the affluent out-of-towners; people hurrying to cocktail parties, auctions, galleries, recitals . . . We heard this lady tell her driver that she wanted to shop at Bergdorf Goodman, a high-fashion Fifth Avenue department store. You can walk there from the St. Moritz in two minutes. Billy turns to me. "Why not?" He was dating a girl named Gretchen. He said he'd like to buy her something nice. So we went.

At Bergdorf's, a private elevator took us up to the third floor.

The sales girl sat us on a divan. Some models slithered out, wearing designer dresses and coats. We lifted our glasses of Champagne off a silver tray, gave them a clink, and smiled, really embarrassed by the whole thing. Yet it was terrific. Sheer fantasy, like we were starring in the movies. I picked an outfit for Merlyn, a beautiful silk dress. Billy selected a pants suit for Gretchen, collar and cuffs trimmed with fur. The girl wrapped both items and had them ready at the desk. We didn't know the prices. There were no tags. Billy gulped when he got the bill. He thought it would be $100, perhaps a bit more. The girl said, "Oh, this is an original, sir. The price is correct." The suit came to $650. He stammered, "Well, uh . . . listen, I've just realized . . . it doesn't match her eyes." For a moment I was tempted to turn Merlyn's outfit back. It cost almost as much. But I felt a helluva lot better after I bought it, imagining her expression when she got it.

On the way back to our hotel, Billy said, "Gee, that sure was a gorgeous pants suit. Too bad I haven't struck oil yet."

It was past midnight. The three of us were still reminiscing about all the things we had done together. Before last call, Whitey started moving around like he wanted to leave. "Well, Billy boy, it's been great. But your life isn't over yet. You go over with Kansas City and make Weiss sorry he let you go."

I guess he thought for a minute.

"Say, I'm pitching tomorrow. Whatever you do, if I throw you a curve, don't hit a home run."

Billy and I closed the joint at five in the morning. By then he had vented his feelings. Casey had let him down. It broke his heart. He said he'd never speak to him again. What hurt most was that he had always looked up to the Old Man, like a son would regard his own father. Now the relationship was over, past, finished and done with. He didn't want to hear his name mentioned anymore. I said, "Billy, you shouldn't blame Casey. It's not his fault. He just works for the club. He can't control everything that Weiss sets out to do."

I would bet that Casey had saved Billy from Weiss several

times before, but this time Weiss was more determined. And I know that Casey was very sorry to see Billy go.

But Billy wouldn't hear me. In fact, he refused to communicate with Casey for five years. I remember Casey coming to me once in a while, asking, "How's Billy? Have you heard from my boy?"

I guess Billy finally came to the conclusion that it was Weiss's fault. He told me that he had seen Casey somewhere, walked up to him, and shook his hand. Casey just started talking to him like nothing had ever happened.

So they made up, and all was forgiven on both sides. It was a very special kind of friendship that lasted until the day Casey died.

Billy attended the funeral. They gave him one of Casey's old warmup jackets and it's still one of his prize possessions.

The first time Billy wore a Kansas City uniform I realized he couldn't be defeated by a trade, the loss of a job, a friend, or anything. Yet it seemed incredible that he was playing against us. Of course, the game must go on and Billy and I didn't keep any secrets from each other. He knew my habits, among them a strong inclination to bunt if a guy had two strikes on me. Which certainly was the case when I came to bat and took two straight fastballs that caught the inside corner of the plate. I looked out to second base. There he was, playing me close to the grass with his glove on his throwing hand, waiting for the bunt. I couldn't help but laugh and stepped out of the batter's box. I swung at the next pitch and missed. The little rat.

Another thing. When Whitey pitched to him, he threw him a curve and Billy immediately hit a home run. He cursed him all the way around the bases.

Chapter 20

I've often thought that a lot of awards you get are made-up deals so you'll come to the dinners. Of course, there are others that have merit. I won the first Fred Hutchinson Award. It's for courage. He was a pitcher and, later, a manager in the majors. He had cancer, but he never let us feel sorry for him. He made us feel good just because we knew him. I truly appreciate that award. It's one of my favorites. The 1956 Hickock Belt is very special to me. And I've been the Father of the Year, the Most Popular Yankee, a Triple Crown winner, and a Hall of Famer. And there are seven World Series rings, twelve American League pennant rings, plus the Silver Bat. When I look at all this, I know I did something. But when you ask if I earned them, well, I don't know if I earned them or not. To me, it seems as if it happened to someone else.

The honor I'm most proud of is the MVP Award. Usually it comes to a guy who is on the pennant winner.

More than the awards, though, I felt good about the fact that the players liked me. When somebody once asked me what I'd want written on my gravestone, I answered, "He was a great team player."

And when I look around now and see those awards in my trophy case, I'm proud; they remind me of the cheers. I still hear them. Like when Hank Aaron hit his record-breaking home run. I watched him on television that night and saw the ball go over the left center field wall in Atlanta Stadium. I can imagine how he felt circling the bases and listening to the gigantic roar. I know the pressure that built up before he hit it. I know what the feeling is. I wish everybody in America could have that feeling just once, to hear all those people cheering and knowing it was for them.

When I won my second MVP in 1957, I batted .365, the highest ever for me. Ted Williams did a little better. He hit .388 to lead the league. It could've been closer. I trailed by a couple of points going into late August. Then—you guessed it—another injury. They wrote it was shin splints and you might've read a whole mix of news stories about how it happened. Forget everything, including the story George Weiss released to the press, which actually filtered down through Casey, who didn't have it right either.

I'll back up a bit. In the beginning Casey installed a rule that we couldn't play golf during an off-day. I never understood why he put such a silly rule into effect. I mean, what is golf anyway? You're out in the fresh air, trying to put a ball in a tiny hole. What is that gonna do? Nothing, except bring you some innocent pleasure. Now, isn't that better than sitting alone in a tavern somewhere? If you don't know, try it.

At the time I didn't take a real interest in golf. I played infrequently, sometimes kidding around with Whitey and Billy. Then Tom Sturdivant and I started to play. One morning he called me and said, "Let's shoot a few holes at the Englewood Country Club." A good course in New Jersey. I said fine and we met there.

The first thing he gives me is his high-pitched hyena giggle. "Hehehehehe," a godawful screech that immediately sets my teeth on edge. But I smile and we decide to make a paltry bet, something like five dollars a hole.

We're on the last green. Tom hits a beaut that comes within seven feet of the cup. My ball lands in a trap—*kerplunk*—and he's going "Hehehehehehe." I'm ready to kill him. Now he squats, measures the distance, scratches his ass, worms his fingers around the putter ten or twelve times, and sinks the putt. I blast out of the trap and the ball dribbles to a stop about twenty-five feet to the right of the flag. I three-putt and he's giggling again, which makes me so mad I take a wild swing at a low-hanging tree branch. It snaps in two and the putter slices down into my shin bone. I walk off the fairway gushing blood.

In the club's locker room, Tom says, "Wait'll the Old Man hears that you did this playing golf."

"Are you crazy? I ain't telling him *that!*"

My cover story was that Tom and I went for a ride. I parked the car, climbed out, and accidentally kicked the corner of the door with my shin.

The story went into the papers. Bad enough I had the shin splints, but worse yet, I kept aggravating myself about the match with Tom. Losing at most ten dollars—naturally that didn't bother me. It was the giggling, the high-pitched hyena laugh—*that* I couldn't take.

Toward the end of the season I was doing my best to catch Ted Williams for the batting title. There was also the pennant. We opened a big lead over Chicago in early September. By then Whitey was pitching, showing good form after testing his shoulder as a reliever. Casey had used him in the middle innings of a crucial game against the Sox. He held them and Slaughter put us ahead with an extra-inning homer. Whitey closed shop in the bottom half—cool, as always. And Slaughter. Last of the Gashouse Gang. A bald-headed, beetle-browed veteran. He never stopped hustling. Enos used to run out for practice wearing a heavy rubber jacket to work up a sweat. He'd run fifteen to twenty minutes on a steamy hot day, then come in and sit down right next to Casey. "Goddamn," he'd say. "What a day for a game. I'm feeling great. I love baseball. Yeah." Making points. And I'd be sitting on the other end of the bench with a hangover, thinking, "Boy, it sure is gonna be hot playing out there today." All Enos had to do was run before the game and pinch hit. That was his thing. His years with the old St. Louis Cardinals were way behind him. I guess he was still longing for the other league and remembering all of his achievements there. Can't blame him, those were great years.

In the final week of September we beat Boston, our green light to the World Series against the Milwaukee Braves. They had a slugger's row of their own: Hank Aaron, Eddie Mathews, Joe Adcock, and Del Crandall. The pitchers: Warren Spahn, Bob Buhl, and Lew Burdette. We played the first two at Yankee Stadium. Whitey pitched the opener and won it 3–1 on a five-hitter, with Spahn taking the loss. Milwaukee evened things up the next day. Our starter was Bobby Shantz. After striking out the side in the first inning, he fed Aaron a ball to his liking. A towering shot that was turned into a triple. I got a late jump and had to chase it to the 461-foot sign. Then Adcock singled Aaron home. I heard the razzing. It was like water off a duck's back. My skin had thickened.

Anyway, Bauer tied the game with a homer. It stayed deadlocked until the third or fourth inning when three straight singles and a miscue by Tony Kubek on Slaughter's relay sent two of the runners home. That ended the scoring. Lew Burdette made the most of it. He gave us nothing but goose eggs through the final innings.

On to Milwaukee. We stayed at a place called Browns Lake Resort, then drove in for the game. County Stadium was filled. I understand they could have filled it ten times over. The crowd was roaring, giving the Braves a thunderous ovation as they took the field. Tony Kubek turned to me and said, "Who'd ever have thought . . . I must be dreaming." He had grown up in Milwaukee and I'm sure he would've been thrilled if the Braves had signed him. Our luck that they didn't. He became a first-rate shortstop. Later, when teamed with Bobby Richardson at second, you had two of the very best keystone operators in baseball.

In the first inning of that game, Kubek hit a Bob Buhl pitch over the right field fence. I came up and walked. Then Yogi walked. I took a good lead off second base as Gil McDougald stepped in. Suddenly Buhl spun around and threw to Red Schoendienst, trying to pick me off. I lunged headfirst for the bag and got my arm over it. The throw went wild. Schoendienst dove for it, missed, and landed on my right shoulder. It was as if someone had dropped a sack of cement on me. I pushed Schoendienst off and ran to third. McDougald knocked me in with a sacrifice fly and Yogi scored on Harry Simpson's single. We had a 3–0 lead. Guys in the dugout were slapping each other on the back. Casey came over. "You okay, Mick?"

"Well, I guess."

He raised his eyebrow. "I saw you wincing out there. Are you in pain?"

"Naw."

The little get-together ended. I stayed in the game and hit a left-handed home run off Gene Conley into the Braves bullpen.

The shoulder stiffened that night. The next day I could hardly swing the bat. I played anyway, though Casey told me in no uncertain terms that he'd send somebody else in if he thought I couldn't make the throw from center field.

It happened in the bottom of the tenth. We had scored the tie-breaker and were up by a run. Now the Braves had a man on second. My shoulder was throbbing so badly I flagged the dugout. Casey called time, took me out, and moved Kubek to center. Moments later I watched Eddie Mathews club one a mile high and into the right field bleachers to win the game.

We lost the Series in seven games. For a while I felt pretty guilty about not being able to help save it. However, the writers named me the season's Most Valuable Player, so would you believe it, early in 1958 I received a contract from George Weiss calling for a $5,000 pay cut. His reasoning was that what you did the year before determined what you would get the following year. Dumb. But that was Weiss's way. To him, 1957 was not a good year for me when compared to my 1956 stats.

Besides this incredible turn of events, I was also getting migraines worrying about my once-flourishing bowling alley. Competition had sprouted faster than a field of wild daisies in springtime. All over Dallas. Alleys that featured all the modern comforts, with special rooms where children could play and be cared for while their parents bowled.

My alley was not luxurious. Even if I wanted to upgrade conditions, lack of space severely limited the improvements I eventually did make, which amounted to a few cosmetic touches that didn't solve anything in the long run. And here I am, holding a five-year lease. At $2,300 a month there were those nights after closing time where I'd stare at the ceiling and imagine myself drilling a hole through the floor of the bank above to let some of their money trickle down.

As for Weiss, once again it would be a case of me having to hang tough. I had no stomach for it. When I refused to report to St. Petersburg, on the day camp opened, I spotted a newspaper story in which Weiss said that if I didn't show up right away I'd be traded. I got on the next plane.

I had to play every game in spring training while still recuperating from an operation on my shoulder, not to mention my aching knees, the shin splints—whatnot. Be there, Mantle, you're a drawing card. We expect your undying loyalty. A George Weiss credo. He could threaten you, do anything he wanted, and he would *never never* allow an agent in his office. He had you alone.

Me? I swallowed my pride and settled for a small raise, which got me up to $75,000.

Early in spring training, Casey has just given the pitchers and catchers a day off. So Whitey is saying to me, "Yes, Mick, I'm gonna play golf. It's a shame you can't go, but that's the way the cookie crumbles, old buddy." I say, "Gee, I sure wish I didn't have to practice. I'd really like to go with you." He says, "Well . . . maybe you can get excused. Tell you what, call the Old Man and say your shoulder is a little sore." Casey did let me off.

Later, as the two of us are coming up to the eighteenth green, I notice a short balding man who's standing in the middle of the green, holding the flag stick. He's looking our way. It's Weiss. And Whitey says, "Let's leave." I say, "Are you kidding? I'm going for par."

We approach the green. I hunch down and start concentrating on my putt. Weiss is standing there. In fact, he's pulled the pin. I putted up and holed out. He says, grim as death, "How's your shoulder, Mickey?" I say, "It doesn't hurt when I'm swinging the golf club, but I can't get my arm up over my head." And while I'm saying it my arm is going up over my head.

He jams the stick into the hole and storms off the course.

I was back on the ball field the next day. But that spring my shoulder kept bothering me. Consequently I had a poor start. It didn't seem to hurt the club, though. Our won-lost record was something like 25–6 going into June. Strong pitching did it. Turley, Ford, Larsen, Ditmar, Shantz, and Kucks. They were uniformly beating the other teams and allowing less than two runs a game. Ryne Duren, working the bullpen, wound up leading the American League in saves, with 20.

Let me tell you about Ryne. He wore glasses that were thick as the bottoms of Coke bottles and he'd throw his last warm-up pitch against the home plate screen, which would scare the hell out of the batters. He even hit the on-deck hitter once. A big powerful guy, always brooding over something or other. Sober on the field and a wild man after hours.

When he got drunk he was tough to handle. I'll never forget one time after we clinched the pennant, we were riding on a train back to New York and Ryne came by the club car where Ralph Houk was sitting and smashed his cigar in his face for no reason.

Naturally Ralph got mad and the next thing you know the two of them were under the table, Ralph choking Ryne. Several players had to pull them apart.

Years later Ryne publicly announced that he was an alcoholic and even wrote a book about it. He spent months in an alcoholic rehabilitation center. I heard some years ago he was counseling others in his home state of Wisconsin.

I used to run around with Ryne a lot. But, thank God, I was lucky enough to have had a greater tolerance or a stronger stomach. I don't know. As I've said elsewhere, I got into the habit of drinking heavily—especially in the off-season—quite early in my career. First beer, then the hard stuff.

In July 1958 the Kefauver hearings were being held in Washington. It was held on July 9, 1958. To me, it was a big waste, nothing more than a means to an end, where the Senators could get their names spread around in all the papers. Anyway, they called in quite a few baseball people, including Ted Williams, Stan Musial, Del Webb, Casey, and myself. When I received the notice saying they wanted me as a witness before the Subcommittee on Antitrust and Monopoly of the Committee of the Judiciary of the United States Senate—man, I thought they were going to put me in prison or something. Casey? He didn't give a shit. So there we were, pulling up in front of the Capitol,

Casey and Edna and me in the backseat of the limousine, Casey dozing, his face collapsed on his chest, his hair tousled, the strands sticking out every which way. Edna took a comb from her handbag and began to tidy him up. Casey slowly lifted one eyelid. He snorted, "Huh . . . huh? Oh, it's you, Edna. Well . . . let me know when you're finished."

The most surprising thing to me, as I moved through the committee room, was that Casey had already found a seat and appeared to be dozing again—or at least not paying the slightest attention to the proceedings at hand.

Then Senator Kefauver called his name. Casey squared around and gave him a lopsided smile. Kefauver said, "Mr. Stengel, you are the manager of the New York Yankees. Will you state very briefly your background and views about this proposed legislation to exempt professional baseball from antitrust laws?"

Casey talked for an hour, starting from the time in 1910 when he played Class D ball in Shelbyville, Kentucky, and was still talking about the price of bananas in Mexico where he tore his pants on a rusty nail and traveled sometimes in three Pullman coaches and when the stores closed on the Fourth of July there you were, sitting at the depot.

Finally Senator Langer wanted to know whether he intended to keep monopolizing the world championship in New York City.

Casey answered that he did get a little concerned the day before because in the first three innings he saw three of his players traded and he had already lost nine and actually called on a young fella in Baltimore who had been doing pretty good and he had to tell the senator that he thought the Yankees were more the Greta Garbo type of success.

Senator Langer thanked him.

I was next. And Senator Kefauver asked me, "What are your views with reference to the applicability of the antitrust laws to baseball?"

"Well, after hearing Casey's testimony, my views are about the same."

"I see. Then can you please tell us what he said?"

Ted Williams and Stan Musial almost rolled out of their chairs. Sure, by nature Casey was a real funny guy. But when they talk about that "Stengelese" and make it a word in our language that suggests a buffoon, a clown with not too much upstairs—forget it. The Casey I knew could match his brains with anyone. When he called you into his office because you broke a rule, he didn't speak Stengelese. He got his message across in clear, crisp English. Beyond a shadow of a doubt, he was a professor in the best sense of the word.

If you wanted to know about Casey's personal side, you'd have to be around him off the field, observe what he did at home during his leisure time. Or watch the way he acted when his wife Edna went along with us on road trips. I didn't see too much of that. Casey never talked about his home life. He talked baseball. He couldn't care less who was listening: ballplayers, plumbers, bakers, candlestick makers . . . His mind was always on the game. The other stuff came second.

He let Edna handle the money. She did all the bookkeeping. Of course, everybody knew her family owned a bank in Glendale, California. There was also common knowledge that they owned apartment houses out there and that Casey had invested in oil wells with some of his old cronies and they struck it rich. Undoubtedly Edna played a big role in getting him involved in the venture. And speaking of roles, at one time she was a silent movie actress. Sometimes Casey would take a breather during one of his speeches and ask Edna to tell the crowd a story or two. "Go ahead, tell them about the time you fell off the horse making a picture with Hoot Gibson."

She was a tall woman, magnificently dressed, very good-looking, and proud of the house she and Casey lived in ever since they got married. It had that old-style California look, with high windows, beamed ceilings, tiled floors. There were flowers and potted plants and every room was filled with antiques of one kind or another, collected from a lot of round-the-world tours. But more than anything, Edna adored Casey. If you ever went against him, she'd cross you right off her list. Yet on their trips together he would often yell and holler at her. She'd just wait till he quieted down. Then he'd get real mushy, trying to make amends.

We were checking into Detroit's Statler Hilton Hotel. I was sitting on a couch with Whitey and Darrell Johnson. Darrell, our third-string catcher, gestured at a couple of guys who were lounging at the far end of the registration desk. "Strange-looking birds, aren't they?"

I nudged Whitey's arm. "What do you think?"

He said, "Detectives. I can smell 'em from here."

Darrell said, "They're watching us over the tops of their newspapers."

Whitey scowled. "I'm telling you, it's getting to be a real drag."

I said, "Yeah, that Weiss—he never gives up. He's always checking, checking. He must really believe he *owns* us."

"Mick, why don't we have a little fun with those two guys?"

A minute later me and Whitey and Darrell crossed the lobby and went out the front door, very slowly, so the two private eyes would be sure to see us. We walked down the street, stopped at the corner, whistled for a cab, and jumped in. They did the same thing and started after us. It was Looney Tunes—we just instructed our driver to circle the block a dozen times, then pull up at the Statler Hilton and let us out.

But what's most amusing is that they finally trailed Kubek and Richardson to the YMCA. The two straightest guys on our team! It was getting too stupid for words. Perhaps it was even getting too ridiculous for Weiss because after the report of our merry-go-round chase appeared in all the New York papers I think the bloodhounds were called off for good.

Anyway, 1958 was the year we beat the Milwaukee Braves to win another world's championship and get our revenge for the previous Series. I got a total of six hits, including a triple and two home runs, but the decisive blows were struck in the eighth inning of the seventh game. Lew Burdette was their pitcher. Yogi lined a double to right field, Elston singled him home, then Andy Carey scored Elston on a single and Moose Skowron hit one into the bleachers, which gave us a 6–2 lead. They had two outs with two men on in the ninth when Red Schoendienst hit a fly ball to center, smack into my glove. A nice way to end the season. Overall, I'd say that most of my personal goals were met. I had a .304 batting average, topped the league in home runs (42) and runs scored (127), and finished fifth with 97 RBIs.

In my first fourteen years with the Yankees, we won twelve pennants and seven World Series. The New York fans expected us to win. I guess we spoiled them. Because in all those years, not once did we get a hero's welcome or a ticker-tape parade. It was the same in 1958. There was no real citywide celebration. I didn't mind. I just wanted to pack my bags and head out to the wide open spaces.

I've hunted birds—ducks, quail, whatever—since I was a kid and I really enjoy it. But I never liked deer hunting. The first time I went I shot a deer in the belly. When we finally tracked him and caught up with him, he was sitting there on his rear end—his legs weren't working because the bullet was stuck in his spine. He was looking at me with those big brown eyes, as if he was saying, "Why in hell did you shoot me?"

And I was trying to figure out the same thing.

But almost every Thanksgiving I used to go out hunting with Harold Youngman, just to be with him. I didn't really care if I got any deer or not. When Billy started going with us, I would let him shoot my quota.

Right around Thanksgiving of that year, Billy and Whitey came along on my annual hunting trip with Harold down near Kerrville, Texas. It meant five days of camping in rocky territory, about fifty miles or so north of San Antonio. We had an old beatup Model A that maneuvered us around pretty good. One day we were riding along. We suddenly spot a buck. Whitey is sitting between me and Billy. He sets his rifle right against my left ear and—*blam*—pulls the trigger. When we stop the car and jump out, I can't hear anything. We all laugh about it later, but Whitey looks a little green because he realizes that if we'd hit a bump he could have hit one of us.

After the hunt, I flew back to Joplin with Harold in his private plane. Merlyn had checked into the hospital the day I left for

Kerrville. The night before she had complained of some discomfort. Nothing severe. She thought it might be labor pains, but I went hunting anyway. Why interrupt the trip? It was important and I figured ten to one she'd deliver after I got back. Besides, she didn't insist on me staying. In fact, she wasn't very upset when I left.

So my third son Billy Giles was born in Joplin. I finally arrived at the hospital and all the odds went out the window. There was my boy and Merlyn was weeping. "You could've waited a few more days instead of taking off like that . . ."

I apologized. Not that it did much good. She felt I had committed a terrible crime. Looking at her side of it, I guess she had every reason to feel that way, alone as she was, then calling her father, and the rush to the hospital, passing cars on the road and barely getting there before the baby was born.

I stood by her bed. She turned toward me, smiling. I said, "Did you pick a name yet?"

"Of course. I named him Billy, after Billy Martin, as we had planned. And his second name is Giles, after my dad."

I bent forward and kissed her. A fine compromise.

Chapter *21*

I'd like to forget 1959 altogether, as far as baseball goes. The whole season seemed to be loaded with mishaps. Actually, my record wasn't that bad, yet too much went wrong. It was only the second time we lost the pennant in the time I had been with the team.

We finished third, fifteen games behind the White Sox and ten behind the second-place Indians. A disaster. And as our fortunes sank, my moods became darker. I'd sit with my head hanging, deep in the dumps, knowing I wasn't contributing as much as I wanted to. Aggravating injuries were part of it. I also worried about my hitting, worried about helping the guys I worked and played with—I worried about everything. I was miserable. As usual, the problems began with George Weiss and his lousy contracts. This one called for a $10,000 cut in salary. I jammed it in an envelope unsigned and sent it back along with a note demanding $85,000. When camp opened I was on the sidelines; a holdout. The next morning Weiss wheedled me into his office. We went at it. Finally he threw in the towel. I got a $2,000 raise.

There were guys who fared worse than I did. They had less bargaining power and signed under the gun. So much for morale. Still another problem was Casey. The old spark seemed to be flickering. He was sixty-nine, getting a bit crotchety. If he'd been up drinking all night he'd let his coaches run the team while he took a quick snooze on the bench, snoring and farting, and everybody would have to move.

It was the kind of season that began with a string of injuries. Larsen and Sturdivant pitched with sore arms. Andy Carey had an infected hand. McDougald was out for a while, having been hit on both hands by a pitch. My number came up in Baltimore. I hurried a throw and reinjured my shoulder. A day or two later

I went out for batting practice. Duke Maas lobbed one in. I waited too long. The ball hit my right index finger and chipped a bone. The following day I got career home run No. 250, batting from the right side. Turned the other way, I couldn't hold a bat without feeling pain. As for the shoulder, it still hurt, but I could live with it. I wasn't about to give in. I had an urge to keep plugging, to maintain a winning spirit, to stay in the lineup and contribute. The urge never left me.

I think of Pete Reiser, a guy who they say was carried off the field eleven times in ten years. They tell me he could've been the greatest if not for the injuries. I don't know. I never saw him play. But if Reiser was all that was said of him, meaning he'd go out day after day, putting everything on the line regardless of the risk, knowing full well that it might cancel his career, then I've got to say he must've been one of the greatest.

I've read about Ty Cobb, supposedly the most individualistic of them all. He was dynamite on the base paths. He played with his heart and his head. And that lifetime batting average of .367 —incredible! For me, though, the greatest thing about Cobb is that he was still ready to risk a broken leg at any time to help his club come in first.

I'll mention this from personal experience. Joe DiMaggio was the same kind of player. In his final season, notwithstanding the sore arms and bad legs and that constantly painful heel, when the team needed him he was there. He gave his all, right to the end.

I cite DiMaggio and think of Moose Skowron. Joe Pepitone told him one time, "They don't call you Moose because you're big and strong. It's because you have a head like one." On the field nobody worked any harder. He was a fine, underrated first baseman, a terrific hitter, could drive any type of pitch out of there. Who knows how great Moose would have been if not for his injuries?

We were in Los Angeles to play a benefit game against the Dodgers. It was Roy Campanella Day, May 7, 1959, with some 93,000 people on hand to honor Campy, who had had a car accident the year before. A great career ended. He was in a wheelchair, paralyzed. During the game they turned out all the lights and asked everyone to light a match. I don't suppose everybody in the stadium had a match because there were so many kids there, but after the matches were lit it was like daylight. Unbelievable.

On the bus going to the coliseum, Moose and I talked about our memories of Campy, recalling those World Series games in Brooklyn, the old Dodgers of Reese and Robinson and all. Gradually we got to talking about other things. Finally Moose said, "I'm gonna shut my eyes a minute" grimacing as he shifted his weight to take pressure off his back. He had a chronic muscle pull and wore a corset. He couldn't lie down on soft beds and often had to sleep in a chair, sitting straight up. Now he leaned forward, nestled his hand under his chin, and, a moment later, conked out.

I was chewing some bubble gum. Gus Mauch, the Yankee trainer, was seated directly in front of me. I was staring at his hair. He had a great big mop, kind of a gray dyed red, like Danny Kaye's. Furthermore, Gus was extremely proud of his hair. He was always combing it and went to expensive barber shops for the royal treatment.

I roll up a little ball of gum and throw it at his hair. He takes a swipe at it, maybe thinking it's a mosquito. I throw another. So it goes. I'm throwing and he's swiping, never once turning around or even suspecting that his hair is getting loaded with little balls of bubble gum.

Now we're at the coliseum, a few minutes before batting practice. Gus comes running into the clubhouse, his eyes darting this way and that way, obviously looking for the culprit. He says in his Bugs Bunny voice, "I wish to Christ I could find the guy who put that gum in my hair." I'm busy tying my shoelaces. Everybody else is either laughing or protesting their innocence. The chagrin on Gus's face turns to genuine anger. His finger sweeps full circle. He yelps, "I hope the guy who did it breaks his legs today!"

Poor Moose. He goes out and rips a hamstring muscle behind his right leg running to first on an infield hit. As they bring him into the clubhouse, I pull Gus aside, point to Moose, and say, "There's the guy who did it!"

Two weeks later we went into last place for the first time since 1940. The whole team seemed to fold. There was an outbreak of Asian flu and other things turned rotten. No hitting, the pitching not much better, and we sent Tom Sturdivant and Johnny Kucks and Jerry Lumpe to the A's for third baseman Hector Lopez and Ralph Terry. Lopez was a Panamanian. He helped us get back into the race that year. A good natural hitter who later became a valuable fourth outfielder and pinch hitter.

Terry was as country as can be. He was from Chelsa, Oklahoma, near Commerce. A likable kid, yet we weren't very close, despite our common background. Anyway, he got to be a top Yankee hurler, peaking in 1962 with 23 wins to lead the league. Unfortunately, he didn't get the big press.

It was also getting harder and harder for me to deal with the press. Especially the New York writers. They'd come in and there'd always be somebody trying for the jugular. Leonard Schecter of the New York *Post* was one of them. He'd ask his questions and the next day I'd read things that didn't sound like me. If I told him he had twisted my words around, Schecter would say, "Oh no, you really said that." It was a no-win situation. As time went by I finally figured, "If that's the way it's going to be, okay, I won't talk to him at all." It slowly developed into a contest of wills, a contest I wanted no part of. I just wished he'd leave me alone.

Naturally I was friendly with some of the writers in New York: Joe Trimble, Harold Rosenthal, Dick Young, John Drebinger— all good people. Ben Epstein was a marvelous man. In the first part of my career, he came to know as much about me as anyone. And in Washington I trusted Bob Addie, Shirley Povich, and Moe Siegel.

Joe King of the New York *World-Telegram* seemed a decent enough guy. He would faithfully report what he saw. The problem there, he'd sometimes *hear* things the wrong way. For instance, in 1965, when Johnny Keane managed us, I was moved by Keane from center to left field. King asked Whitey what he thought about it. Whitey said, "I've been pitching fourteen years for this club, trying to keep guys from hitting the ball to Mantle in center field. Now I'm gonna have to keep them from hitting it to left."

It was an inside joke. Nobody could possibly misinterpret Whitey's remark. That is, unless you were Joe King. He wrote that Whitey was "boiling mad" because I had been shifted over. Once again, a case of the accurate quote and the inaccurate interpretation.

However, to the best of my recollection, I'd say the press was more than fair with me. They wrote the stories. Hits, runs, and errors. An article here and there about some problem an individual had to face. There was little written about me and my family, except the usual nice things. You know, the Commerce Kid and the Oklahoma background, the struggles and such. During the fifties that's what they wrote. Movie stars and ballplayers were still being held up as heroes. As in Babe Ruth's heyday, when they made him out to be a fun-loving big old happy guy. Today they would rip him apart. He'd be crucified because the norm is sensationalism. At least in the fifties they primarily mixed fact, fiction, and fancy in the coverage of games. Psychology was confined to how you did as a player. And at that stage of my career, I had not yet broken loose from the DiMaggio comparison.

Notwithstanding the two MVPs, they were still saying I was only out for myself, uncooperative, testy, a miserable pain in the ass. Now, if a writer had said I booted a ball and let the winning run in, well, if it was true, I would never complain. But the booting of a ball has nothing to do with instinct, purpose, desire, zeal, and all the other things that determine a ballplayer's psyche. Mine must've been fairly strong. I withstood the abuse.

Meanwhile the team slump continued. By the middle of June we were only in fifth place and I was pressing. This added to my frustration. The pressures built up on all sides. And the fans got on me worse than ever. One game it got so bad I ran into the dugout, boiling. Casey gave me one of those "Watch your step" looks, as he was under enormous pressure himself. Evidently the owners were not happy with the way he was running the club. I know Dan Topping had criticized him publicly, saying he had overworked the platoon system. Then there were the rumors about Casey and George Weiss having serious differences.

True or not, I know that Casey was starting to get on some of the players through the press. I remember when Ralph Terry lost a game on a home run pitch. Casey called in the writers and said the only thing wrong with Ralph was that he didn't have enough sense to cross the street.

One day he told me, "I'm gonna buy you some paper dolls to tear up. Maybe that'll curb your temper." Darned if he didn't buy me a whole bunch of paper dolls. Then he got me one of those Joe Palooka bounce-back punching bags. "Hit that the next time you strike out," he growled.

But whatever Casey did, he thought he was doing right. Nothing he could have done would have provoked me to show him up in public. Even if he had slapped me in front of the whole team, I would have taken it. That was the relationship; that was the understanding.

The fans in Baltimore were the toughest on me when I had a bad day. On the way there, Casey said, "I'm going to have to fine you if you kick the water cooler or do anything like that anymore . . ." The following night we play the Orioles and the first thing I do is strike out. The fans are yelling, "Hit the water cooler! Hit the water cooler!" I'm taking a drink and hear this.

Now in Baltimore the water cooler is one of those big inverted glass bottles. Before I know it I've got it in my hands, haul it out in front of the whole stadium, and smash it on the ground—*blam!* And Casey goes nuts.

I was disgusted. Mad at the fans, mad at the pitcher, mad at Casey, myself, everybody. But I had no intention to do what I did. What I had was a rage to succeed. A blind rage. I'll say it once more—I can't stand to be beat.

As the Chicago White Sox went into the World Series to play Los Angeles, I went home to Dallas, bitterly disappointed over our third-place finish and far from happy with my .285 batting average, 31 homers, and 75 RBIs. The only pleasing thing was knowing I had topped the league in fielding percentage.

That December there was another trade. Hank Bauer, Don Larsen, Norm Siebern, and Marv Throneberry were shipped to Kansas City. They sent us Joe DeMaestri, Kent Hadley, and Roger Maris.

Though I lost a lot of good friends in that trade, especially Hank, I consider myself lucky to have found a new friend in Roger Maris. He came to the Yankees virtually unknown and nobody paid any real attention to him until he hit the 61 homers. But I had seen him in early 1957, his rookie season. We were playing Cleveland. One look and I knew. He hit line drives, had speed on the base paths, a great arm, excellent range in the outfield. Then later that season he busted a couple of ribs trying to break up a double play. It knocked him out of the running for Rookie of the Year honors. Another problem he was having was the platooning. Bobby Bragan, the Cleveland manager, had been shuttling him back and forth with Rocky Colavito, a situation that made Roger very unhappy. So the following year general manager Frank Lane sent him on to Kansas City. There he played under Harry Craft.

Sometimes after a game I'd meet Harry at his hotel. We'd talk baseball at the bar downstairs. The usual stuff. Harry would mention certain players around the league and I remember a night when he said that Roger would hit a lot of home runs if he played for the Yankees. "The stadium is tailor-made for him. My gosh, it's only 296 feet down the right field foul line. With his ability to pull the ball, he'd have a picnic." My instinct told me that Harry knew what he was talking about. And he laughed and said, "It's one thing to speculate, but the fact is we want Roger in Kansas City. He *could* be another Mantle."

I smiled.

Then we got back to discussing somebody else.

Chapter 22

It's been said that baseball is only a game and the fate of the world doesn't rest on winning or losing a pennant. But when you watch baseball at its best there's a tendency to forget the real world: wars, famine, natural disasters, the day-to-day problems. People would rather think about Babe Ruth, Willie Mays, Hank Aaron, and Stan Musial. Who wants to be reminded of Attila the Hun? What really counts is the dream to be as great as the guy with the big batting average, the big strikeout record, the big fat contract he gets for playing a simple game. It's how we see the American success story. Everybody loves a star.

Take George Weiss. He loved me so much the first thing he did in 1960 was forward my contract by special delivery. I was not prepared. I figured, "Gee, this must be a misprint. Nobody in their right mind would offer me a $17,000 cut." But I was dreaming again. When I woke up I called him. He said, "It's no misprint. Your performance last year was poor. The best we can do is $55,000." I said, "Mr. Weiss, it's an insult and I won't go to camp under these circumstances."

There was a deafening silence on his end of the line. I slammed the phone down. Hard to believe. As far as he was concerned, if I showed up, fine. Otherwise things would go on as if I had never existed.

Ten days after camp opened, I flew to St. Petersburg. He seemed pleased. He said, "Let's talk. I'm a reasonable man." I had little to say beyond the refusal to accept his initial terms. It ended in a compromise. I took a $10,000 cut, then came out feeling like a prisoner of war.

The reporters were waiting. They got what they wanted: a shattered ballplayer trying to put up a brave front. And to face them was the bitterest pill of all.

I didn't do much in the spring training games. There's no question that emotional stress led to a lot of negative reactions. I'd scream out my disgust and Casey would look at me with sparks flying from his eyes. Meanwhile the rest of the club wasn't doing too good either. We finished the exhibitions at the bottom of the American League barrel.

Then Opening Day and we beat the Red Sox. Roger Maris got off to a helluva start. He hit two home runs and knocked in four. He also played aggressively in right field, hustling all the time. You could tell he'd have no trouble making the switch from Kansas City to New York.

By the end of May I probably had a .250 batting average. At this point I realized that a very thin line separates self-assuredness and absolute uncertainty. I found myself on the other side of the line. I had allowed the humiliating pay cut to affect my attitude. From the moment I had suited up at camp, that above everything else was the needle. And behind it was Weiss, a coldhearted, calculating old buzzard whose visions of baseball sat at opposite poles from mine.

Realizing this, I finally understood my problem. To correct it took a little time.

Because one day I walked away from a third strike, not bothering to notice that the ball had skipped past the catcher. Ordinarily I would've sped to first like a panther, but now I'm halfway to the bench, watching the putout, mad as hell, knowing I might've beaten the throw.

Later in the season I really screwed it up.

It happened at the stadium during a game with the Senators. Roger was on first base, the score tied, and one out. I bounced a ground ball to the infield. Believing there were two out, I quit running after a few steps. It's like a betrayal, totally ignoring a basic rule. In this case, the rule says you run on everything. Nowhere in the fine print does it say ". . . with the exception of . . ." To make it even worse, I didn't give Roger a fighting chance to spoil the double play, although he slid into the bag so forcefully that he bruised his ribs in the process.

That's when the fans let me have it. They booed and kept

booing. The loudest, most venomous eruption of noise I had ever encountered. Who could blame them? I had it coming and Casey did something any good manager would have done under the same circumstances. He benched me and sent Bob Cerv in to play center field. It stung almost as much as the boos. What *really* blew my mind was that Roger nearly wrecked himself trying to keep the inning alive.

The following night we played Baltimore. Man, how I ached to get into the game. And how the fans poured it on when my name was announced. No sooner done than their shouts rolled in from the bleachers and formed one big continuous roar of abuse. I shut my ears to everything, even to the catcalls that trailed me to the bench after I grounded out in the first inning.

The Orioles came up and Ron Hansen hit a home run to put them ahead. On my second trip, batting left-handed, I laced a pitch over the right center field fence into the bullpen. As I circled the bases, the jeers slowly receded. A ripple of applause broke through, then some cheers, getting louder and louder still. I crossed the plate, then tipped my hat to the crowd— something I almost never did. That home run sure gave me a wonderful feeling.

Then Baltimore grabbed the lead again, coming off a home run by Jackie Brandt. In the bottom of the eighth they had Hoyt Wilhelm pitching. His special pitch was a knuckleball that would dance in and go right by you. After waving my bat at the first one, I popped a high foul behind the plate. Clint Courtney dropped his mask and ran over to gather it in. He wore this huge glove, large enough to cover a manhole. The ball dribbled out and landed at his feet. Now, with a two-strike count and lucky that I had another chance, I hit the next knuckler into the upper deck and we won the game.

The next day they're writing about my courage in battling back. All the papers were congratulatory. There's not a bad word anywhere. Everybody was with me again. The lesson: Things get turned around if you give them enough time.

In 1960 I played just about every ball game. Though my batting average dipped to .275, I hit 40 home runs. It led the league. Roger hit 39, took the RBI title with 112, and was so outstanding that he won the Most Valuable Player Award. Moose had a great season, too, shrugging off his injuries to provide additional firepower. He hit 26 homers and played the best ball of his career. And Yogi was still doing a helluva job for us. Most of the time Casey played him in left field. Yogi expected it. He was thirty-five years old, past his prime as an everyday catcher, the most physically punishing position of all.

Now, Yogi was not a stylish catcher. Far from it. But in my opinion nobody ever called the games any better than he did. However, when I first joined the club, either Casey or Jim Turner would meet with him and tell him which pitches to call. After a year or two he was left on his own. They trusted his judgment. But some people couldn't resist trying to second-guess somebody else's mistake.

I remember a particular game up in Boston in the early fifties. It was one of those heart-thumpers, a succession of zeroes on the scoreboard. In the seventh we added another zero. In the bottom half the Red Sox had a couple of guys on base with two out and the batter was Walt Dropo. The man stood six feet five inches tall and was built like a Mack truck. He could really whack the fastball, but show him a slow curve and you'd have a much better chance to get him out.

Well, Dropo takes a swing at Raschi's first pitch. A fastball. He goes completely around and staggers back. Casey calls time. He's at the mound, jawing with Raschi and Yogi, then stomps off, letting out these loud grunts, meanwhile wagging his finger at Yogi, who's nodding his head like, "Yeah yeah, I understand. Don't worry about it . . ." But all the time he's pounding his glove as if the Old Man's head is stuck in the pocket.

Another fastball and Dropo kisses it goodbye. The score is 3–0. Raschi gets the next guy on a soft liner to Rizzuto. After the game we go into the clubhouse.

Casey starts hollering at Yogi. "Why did you call for a fastball? Didn't I ask you to call for a slow curve? Huh, huh? Well, the son of a bitch didn't hit the curve because you didn't call it and if you called it we would've been out of the goddamn inning instead of down by three runs!"

Yogi says, "Ah now, Casey . . ."

And Casey starts hollering again.

Finally Yogi gets all red in the face and says, "That's it. You call the pitches from now on. I ain't gonna call them no more."

"Oh, *you're* not gonna call them no more. You mean little Yogi ain't gonna call the signals? *B-u-l-l-s-h-i-t!* You'll do whatever the hell I tell you to do!"

Now in 1960 Yogi was making the transition from catcher to outfielder. I'll admit I was getting on him for calling games, in other words telling the best handler of pitchers in history what signs to give against different hitters. One day he says, "Okay, I'll let you run the show."

Very clever. Also kinda silly to anybody who knows I never called a game in my life. Despite this, Yogi and I get together on it. I say, "When I stand straight up, it's a fastball. When I bend over and put my hands on my knees, you'll know it's a curve." And so forth.

Now, a couple of days later, Whitey is pitching a helluva game. But we're not getting any runs either. Going into the eighth inning, there's no score and I'm nervous, actually afraid I might call a wrong pitch. "Geez, what if I call a fastball and the hitter knocks it right out of the park?" Suddenly I begin to realize what Yogi has to go through. Nonetheless, it's coming down to the crunch, the ninth inning, and I'm saying to myself, "Damn, we better get ourselves some runs because I don't want this kind of responsibility."

Just then the leadoff batter steps in. A nothing. The guy is absolutely terrible, the worst excuse for a ballplayer I've ever seen. Only, by now he looks more and more like Babe Ruth. I'm worried that he's going to hit one clear over Babe's monument and we'll lose the game.

Meanwhile Yogi's waiting for the signal. He gets off his haunches and stares at me. I turn my back. Enough of this nonsense. He, in turn, trots to the mound. There's a short conference. Whitey takes off his cap, his signal that I can rest easy.

After the game I questioned him. "What were you and Yogi talking about while Whatzisface was up?"

He explained patiently. "We figured that if he hit one you would've had a heart attack. We didn't want the responsibility."

We won the game, 1–0.

The first and last time I ever called pitches by remote control.

I also gained a lot of respect for Yogi.

The 1960 season was particularly enjoyable because the team meshed in late summer, everyone pulling together, nobody slacking off. We had a superb bullpen, bolstered even further by Luis Arroyo, who came over from Cincinnati and saved a few games for us. Then Bill Stafford was brought up from Richmond. A gritty kid. He went 3–1 in the final weeks and had a low ERA. Our frontline pitchers were Ford, Ditmar, and Turley. Jim Coates did a good job during the early sledding, at a time when Ford and Terry were having their problems. With Whitey it was the tendonitis. One game he'd throw a shutout, the next would be a struggle. In September he was never better, winning his last three starts. Terry's problem corrected itself once he stopped experimenting with an assortment of new pitches. I know Casey used to get hopping mad whenever Terry threw the slow curve as a sort of test against the hitters. At any rate, Casey demoted him to the bullpen and kept him there until he agreed to forget the experimenting and rely on his mainstay, a blazing fastball. The following spring Johnny Sain became pitching coach and under his direction Terry went from 10–8 to 16–3. So a fresh approach really made the difference.

Without a doubt those teams from 1960 to 1964 were the strongest I had played on. In 1960 we had a great infield: Skowron, Richardson, Kubek, and Boyer. Boyer was a class act at third, a real magnet for line drives. Richardson was flawless; Kubek played short with skill and determination. Skowron might not have been the greatest defensive first baseman who ever lived, no argument there. But he did the job better than most. In fact, he led the league in putouts and I know he played first base thinking he was the best. So maybe he was, after all.

People don't remember our pitching staff being really overpowering. But they led the league in saves, team ERA, and shutouts and Bobby Shantz won the Gold Glove.

To complete the picture, we had Berra, Howard, McDougald, Maris, Lopez, Cerv, and I'm not about to skip over our center fielder, either. Altogether the offense generated 193 home runs to set a new American League season record. Maris led the league in RBIs and slugging average and I had the most home runs and the most total bases.

When the season ended we were in front by the proverbial mile, which came off a fifteen-game winning streak. From mid-September right to the wire everybody was keyed up and ready for the Series against Pittsburgh, absolutely sure that we couldn't lose.

Then a real mysterious thing happened. Casey didn't start Whitey in the opener. Here's the number-one all-time pitcher for World Series wins and our manager goes with Art Ditmar. Fate, circumstance, whatever—the decision either blows up in your face or makes you into a genius. I have always said this and I never second-guessed Casey in my life, but I believe the whole Series revolved around that decision. My hunch is that he was saving Whitey for the stadium. Of course, you can't go back. Casey never explained why he started Ditmar. I don't think anybody knows. If he *did* make a mistake, you could wait a million years and still not get him to admit it.

So we opened at Forbes Field and Ditmar got beat. Going into the sixth game, the Pirates were one up after Harvey Haddix and Elroy Face held us to five hits and two runs. Meanwhile Ditmar took his second loss. Game six had us in Pittsburgh, where Whitey threw his second shutout and we bombed them, 12–0.

The next day was the day of the Mazeroski home run. Nothing ever hurt as bad as that one. I remember Bobby Shantz pitching brilliantly in relief of Bill Stafford, who had relieved Bob Turley. We were ahead when Gino Cimoli came to bat in the bottom of the eighth inning. He singled. Then Bill Virdon hit a sure double play ball to Kubek, only, it took a sudden hop and struck him in the Adam's apple. He was knocked dizzy. The ball trickled away. Cimoli went safely into second and Virdon made it to first. Meanwhile Kubek's on the ground, choking. What a scene. Gus Mauch out there with his first-aid kit, Casey yelling, "Give him room! Give him room!", and the rest of us walking around stupefied until Kubek got to his feet, appearing as though he had just disgorged a rock from his throat.

Joe DeMaestri replaced him. The next batter was Dick Groat. He singled past Boyer for a run. We still held the lead, 7–5. Then Casey brings Jim Coates in from the bullpen. He pitches to Bob Skinner, who bunts the runners along. Rocky Nelson flies medium-deep to Maris. Virdon stays glued to third, knowing better than to challenge Roger's arm. Two out and Coates slows it down a bit, pitching carefully to Roberto Clemente, who hits a chopper to Skowron. I'm already on my way in from center field, thinking the inning's finally over as Skowron moves to his right, fields the ball, and turns.

Hey! What the hell is Coates doing! I see him stop dead in his tracks between the pitcher's mound and first base! He didn't make the play. He *presumed* Moose would cover the bag. But Moose is standing helplessly by as Virdon scores. Right then and there—no question in the world—Casey should have pulled Coates out of the game. The situation demanded it. He was fidgeting like a man with ants in his pants. You don't let the man pitch.

He worked a full count to Hal Smith, cranked up, eyeballed Groat at first, and threw a lovely fastball. Smith's bat whipped around and the ball jumped over the 406-foot cement wall in left field. They had three runs and a 9–7 lead.

Then Casey brings in Ralph Terry, who holds off the inevitable by getting Don Hoak on a fly ball to end the inning.

Bobby Richardson opens the ninth with a single. Then Dale Long pinch-hits a single, which sends Bobby on to third, and McDougald comes off the bench to run for Long. Next Roger fouls out. My turn and I single to right center, scoring Richardson.

Yogi is our next hitter. He grounds hard to first. Fortunately, I'm leaning in and dive safely under Nelson's tag as McDougald scores the tying run.

Bottom of the ninth. Bill Mazeroski is at the plate, taking the first pitch, a high slider . . . And the vivid memory of Johnny Blanchard going out to tell Terry to keep the ball down and me glancing at Yogi and Roger, the three of us breathing heavy sighs when Blanchard hunches down, gives Terry the sign . . . And the most tearing moment of all, seeing Mazeroski's hard line drive heading for the left field wall. Yogi moves toward it, me backing him up, but it keeps going, going, going . . .

There's a sick sensation in the pit of my stomach. There's that unforgettable look on Yogi's face when he turns around, grim acceptance, expressed by a slow shrug of his shoulders. We walk off the field, a mob of fans already streaming past, and as Mazeroski crosses the plate his hysterical teammates grab at his uniform.

In the locker room, all of us are wandering around in a trance, muttering, "What happened?" I'm slumped on a stool, feeling so low I can hardly peel off my uniform.

In all my World Series experience, that was the one time when I really thought the better team had lost.

Two days later the Yankees dismissed Casey. They needed a change, I guess. At the press conference in New York, Dan Topping said they were letting him go because of his advanced age. To me, it seemed like a cruel thing to announce after all that Casey had done for the club. Don't get me wrong, I felt—I feel now—that Dan Topping was a gracious individual. I won't say anything against him or against Del Webb, for that matter. I just believe they were too far removed from the scene up in their private boxes. You can't see very much from that distance.

With Casey it was age. With Billy it was the detective reports. Bad for the image. Nothing personal, you know, just good business practices. Maybe so. But I felt Topping should have taken a different course. I mean, there is such a thing as consideration for services rendered.

A month after Casey was dismissed, George Weiss retired. The irony is, George Weiss, the classic example of a man who had dollar signs in his eyes and ice in his blood, actually cried at the press conference announcing his retirement.

Now, when a man like George Weiss sheds a tear, what can you do? I know what I did. When I read the announcement, I poured me a drink, lifted the glass, and said, "Goodbye, George, you tough old bastard."

Chapter 23

Ralph Houk first managed the club from 1961 to 1963, then again from 1966 to 1973. During his first stint, he had a perfect record, winning three pennants. So people ask, "How would you compare him to Stengel?" And I say, "They were both great." In fact, Ralph patterned himself after Casey. He ran along the same lines. No pets, good with the rookies, and had an excellent coaching staff.

But there was a difference. Where Casey relied heavily on the platoon system, Ralph went for the set lineup. Where Casey saved his best pitchers for the top contenders, Ralph stuck to a regular rotation, no matter who we played. The only other thing that separated them was the manner in which they did their jobs. If necessary, Ralph could be tough, yet he never questioned a player's ability, at least not while I was around. His approach was based on a simple premise. "Don't be discouraged, I'm sure you're doing your best."

The day he took over the club, he came to me and said, straight out, "I'm naming you team leader."

I felt relieved.

He grinned. "Well, what do you say?"

"Gee, I don't know. What will I have to do?"

He said, "I don't want you to do anything more than keep the guys fired up by your own actions. I know you can."

You have to understand that Whitey and Yogi were the only other regular players from the old days who were still with the Yankees. We were older, looked up to. Why, they even called Whitey the Chairman of the Board and he would step in to settle disputes.

So I was flattered at the time by what Ralph said to me. But looking back, I'd bet that he made the same speech to Whitey and Yogi.

It was some year. Under Ralph's leadership, we set a new Yankee record for wins and ran away with the pennant. The Tigers finished second. They had a powerhouse team. Norm Cash won the batting title and hit 41 home runs. Rocky Colavito hit 45, Al Kaline 19—that's a total of 105. But Mantle and Maris did better, hitting a combination of 115, an all-time event in itself. It broke the Ruth–Gehrig mark. A baseball highlight, certainly, and there are enough of those to fill an encyclopedia: Cookie Lavagetto busting up a World Series no-hitter, Carl Hubbell's All-Star masterpiece, Gabby Hartnett's "homer in the gloamin'," Joe DiMaggio's 56-game hitting streak, Don Larsen's perfect World Series game . . . Well, the single greatest feat I ever saw was Roger Maris hitting his 61 home runs to break Babe Ruth's record. I was with him practically every step of the way and know the dues he paid to get there.

Remember, in 1956 I came close. Into the final month I was ahead of the Babe's pace, so I felt the same kind of pressure that Roger went through. People taking your picture, reporters bombarding you with stupid questions, speculations and false accusations without the least concern for your own human needs. Okay, I could cope, I had been in the center ring since my rookie year. Not Roger. He had never been subjected to anything like this before. It really got crazy. Every day you'd read what Mantle and Maris did. Nothing else seemed to matter except the Home Run Derby. Whitey went 25–4 that year and hardly anyone noticed. The rest of the guys were forgotten soldiers. But instead of resenting the publicity we were getting, they teased us about it. A cry would go up in the clubhouse. "Hey, what did Mantle do?" "I don't know. What did Maris do?" Laughing, joking—hell, the guys were great!

Meanwhile there was the press—a lot of antagonists out there saying Roger and I didn't like each other. Pure fiction. Furthest thing from the truth. During our race to catch the Babe, we shared an apartment with Bob Cerv. Now the three of us lived in Queens, close to Kennedy Airport. Between games we'd hang around and read, relax, listen to country music. Sometimes we'd go out to eat in a nearby restaurant and we talked about the home run duel quite often.

Roger was very private. He hated public attention. He got a bad rap from the writers and fans alike, mostly because he was still new to the team and pressing in on the record.

Through it all we remained close. There was never any jealousy. I rooted for him and definitely rooted for myself. Besides, with Roger hitting good it made me try harder. So, if there was a rivalry it was a friendly one. In fact, when we did hear some rumor about us not getting along, we used it as a running gag. Like, we'd sit in the apartment, reading the paper. I'd put mine down, look over at him, and say, "I hate your guts." He'd laugh. Some feud. All my feuds should be as nice as the one I had with Roger. Believe me, I'd have no enemies.

The point is, I understood him, his reactions, even at a distance. How he stood up I'll never know. A writer once asked him, "How come a .260 hitter like you manages to get more home runs than Babe Ruth?" And Roger answered, "What are you—a newspaperman or a goddamn idiot?" A while later he came to me and said, "Mick, I can't take it anymore." I had to tell him, "Just hang in there. It'll be over soon."

Toward the end of the season, patches of Roger's hair started to fall out because of nerves. I remember. We were in Baltimore and Bob Turley invited a bunch of Yankees out to his house for cocktails and dinner. A bit of relaxation around his swimming pool. Late that afternoon we sat out by the pool in bathing suits borrowed from Bob.

I'm telling Roger I used to be the Oklahoma state swimming champion. His eyes open wide as saucers. I keep bragging about all the diving medals I've won doing triple back flips, besides my unbeatable records in the 200-meter breaststroke and the 400-meter butterfly. Roger doesn't know I can't swim. He swims like a fish. He must have been born in a swimming pool, that's how good he is. Well, I'm going on and on and finally Roger says, "Okay, let's see how well you can do against me." Bob is all excited to stage this great big swimming meet between Mantle and Maris. Meanwhile old Slick is two steps ahead of everybody.

He gets one of those long brooms that you clean the pool with. The handle is maybe ten feet long. So I line up with Roger at one end of the pool. Turley signals and we dive in. Soon as I hit the water, Whitey has the handle waiting. I catch hold and he runs.

Suddenly Whitey veers off and starts pulling me along the side of the pool, scraping the skin off my arm. But I won't turn loose for anything.

I'm hanging on to the end of the pool sweep. Whitey is running so fast I'm leaving a wake. He pulls me up to the other end real fast and I jump out. And here comes Roger like an Olympian, breaking all the international records. He touches the edge, blinks, and sees me sitting on a lounge chair, legs crossed, sipping a drink. He says, "How the hell did you get here?" Then he sees my bleeding arm. Finally he puts two and two together and grins.

"I'll be a son of a bitch," he says.

Around mid-August we were even in home runs with 45 and drawing capacity crowds. We needed special cops to escort us in and out of the ballparks. We couldn't enter a dining room or a hotel lobby without having a horde of writers, photographers, TV and radio people—everybody—breathing down on our necks. The tension was unbelievable.

On September 3, I hit a pair of home runs at Yankee Stadium and trailed Roger by three. A week later he hit his 56th home run off Mudcat Grant in Cleveland. The next day I hit No. 53 off Jim Perry. We had eighteen games remaining. I felt sore and stiff, my legs bothered me, and I also developed a real bad head cold. Regardless, this was the big push.

On the way back from Boston, I was still suffering with the cold and Mel Allen, the Yankee broadcaster, said, "I have a doctor. He'll give you a shot that'll fix you right up."

The doctor's office was somewhere on 79th Street, off Central Park. His patients included people like Eddie Fisher, Tennessee Williams, and Elizabeth Taylor, just to give you an idea of his reputation. "He's above reproach, the best there is," says Mel. He picks up the phone and makes an appointment for me to see this doctor, Max Jacobson, that very evening. I can't wait to get there.

Dr. Max. He greets me at the door wearing a white smock with bloodstains all over it. Like a lamb, I follow him into his office. Now I'm watching him prepare a syringe and needle. He's mixing the stuff and so help me his eyes are literally rolling in his head as he draws a smoky liquid from the vial, squirts a little in the air, and tells me to pull down my pants. I oblige. He walks around. "All right, here we go. This might hurt, but then again it may not."

As soon as it hits the skin, I scream. "Goddamn, that hurts!"

He stuck the needle up too high. It felt as though he had stuck a red hot poker into me. I'm paralyzed. He slaps me on the back. "Walk back to the hotel. Don't take a cab, you'll be fine."

I don't know what he put into the needle, but a few minutes later I find myself on the sidewalk, trying to make it back to the St. Moritz, feeling that at any minute I'm going to faint from the pain. A little old lady comes by and says, "Mister, are you okay? Should I call you a doctor?"

"No, thanks. If you don't mind, I'll lean against the building until you can call me a cab."

The next morning I wake up in my hotel room and realize I'm sweating, sick, burning up with fever. What's more, Merlyn is coming in by train from Dallas and I'm supposed to meet her in a couple of hours. I can't make it to the toilet, let alone to Penn Station, so I call down to the manager of the hotel, asking if he would kindly send somebody to get her because I'm not feeling too well. The manager says there's no problem, he'll take care of it.

A couple of hours later my fever is worse. I'm really dizzy and there's Merlyn at the foot of my bed.

"What happened to you?"

"Nothing much. I just got sucked dry by a vampire."

I finally had to call Ralph Houk and tell him I couldn't play ball that night. It nearly broke my heart, but there was no choice. I ended up in Lenox Hill Hospital, where they lanced the wound, first cutting a three-inch star over the hip bone, then letting it drain. It left a hole so big that you could put a golf ball in it.

P.S. The Yankee front office was furious.

P.P.S. Dr. Max sent me a bill. I never did pay it. I wanted to sue him. A few years later he stopped practicing.

I only started two games after the shot. In Boston I hit my 54th homer. That finished my season and a chance at the record.

Roger got No. 61 on the last day against Tracy Stallard, the Red Sox pitcher. A bunch of the guys pushed him back on the field so he could wave his cap at the stadium crowd. I watched it on TV from my hospital bed.

Now Roger is listed with the Babe. I'll tell you, he did it like a true champion. He never cracked, not once during the whole ordeal.

We played the Series, routing Cincinnati in five games. I got into it long enough to contribute a base hit at Crosley Field. I stood on the bag: My wound had opened, blood oozed through my uniform, running into my stocking. I couldn't go on. Ralph Houk sent Hector Lopez in to run for me. And we eventually won.

But breaking the record became a haunting experience for Roger. Commissioner Ford Frick attached an asterisk next to the 61 homers in the record book because Roger failed to hit them within the first 154 games, which happened to be the schedule when Ruth got the 60. I thought it was a ridiculous ruling. It made no sense at all. Check further and you'll note that the same year, 1961, Sandy Koufax broke Christy Mathewson's National League strikeout record. Mathewson set it in 1903, when they played a 140-game schedule. But you won't find an asterisk attached to Koufax.

As for Roger, in 1962 the fans gave him the worst beating any ballplayer ever took. From April straight through September they stayed on his back. I guess they expected him to hit 62 home runs. They weren't satisfied with 33. So they booed him in every ballpark. At Briggs Stadium he had to walk off the field after a shower of soda bottles came hurtling down from the stands. Detroit was bad. One night somebody heaved a flashlight. Fortunately, it didn't hit Roger. If it had, it could've been fatal.

Well, maybe if I had beaten him in the Home Run Derby, the fans wouldn't have liked me either. But I always felt that people somehow continued to support me because I was from a small town in Oklahoma, that I had played despite injuries for several years, and I had done pretty well.

After Roger set the record, then the ovations came my way. That's when they turned on him and started cheering me. I was human, frail, like them. They could see the cracks in the armor.

So I didn't lose. On two counts. I won over the fans and out of it came a beautiful friendship between me and Roger.

Chapter 24

One of the worst things about baseball is all the traveling. From March to mid-October you hardly ever see your family. By 1961 I had four boys and I hardly knew them. Merlyn was raising them and I didn't get to see her a hell of a lot either. After Billy had been traded, and when Whitey wasn't around, I spent a lot of time alone in hotel rooms, looking down at the lights in some city—Chicago, Minneapolis, Detroit, Los Angeles—thinking about my kids.

I missed them, and I'd remember certain days, like the time I took them to the stadium. They had good seats behind first base and really seemed to be enjoying themselves. Between innings I came back to the clubhouse for one reason or another, just to see how they were doing. During one of the visits, big Pete Sheehy, the equipment manager, drew me aside. He put a finger to his lips. "Shhh . . . you gotta see this." We went into the players' lounge. The kids were curled up on a divan, sound asleep. Mickey Jr. with a ring of strawberry soda pop around his mouth, David holding a half-eaten hot dog, little Danny nestled against Billy's shoulder—just the four of them, sleeping, mustard smeared all over their faces. I'd give anything to have a picture of that today.

I found it hard to keep such moments in focus. Too often I cared more about hanging out with friends after a game. There were too many nights on the road, too many lonely hotels and bars.

My youngest son, Danny, had been born at Baylor Hospital in Dallas in March 1960. But I didn't get to be there for that either because I had to be at spring training in Fort Lauderdale. Baseball came first. It was my life; it had always been my life. When I played, there was no other world. Accordingly, I felt no urgency to leave camp and attend my son's birth.

It's taken a lot of years, but now I can finally admit to myself that I gave Merlyn everything she wanted except having me around enough. I was no better father than I was a husband. I've been to my kids just about like I've been to Merlyn. I didn't spend the time with them that my dad had spent with me.

Merlyn's big complaint has always been that I would never want to come home. Off the road—and it was seldom—I would go to bed late and I wouldn't talk to my kids very much at all. When I was home, I would get up early and go out to play golf, go fishing, or whatever. I couldn't wait to get out of the house.

I did love to play with my kids, though. Some of my best times with the boys—and there weren't very many of them—were weekends spent playing touch football in the backyard. When they were little, I would let them run into my arms like they were carrying the ball and I was tackling them.

One time, shortly after we had moved to Dallas, David discovered that a lot of people wanted my autograph. He didn't know why, but he figured it must've been worth something. I'd sign a batch of pictures and set them aside for my next speaking engagement, then find them missing. He was taking them around from house to house, selling them. I said, "No more. We don't need the money." That's David. Always enterprising.

If I could go back and do it over, I would never have named my first son after me. First day of school, he would stand up in class and give his name and some of the kids would snicker. Also, I recall Merlyn telling me about a plane flight from Florida to New York after spring training. Mickey Jr. got restless, as little boys do, and began to run up and down the aisle. A guy leaned toward him, saying, "Hey, you're cute. What's your name?"

"Mickey Mantle."

The guy throws his head back and roars. "Ho ho ho, this kid thinks he's Mickey Mantle!" Mickey ran back to his seat, his lower lip trembling.

In spring training in 1962, Roger and I were still reaping the benefits of our home run race. Among them was a movie deal.

Three days' work and a guaranteed $25,000 apiece for playing ourselves in a film called *Safe at Home!* It had a Little League theme. A tearjerker. They shot our sequences at the new Yankee camp in Fort Lauderdale. The director was Walt Doninger. He cast Mickey Jr. and David in secondary roles. I flew the family down the day before they began shooting. We were on the practice field. Doninger had his crew in position, checking light values and setting up equipment while the Little League actors got ready for their scene. I was squatting against the fence behind home plate. Doninger was nearby, talking to David.

He says, "All right, now you go into the dugout and I'll be along real soon to explain your part."

David tips his cap. "Yes, sir." Later. I'm bending an ear as Doninger tells him, "The score is tied and a batter on the other team has just smacked a ball that looks like a sure home run. It's going out, farther and farther, and you feel terrible. You want to cry. If the ball goes over the fence, the other team wins."

David shuts one eye, puzzled.

"When you see me give the signal, start cheering. Jump up and down and throw your glove in the air. David, isn't it great! Your center fielder has made the catch! Backhanded—just like your father!"

David looks around. "There's nobody on the field. And my daddy is over there . . ." He points straight at me. I turn my face away, about to bust.

"You're right, David. There's no batter and no fielder. And there's your daddy. But you see, we're just pretending there's a batter and a fielder. So, when I say 'Action,' you start groaning and follow the ball . . ." It's a take. David carries off the role perfectly. He's a big hit. Doninger congratulates him. And David says, "Can I go sit with my daddy now?"

My twelfth year as a Yankee was 1962. Not yet a grind, but getting there. Camp, scuttlebutt, taping the legs, practice, another exhibition season and a new crop of rookies: Joe Pepitone, Tom Tresh, Phil Linz—the Now Generation. To them, a ballplayer was a ballplayer. They wouldn't hesitate for a moment to go out and have a drink with me during spring training. I liked it that way. As a rookie I never felt neglected, just uneasy, always in awe of DiMaggio. I didn't want these kids to feel the same way about me. I wanted them to slap me on the back, pull a joke, whatever—better than to hear someone whisper, "Hey, that's Mickey Mantle. You can't fool with him."

Joe Pepitone? A wisecracking, flashy type. He was the sort of kid who preferred to run around on his own, his hair all blown-dry (the Italian Stallion look), and when he hit the bars—first thing, he would check out the ladies. To make sure his presence was known, he'd shout at the bartender, "If you get any phone calls for Joe Pepitone of the New York Yankees, he's right here."

Always a joke, one adventure after another, every day something brand-new. If he had just cared about *anything,* he could have been on top, among the very best. He had all the tools. A natural home run hitter who played center field better than I did and he was a great first baseman. His downfall? Strangely enough, he never took the game seriously.

Of course, Pepi had a vivid imagination. A while back he wrote a book, *Joe, You Coulda Made Us Proud.* There's a story in it, telling how we went to play the Army. Part of the story is true.

I hired a limousine because we missed the bus. So off we go and I'm carrying along a bottle of vodka and a quart of orange juice. Finally we get to West Point. As Pepi sees it, by now I'm so loaded I instruct the driver to pull up at home plate. Then I stagger out of the limo, hold up the two empty bottles, and yell, "Play ball!"

Cute. But can you imagine me doing a thing like that? Why, Ralph Houk would have kicked my ass clear across the Hudson River all the way back to New York City. This is what I mean about telling a bullshit story that somehow, over a period of time, becomes an accepted fact. It may be funny or sad, but it's simply not true.

Now, when I was a rookie, rooming with Hank Bauer and Johnny Hopp, I did what they told me—almost like a servant. If they wanted a sandwich from the deli downstairs, I would fetch it.

And the same rules applied for a few years after I became a veteran. But by the time Pepi and his bunch came along, the rookies seemed less willing to play by those rules. Still, Whitey and I waited for a year or two before we would let Pepi come along with us after we left the ballpark. And when we did let him join us, the deal was that he would find the cab, open the doors, pay the tip, that sort of thing.

Pretty soon, though, Pepi seemed to get too big for his britches, so we decided to play a little trick on him. One time in Detroit I asked Pepi and Phil Linz if they'd like to have dinner with me and Whitey.

"Yeah, yeah . . ."

"Okay," I said. "There's a swell place called the Flame Lounge. Do you know where it is?"

They shrugged.

"Well," says Whitey, "I'll give you the address. It's not far. Only a couple of bucks by cab. Mick and I will meet you there at eight o'clock. Just ask for our table."

They went for it—hook, line, and sinker.

The next day here's Pepi and Linz, stepping into the team bus. They look very subdued and on the trip to Briggs Stadium both of them say absolutely nothing to either me or Whitey, which naturally heightens my curiosity. At last, Pepi turns around. "Listen, Mick, about last night . . . well, we got delayed and then something else came up and—look, I hope you guys aren't mad."

Whitey says, "What do you mean we aren't mad? You ruined our evening. We waited at least an hour before ordering dinner."

I agree. "And besides, we lost our appetites when you didn't show."

Pepi sees that I'm ready to explode. He says timidly, "You weren't at the Flame Lounge, were you?" Whitey and I howl. Now Phil reacts. "I knew it, I knew it—it's what I kept saying to Pepi all the way over there. I said, 'This is crazy. They're sending us on a wild goose chase!' I mean, the meter was clicking and clicking and the streets got darker and darker—"

Fact is, the joint was on the other side of town. A dilapidated neighborhood—poverty row, a bleak ruin. In the heart of it was the Flame Lounge. You could sit there and watch the strippers and, for sure, a lot of other customers would stare at anyone who happened to be white. I knew about the place because Bobby Layne, the old Detroit Lions quarterback, took me there.

Anyway, I can still picture Pepi going in and asking for Mr. Mantle's table.

In 1962 we played the Giants in the World Series and took it, but not with much help from me. I got three hits in seven games. My strongest effort was a double off Jack Stanford. The big bright spot for me was winning my third MVP Award. The bad memory was of a game against Minnesota, sometime in the middle of May. I was sprinting to first base on an infield hit. The shortstop made a great stab, so I had to pour on a little extra speed. I pulled a hamstring on my right leg—my bad leg, I took a few hops and tore two ligaments and some cartilage in my good leg.

I was out for a month. When I finally returned, it was to pinch hit in Cleveland. I got a long home run off Gary Bell, which put us ahead. The icing on the cake was hearing those fans cheering me around the bases. After that, Ralph Houk used me in a few more pinch-hitting roles. It's a hard job. You come in fresh off the bench and there's only one chance to show yourself. You strike out, you're a bum. Get a base hit and win the game, you're a hero. No in-between. Anyway, I take my hat off to the likes of Johnny Blanchard, who tied the record for World Series pinch hits and who once hit four home runs in a row, two as a pinch hitter. The other successful Yankees were Johnny Mize, Johnny Hopp, Enos Slaughter, Bobby Brown. The best of my time. Then you have Dusty Rhodes of the old Giants. In 1954 he hit 15 homers in 164 plate appearances and batted .341! I'll also mention Smoky Burgess, who played his final years with the White Sox, and Manny Mota, who had the most pinch hits of anybody. I was a fair pinch hitter. After the Minnesota mishap, my problems pinch hitting were running on weak pins and striking out a lot.

I was known as a home run hitter. However, my ratio of home

runs against times at bat is seventh on the all-time list. If I had gotten to bat more times over the eighteen-year period of my career, say 11,000 instead of the actual 8,000, that would give me about 250 more home runs than the 536 I actually got.

Also Yankee Stadium was tough for me because center field was so deep. Today, with the drawn-in center field, there's no telling how many I would have had. And certainly my average would be well over .300.

The big ifs. Tony Kubek once said that if I had played in Atlanta, I'd have hit 1,000 home runs. I believe him. I was in the Old-Timer's Game there. No batting practice in five years and I hit a pitch that was in on my fists over the wall. What could have happened *if* I were an Atlanta Brave or a Brooklyn Dodger. Things like that. What's the sense of it? You get nowhere. What happened, happened.

I was glad to be a Yankee.

In 1963 in a series at Baltimore, I was on the disabled list, probably with a broken toe or foot. Who knows what it was? Whitey had just pitched a good game. We were both happy because neither of us would be working the next day. So we went out to eat with some friends of mine who owned this farm in Maryland. Whitey, Dale Long, and I met them at a seafood restaurant. We had dinner. After that, the maître d' filled up goat bags of wine for everybody and we left.

Now, at the farm, somewhere deep in the countryside, the whole gang sat around talking and drinking till 2 A.M. My friends suggested that we stay over and head back to Baltimore in the morning. Whitey slept upstairs, Dale folded in the living room, and I must've been a little sick or something, as I found myself shivering on the porch swing the next morning at 10 A.M. I went inside and woke up the house. We went straight to the ballpark. When I got out of the car, my feet were wobbling. I didn't care. I wasn't going to play anyhow.

Well, Hank Bauer was coaching the Orioles then. He took one look at me and said, "Oh my God! Has Ralph Houk seen you yet?"

"No."

"Phew. I advise you to get out on the field so he *won't* see you. And while you're there I'll have my batboy slip you a bottle of Lavoris."

So here comes the kid. I grabbed the bottle, swished the Lavoris around my mouth, spat it out, and thanked him kindly.

The game went into the seventh inning. Whitey and I were way down at the end of the bench, the sun bearing right into the dugout.

I'm leaning on Whitey's shoulder and suddenly I hear him say, "Get up, get up! It's Ralph."

Ralph walks over and asks, "Can you hit?"

"What are you talking about? I'm not even on the active list."

He moved in. "Yes you *are* . . . starting today."

"Sure . . . I'll try."

I searched for my ball cap. It was crushed under Whitey's ass. Finally we got everything straightened out and I walked up to the plate, the last place in the world I ever thought I'd be in that day—going to bat in this game. The fans were jeering me something awful. A left-handed pitcher was on the mound, probably Mike McCormick, though it might have been Dave McNally. Who knows? I was feeling so terrible from the night before, I couldn't tell the difference. Anyway, Bauer goes out to talk to the pitcher. I know what he's saying. "Whatever you do, don't walk this guy. Throw strikes. He's out of it."

The last thing I remember Whitey saying before I left the dugout was "Swing at the first fastball."

The first pitch was a high fastball up around my eyes. I hit it over the center field fence. Barely felt my feet touching the ground as I rounded the bags. And I was so tired I could barely run. I came around second, aiming for third, and saw Brooks Robinson standing on the bag, his hands on his hips, shaking his head in utter disbelief.

It was here, in the early sixties, that my fun with drinking caused an accident that really scared me. Merlyn and I were having dinner with Yogi Berra and his wife Carmen. Now, Yogi always drank straight vodka on the rocks. He'd have a limit, maybe three or four, and that was it. Me, I'd be just starting. On this particular night I was drinking fast and furious. At the end of the dinner, when it was time to leave, Merlyn got in the passenger side of the car and I got in the driver's side. Yogi hollered, "Merlyn, I wouldn't ride with him!" Good old sensible Yogi.

On the way home I'm going about sixty or seventy miles an hour and Merlyn is trying to get me to let her drive. She's going, "Oh oh, you're driving too fast. Slow down, will you?" Then she hits me with her purse.

I reach over to take her purse away. Then I see a telephone pole coming right at us. We hit it head on; Merlyn went through the windshield; the rearview mirror just creased the top of her skull.

The policeman who had come to investigate was our next-door neighbor. He put us in his car, called in the accident, and drove us to the hospital.

Merlyn needed a lot of stitches in her head, I was well enough to play in a doubleheader the next day. Of course, there was a police report. I had to pay $400 for the telephone pole, though there weren't any charges filed for driving while intoxicated. And it never made the papers. The cops covered for me. But I realized right then and there that I might have a problem.

So, while I'm proud of everything I accomplished in my career, if I had to do it over again I would definitely have cut down on the booze.

I'll say this. In the last few years my drinking has been confined to social occasions. Merlyn has been highly successful in reminding me if I forget. As a matter of fact, if it wasn't for her I probably would have wound up an alcoholic like so many other ballplayers who did come to a tragic end that way.

But not all ballplayers spent their leisure time in hotel bars.

One of my friends and teammates during those years was Bobby Richardson. He came from the Bible Belt of South Carolina. Bobby was a clean-living, practicing Christian who used to hold religious services for the team when we were on the road. I helped to round up some players who wouldn't ordinarily go: Pepitone, Boyer, Maris, and a few others. We probably had ten or fifteen guys attending.

Bobby would rent a room at the hotel on Sunday mornings and would usually choose the readings himself. But one time he turned to me and said, "Why don't you recite the Lord's Prayer, Mickey?"

I didn't know the Lord's Prayer—as I told you, our family hardly ever went to church when I was a kid. I felt terrible and it was the last time I attended one of Bobby's prayer meetings.

Chapter 25

In 1963 I was up in the clouds, having signed my first $100,000 contract, then hitting real well through the first months of the season, and reaching a new high in May when I tagged one off Bill Fischer that hit the façade on the right field roof of Yankee Stadium. A couple of feet more and it would have cleared the top. As hard a ball as I had ever hit in my life.

One night in June we played at Anaheim Stadium, left town around 3 A.M., and landed in Baltimore for a doubleheader against the Orioles. There was barely enough time to take batting practice. I will never forget the second game. Brooks Robinson hit a fly ball deep to center field. I chased it past the warning track, leaped, and hooked my toe on the chain-link fence. They carried me off on a stretcher.

The instep of my left foot was broken. I went home to recuperate. It took a long time before there was any improvement and some mornings I'd wake up wondering, "Gee, why am I punishing myself like this? Maybe I'm kidding myself into believing I can make it back." But my worries were needless. After missing sixty-one games I rejoined the team.

On August 4 Ralph Houk sent me in to pinch-hit against Baltimore pitcher George Brunet. They had a 10–9 lead and the crowd noise in Yankee Stadium turned into a big welcoming roar when I came off the bench. I was hoping to hit a hard grounder, a single, *anything,* long as I didn't strike out. Brunet's first pitch was a fastball below the knees. Then he threw a curve. I pulled it into the left field stands. As I touched home plate, I tipped the bill of my cap, responding to the fans. They were up on their feet, cheering and whistling, a whole chorus of yells, "Mick . . . Mick . . . !" My teammates surrounded me in the dugout, everybody showing how happy they were for me.

Bobby Richardson had tears in his eyes. Yogi stuck out his paw, saying, "Nice, nice . . ."

We made it to the World Series. It was short and sweet—for the Dodgers. Sandy Koufax won the opener, striking out fifteen, a record. Johnny Podres beat us in game two, then Don Drysdale pitched a shutout. Whitey tried to stop them in the fourth game. He allowed just two hits. We got six off Koufax and lost. The score was 2–1. I hit a solo shot in the seventh inning, my fifteenth in Series play. It tied the Babe's record.

Before the fourth game, Ralph Houk held a clubhouse meeting. All he said was "Remember, boys, even if they win today we've had a hell of a year. I just want to say one thing. We'll take no prisoners."

Life is like that. It's filled with unexpected events. Not more than a week later Yogi put his catcher's mask in mothballs to become our manager and Ralph took over Roy Hamey's spot as vice president and general manager. I was really surprised because Ralph had done such a terrific job in the dugout. On the other hand, I had confidence in Yogi. True, he had never managed before and he wasn't a forceful personality. But he'd been in baseball all his life, calling balls and strikes and running the defense for our team for eighteen years.

Under Yogi's direction, we won the pennant in 1964. Certainly there were a host of reasons. I think the essential one came about after he had taken a bellyful from the younger players and decided enough was enough. Until then Yogi just floated through his job, happy to oblige, willing to forgive and forget, and saying things without really meaning it.

His style was casual. I remember one occasion when he was waiting on the sidewalk as we came out of our hotel to catch the team bus. I hear his voice, saying rather sheepishly, "Been waiting for you guys. We leave at five o'clock, y'know."

A few players straggled on. I'm very well aware of the time. It's already ten past five, but I'm hanging back anyway, playing dumb. At last I go by, glance over my shoulder, and say, "Hi Yog. What time is it?"

He says, "Well, yeah . . . the time. What do you mean? Right now?"

A gentle soul. He didn't have the heart to bawl out the players who deserved it. Plus it was especially hard when he got around to me and Whitey. We had played with him all those years and when the chips were down he could count on us to give him whatever help he needed. The thing is, he never demanded it. He was too proud. He'd come over to me in the dugout, still acting like the old teammate. "Aw, Mick, you know better than that. We gotta pull together and win this game." He wouldn't say, "You better do this or else." It was always, "C'mon, let's do it, huh?"

There was a time in Chicago when he comes over to the Playboy Club. It was a few days after he'd talked to some of us about staying out too late because we were falling behind in the pennant race.

He knows something is up and when he walks into the Playboy Club he's sure. The first thing, right in the entranceway, he runs into me staggering down some stairs, drunk. He grabs me and shakes me. "Hey, what the hell are you doing here? You better get home right now."

So I left. But he stayed to find a few more players and sent them home.

The point is, Yogi could exercise his authority when he wanted to, just like Casey did.

There were no meetings to speak of. Mostly, he'd take the pitcher and catcher aside before each game and discuss strategy, how he wanted certain batters pitched to. Or he'd express his views on how the outfielders should play the hitters; this one shaded to the left, that one shallow or deep. Things like that, always privately. In front of the whole team, though, he'd just stroll around the clubhouse, smiling, nodding his head, encouraging us all to go out and win. So now you've got a fair idea of Yogi's makeup when he first took the reins.

I recall we had blown four in a row to the White Sox in late August. Everybody figured us out of the pennant race. I was beginning to believe it, for here we were, going to O'Hare Airport from Comiskey Park—changing towns—and I was listening to a bunch of guys bitching and griping about the defeats.

I had sneaked a couple of beers on the bus. Probably a few other guys did the same. Now, Yogi had rules, like no beer on the bus. Only he didn't enforce them. Therefore, between the drinking and the complaining, there wasn't a dull moment while we inched along in heavy traffic.

Through the long miserable ride, we're slumped in our seats, trying to forget our problems. All of a sudden I hear a harmonica being played. It's Phil Linz, who's sitting in the backseat with Joe Pepitone.

He says, "I'm learning how to play this thing."

Joe says, "You're kidding."

The more Phil plays the lousier it gets. The tune creeps over our heads and carries to the front of the bus where Yogi is sitting in tortured silence.

We'd just lost four games. So we're dumbfounded, taking whatever comes along, going to get on another airplane. And the music, even though it was pretty bad, kind of breaks the monotony.

But Yogi's mad. He whips around in his seat.

"Hey, Linz! Go stick that harmonica up your ass!"

Phil hesitates, then leans forward and asks me, "What did Yogi say?"

"He said if you're going to play that harmonica, play it fast."

So Phil keeps playing.

Yogi jumps up, storms down the aisle, and slaps the harmonica from Phil's hands with such force that it bounces up and hits Pepi's knee. Whereupon Pepi falls out of his seat, screaming. "Oh my God, I'll sue him! He broke my knee! Get a medic! My knee, my knee!"

In our eyes that was the first time Yogi showed all of us his leadership qualities. It was the turning of the tide. From then on we played great, made it to the World Series, and came within a game of beating the Cardinals.

When it ended, he said to me, "Take care of those legs. We want you healthy at spring training."

"Sure, Yog. I'll see you there."

He was fired the next day. I still can't believe it. No matter what anyone else said, I enjoyed playing for him. And I know he deserved a whole lot better than he got.

Johnny Keane came over from the Cardinals as Yogi's replacement. We were used to Casey and Ralph, who didn't even have a curfew, and Yogi, who didn't really enforce one. Now, all of a sudden, here's this guy coming in like a drill sergeant, with a curfew and everything. Keane was determined to change things. There would be no more drinking, no more late nights for the Yankees. Under him we took a nosedive, going from first place in 1964 to sixth place in 1965.

I kept my distance. When we did talk, there were no arguments. More often than not, we had staring contests. Eventually the situation got so bad that if I had been financially set, I would've retired at the end of the season.

Right off at spring training, Keane went after me. After a night when he knew I'd been out late—I had a hangover—he sent me out to center field. He grabbed the fungo stick and a bag of balls, about fifty of them, and started hitting them out— to my left, to my right, behind me, until the bag was empty.

Now, I had been playing center field in the major leagues for about fifteen years. I knew how to catch fly balls. I knew he wasn't providing instruction. He was trying to make me sick, trying to set an example. And I didn't like it.

The day of reckoning came in St. Petersburg. Keane was at it again. For over an hour I ran all over the field, shagging his fly balls. My tongue was hanging out. Suddenly he hit one real short. I dashed in, picked up the ball, and threw it as hard as I could. Right at him. He ducked.

After the season, he was the only manager that I ever felt I should apologize to—not just for trying to bean him, but for everything.

Keane might have been a very good manager, but he wasn't right for the Yankees. He brought a coach with him and the two of them kept to themselves. Almost as though we were on opposing sides. Instead of being our leader, he seemed to be working against us.

So, after all those years in the major leagues, I was too old to knuckle under Keane's regimentation and his silly little high school rules. I knew that if he kept doing things his way, there would be nothing but trouble down the road.

It caught up with Maris. He had a broken bone in his wrist and Keane tried to play him. Maris couldn't believe it. He threatened to leave the club. He was prepared to stay out until he was either traded or another manager came in. As it was, he missed a good part of the season because of the injury.

Meanwhile my right leg got worse and worse. There were treatments, of course. Dr. Gaynor would give me cortisone shots and they provided some temporary relief. But in a game against Kansas City, I pulled a hamstring trying to score from third on a passed ball. It finally healed enough for me to get back in the lineup. Actually, I was in and out. The right knee always felt like it was going to give on me; that's why I uppercutted so much when I batted left-handed during my last four years. My arm was also getting worse and Keane moved me from center to left. To make a long story short, I ended up real unhappy about the whole season. Playing 122 games, I only hit .255. The lowest point of my career by far.

That was the season Bobby Murcer joined the club. They had already pinned a label on him: the Second Mickey Mantle. And we were alike in many ways. We came up young, both of us from Oklahoma, both shortstops, both converted to the outfield. I'll say this for Bobby: he grew into his major league shoes faster than I did—more advanced, more mature at about the same age. We palled around and I sorta looked after him.

But by this time, most of the old team was gone. Only Whitey and I were left and we were witnessing the team's decline. Things had changed. The old days were over.

In early 1965 I realized I'd have to find a new outlet. Something to do after my playing days were over. That winter I joined a brand-new country club, Preston Trails. It's the best investment I ever made. I can roll out of bed and be there in ten minutes. I love it. I'm one of the guys. When I'm home in Dallas, that's it. I'm at the club from 11 A.M. to 6 P.M., Tuesday through Sunday. Never miss.

When I first played at Preston Trails, I was about a twelve or thirteen handicap. I could shoot 85 on a lucky day. Now my handicap is eight. I think without question that one of my greatest thrills in sports, including my World Series homers, was the time I made a birdie on the ninth hole. I made the putt and saved me and my partner $1,200. We didn't win anything, but sinking that putt, boy, that was an electrifying moment.

You don't necessarily have to be an athlete to be a golfer. Young or old, fat or skinny, short or tall, you can play the game. However, logic dictates that the people who take care of themselves the best are the ones who are the most likely to succeed. Gary Player runs all the time. He's always in tip-top shape. Jack Niklaus, in his forties, has the same regimen going. They're athletes. Arnold Palmer is another. All three would have made good ballplayers.

I saw Sammy Snead put on an exhibition for us in the fifties. We were playing a doubleheader at Griffith Stadium. Between games they drew a big circle in the outfield with a flag stick planted in the middle. Sammy stood at home plate with a wedge and hit ten or twelve balls into the circle. Then he took a wood and started hitting balls right out of the park, just like a handful of my home runs. Allie Reynolds, the best golfer on the team, also tried with the wedge, but he could only hit one or two into the circle.

Then they changed sports. The plan was that Allie would stand on the mound and throw the ball in for Sammy to hit. But Sammy couldn't seem to connect. Allie kept moving in toward home plate, tossing them underhand. At last, he was about thirty-five feet from the plate and a few balls finally dribbled off Sammy's bat.

Which proves something. It's a lot easier for a ballplayer to be a golfer than a golfer to be a ballplayer. Hell, that little white ball isn't going to jump up and hit you in the head at 100 miles per hour.

I know that Sammy and Ted Williams used to argue over which of the two sports is the hardest. I get a kick out of people who do that. When I'm playing the Pro-Am matches and I hit a bad shot, somebody is bound to yell, "Hey, Mantle, it's a lot easier to hit the baseball, ain't it?" And I want to say, "Bullshit!" The hardest thing in sports is to hit a baseball. How would you like to face Don Drysdale after me and Roger Maris have already hit home runs off him? "Oh damn, I'm coming up next." And Don's thinking: "This son of a bitch isn't going to hit another one off me. I guarantee it."

The challenge in golf? A few warm-up strokes on the practice green, stepping up to the tee, that little white ball just sitting there waiting . . .

If I get beat, I come in and slam my locker, throw my shoes down. So the guys will be at my house later on, looking around my trophy room, winking at each other and cackling. "Where are all those good sportsmanship awards, Mick?"

I'd laugh because they know when I play golf it's a World Series game every time.

Nothing has really changed.

Chapter 26

In November 1965 I was in the backyard playing touch football. My brothers Ray and Roy and Butch were going against me and Mickey Jr. He had the ball and I was running out for a pass when one of the twins blindsided me. My shoulder was hurt. I knew it was serious. I knew right away it was going to affect my career.

Only, general manager Ralph Houk was not about to agree. After he heard my story, he said, "Before you decide anything, let's have somebody look at it."

At his insistence I went out to the Mayo Clinic, where they told me I had bone chips and calcium deposits in the shoulder. I was operated on that afternoon. Later, still a bit groggy, I looked up at the doctor. "Well, what's the verdict?" He said, "The shoulder's all right. Give it a little rest and with any luck you'll be knocking them over the wall again."

I wasn't so sure, but I could throw and swing a bat well enough by February to sign a Yankee contract and report for spring training.

Johnny Keane started his second year as manager just about the way he ended the first year, knotting his eyebrows and gnashing his teeth during an April slump that stretched into May. We lost sixteen out of twenty games and at this point he was fired. Ralph Houk stepped down from the front office to take over the job. Lee MacPhail became general manager.

And Johnny Keane? Poor guy. He died of heart failure some eight months later.

I do know that when you have to go the full route of a 162-game schedule, along the way you'll find plenty of things you can torture yourself about. I got into 108 and hit 23 home runs. They came sporadically, in clusters, two of them off Jose Santiago, the Boston pitcher. That was on June 28. The next day at Fenway Park I got two more off Rollie Sheldon. It went on. Eleven home runs in eleven consecutive days. The streak was finally broken at the stadium.

We were playing Washington. I hit homers off Dick Bosman and Jim Hannan for my fourth two-homer game in the streak, then tore a hamstring later in the game, trying to score from second. When I came into the dugout, Ralph was shaking his head. I thought, "Gee, maybe this is it."

With all the injuries, coupled with the deteriorating legs, no doubt I could have called in sick and stayed away from the ballpark. Yet somehow I'd get myself up one more time, and still another, thinking that by some miracle it would all come back. No more hurting, no wobbly knees, no sore shoulder, no aches and pains anywhere. Foolish, but that's how it was.

There were some good moments ahead. Like the home run I got off White Sox pitcher Bruce Howard. My 494th, which put me in front of Lou Gehrig and into sixth place on the all-time list. There was also a day when I came off the bench after being out two weeks with a pulled muscle and put Hank Aguirre's second pitch into the right field stands. It won us a ball game at Yankee Stadium.

On the downside, in Chicago for the final series we lost an extra-inning game to clinch last place. Mel Stottlemyre was our pitcher. He took his twentieth loss. I can't imagine him losing that many after having won twenty games the year before. It shows how bad he and the team went in 1966.

It's unfortunate that Mel came up at the very end of our long reign as world champions. Though he eventually compiled a great winning record, he did it while playing for a mediocre ball club.

Mel was one of the nicest guys I ever met. If I had twenty-five like him, I wouldn't mind managing. You could make an error behind him and he'd say, "Don't worry about it. We'll get the next one."

He tended to business. He'd have a drink with you to be sociable, but most of his free time was spent with his family. He had a real feeling for hearth and home and I always think of him in that light.

Sometime after my retirement I was assigned by ABC-TV to work the Little League World Series in Williamsport, Pennsylvania. Jim Fleming was the play-by-play announcer. I handled the color commentary. Well, the Japanese team had this pitcher, a little kid of twelve or so. The spitting image of Stottlemyre—the ears, the way he wore his cap, the whipcord body —a pint-sized Oriental duplicate. He threw just like him, too: sliders on the outside corners, sinkers on the inside corners, a good fastball—I mean, *exactly* like Mel.

So up in the booth I'm raving about the uncanny resemblance. "It's incredible . . . Yeah, the kid is cut out of the same cloth . . . Say, I wonder if Mel has ever been to Japan—oops!"

Jim responded with a nervous giggle. "No no—not *Mel!*"

So at the time Mel joined the Yankees we were going down the tubes. Meanwhile a lot of owners in both leagues started to buy up the desirable prospects for big bucks. Topping and Webb didn't get into that kind of situation. They sat on their money bags and as they sat we lost our minor league teams one after the other. Thus, we didn't have the great potential stars coming into the system. Instead, everything sort of drained off. By then the free agent draft had been adopted and the more aggressive owners began claiming the rights to high school and college kids not yet signed to professional contracts. For example, in 1964 the California Angels shelled out $250,000 to sign Rick Reichardt. He was from Wisconsin. Given the choice, he probably would have preferred to play for the Milwaukee Braves. I really don't know about him, but when I signed with the Yankees, that's the team I wanted to play for. The St. Louis Cardinals never entered the picture, although I rooted for them as a youngster, mainly because of their close proximity to my hometown of Commerce. But at seventeen my thinking was no different from any other high school football star who hoped to get a scholarship to Notre Dame or UCLA or Penn State—and not to Podunk U. He had options, just as I had. The free agent draft took those options away. You went to the team that selected you. The rub there was that the worst team got the first shot.

I belonged to the Yankees. I had signed a slave contract. Who cared? I was happy to be playing for the greatest team on earth. Today under George Steinbrenner I could play out my contract and split. Back then, with Webb and Topping at the helm, I might as well have been a cow or a horse. They owned me—lock, stock, and barrel.

Remember when Weiss said I could stay in Dallas and run my bowling alley? He didn't give a damn, he'd just trade me for Herb Score and Rocky Colavito. And for a moment I was so mad at Weiss that I felt it would've been a pleasure to play in Cleveland. Once out of his office, though, a pressing realization hit me: "God, I don't want to be a Cleveland Indian, I want to be a Yankee." Having this seared into my brain, I doubt if I ever would have left by choice.

But then again, if Frank Lane, the Indian's general manager, had pushed a million dollars in front of me and said, "Here, you are now free to leave the Yankees and come with us," boy, you gotta think about your family and the security that comes with it. Hell yes, I probably would have grabbed the money and said, "Thank you, sir. It will be an honor and a privilege to play in Cleveland. You have a great city there and . . ." Blah blah blah.

You'll recall that I once took a $10,000 pay cut to remain a Yankee. Glad I did, too.

The only regret I have is that in my day we were so dumb we didn't know how to handle our financial dealings with the front office. They told me $32,500 was a lot of money and I thought it was. When you go from making $35 a week in the mines to playing for the Yankees and within five years you've signed a $32,500 contract, it's pretty hard to believe you're worth more than that.

Nowadays you see guys coming to the ballpark attended by businessman types who carry Gucci briefcases. I came with my bat and a glove, ready to play ball. Now there are too many guys around who shouldn't even be playing in the major leagues, yet they are and they're getting $600,000 or $700,000 a year. I'm not faulting them. I'm all for free enterprise, except when I see certain players in the starting lineups sporting astronomical salaries and crummy batting averages. It gets my back up because I know that off the field they're grumbling, bitching all the time, not concerned in the least to be part of the total team effort. They can afford to say, "Trade me. I don't like the team, the manager, the other players, the owner, *or* the fans." They can afford to sit out games with only minor injuries.

They can say what they want. They can do what they want. They're secure for life, no matter what. In my playing days I couldn't stand to sit out a game. I'd keep telling myself, "There's Whitey out there, working, trying to win this thing. I might be able to do something to help him. What am I doing on the bench?" My conscience would be telling me: "What about incentive? What about pride? What about the hand that fed you, Mantle?"

Chapter 27

In September 1966 Dan Topping sold his remaining stock to CBS and they made Mike Burke the Yankee president. I liked him. I can't think of a minute's trouble from him. He was a tall, good-looking guy, a great promoter, and smart enough to let Lee MacPhail and Ralph Houk run the Yankees.

Lee had a lifetime background in baseball. His father, Larry MacPhail, was part-owner and general manager of the club back in the mid-forties. I've always thought that the greatest business deal I've ever heard of was when he and Dan Topping and Del Webb bought the Yankees from Jake Ruppert's estate for $2.8 million and then drew over 2 million people the first season. So they got their money back in less than a year. And when Webb and Topping sold the team to CBS, it was for $14 million. Unbelievable.

Larry had a flamboyant personality. An innovator, wildly imaginative, a man who made things happen at the snap of his fingers—or so I'm told.

As for Lee, we had always gotten along and he became a good friend of mine. But shortly after he filled Ralph's chair as general manager, the Yankees got worse. Right before the 1967 season, I was surrounded by new faces. Kubek and Richardson had retired, Whitey was about to retire, Maris got traded to St. Louis for Charley Smith, and Clete Boyer went to Atlanta in exchange for outfielder Bill Robinson. Actually, Roger was happy to go to St. Louis because he just didn't see eye to eye with Houk and MacPhail.

With all my old friends gone, it wasn't the same.

Most of the newcomers lacked the talents of my former teammates. I'll call them the extras; I don't want to say losers. Until then almost everybody came through our organization, all of us climbing the ladder, step by step, up from the farm clubs, at last reaching a point where the Yankees would either make room for us at the top or send us to another team. Now we were getting ballplayers from everywhere. Guys named Reuben Amaro, Jake Gibbs, Horace Clarke, Charley Smith, Steve Whitaker, Bobby Cox, Junior Kennedy, and Bill Robinson.

Bill Robinson was another story. He had great credentials, but Yankee Stadium is tough on right-handed power hitters. Hell, if DiMaggio had played anywhere else he could have hit way over 500 home runs, at least more than his career total of 361. But when Robinson arrived he was young and inexperienced. It took a long while before he got on the right track. Later at Pittsburgh, he finally found the range and began to hit home runs. Except by then he was into his thirties. His best days were already behind him.

Anyway, the overall lack of talent made things a little easier for the opposing teams. In those years it seemed I never got a good ball to hit, especially when men were on base.

One night at the stadium against Minnesota, we were in the last of the ninth inning, the Twins ahead by a run, two out. Jim Kaat was pitching and I came up.

All of a sudden the ballpark was lit up even further by a bolt of lightning. Twins coach Billy Martin ran out to the mound for a conference with Kaat. A big powwow ensued. And then the umpires gathered around, sniffed the skies, and started yelling at Billy, "Hurry up, willya? It's gonna rain any minute!" Billy ignored them. I know he wanted Kaat to walk me. Good strategy. For one thing, it delayed the game. Secondly, there wasn't another home run hitter on the roster. In either case, the situation was definitely to the Twins' advantage because it started to sprinkle more heavily. So Kaat cranked up and delivered his first pitch. A fastball, right across the plate. I hit it into the left center field stands and tied the score.

Meanwhile the skies split open and we were in the midst of a veritable monsoon. The umps didn't even wait for the tarps. They suspended the game. The run counted and we played the rain-out late in the season.

The Twins lost. We were in seventh place at the time, but

they'd been battling like mad for the pennant, so Kaat's home run pitch really hurt them. They might have won by pitching around me.

Look at the statistics. The last two years I was walked at the rate of once every four times at bat. They had me in there for power and the pitchers were walking me so damn much we couldn't score. The stats will also show that I struck out a lot. What it doesn't reflect is me trying to hit all those bad pitches. As long as I had a bat in my hands, I wanted to be boss.

But then the body starts to go and the mind can't force it to respond. And before you realize it—*poof*—the enthusiasm is gone. It happens to all of us.

At spring training in 1967, I switched over from the outfield to first base. It took the strain off my legs and after a few workouts I settled into the position. I wasn't great, just adequate. I should have been happy with that, but I had spent my whole career shooting for perfection.

In May 1967 Whitey retired. He had a circulatory problem in his left shoulder. At first his doctor thought it was a minor injury to an artery. He prescribed a little rest, saying it would heal itself. It didn't. Whitey's hand went numb. Finally the artery was blocked. So he had an operation. They took a vein out of his leg and grafted it into his shoulder, which got the blood circulating again. Before this, Whitey's fingers would become stiff and cold everytime he pitched.

Whitey had a nose spray bottle filled with hot water that he used to warm his fingers. One time we were playing Detroit and Whitey brought the bottle out to the mound. Charlie Dressen was the Tiger manager then. A tough old bird who'd been through all the wars. He said, "Whatever the hell you got there, you can't use it. It ain't legal."

Whitey explained the deal, but Dressen wouldn't buy it. "The _____ rules don't give a _____ about those _____ explanations!" I guess he figured that Whitey was going to throw a spitter. Finally Whitey had had it up to here with Dressen. He said, "Charlie, the day I have to use a wet ball on you humpty-dumps, that's the day I get out of the game." And he finished Dressen off with a couple of choice profanities of his own.

Whitey developed a bone spur in his left elbow. The pain got so bad that he couldn't pitch. After a one-inning stint he told Ralph he couldn't go on any longer and the following day the Yankees announced his retirement.

A sad time. I knew I was on my way out too. I'm watching Whitey and saying to myself, "How is it going to be when I quit? What will I do?" As badly as I felt for him, I felt just as bad for me.

While you're playing ball, you're insulated. All the ballparks and the big crowds have a certain mystique. You feel attached, permanently wedded to the sounds that ring out, to the fans chanting your name, even when there are only four or five thousand in the stands on a Wednesday afternoon. You could hear every one of them, particularly in St. Louis. They'd really get on you at Sportsman's Park because it was almost always empty. And in my later years, there were ovations everywhere.

Sometime in June, at the stadium, I led off the ninth inning with a home run to beat Detroit. It was my eighth game-winning hit and seven of them were homers. I wanted more. I still had goals to reach. I had just passed Gehrig, now Mel Ott was dead ahead in fifth place, right behind Ted Williams. Then there was Jimmie Foxx in front of Ted, and Willie Mays led Jimmie. Then the Babe—all by himself. Who would ever have thought that anybody would catch him?

On Independence Day the crowd began whooping it up when I hit a home run off Mudcat Grant, the Twins pitcher. It tied Ott at 511. A few innings later they really went wild after I put another one into the seats.

There was one more season, 1968. At the end of the season my lifetime average had dipped under .300. The most disappointing thing ever. I could hardly stand to think about it. Even after my second year with the Yankees, when I hit .311 and finished third behind Ferris Fain of the A's and Dale Mitchell of Cleveland, even then it was almost impossible to accept. I felt I should've led the league and I only did that once in my major league career. But goddamn, to think you're a .300 hitter and end up at .237 in your last season, then find yourself looking at a lifetime .298 average—it made me want to cry.

Not long ago I was on a dais in Louisville, Kentucky, with some great stars: Joe DiMaggio, Terry Moore, Enos Slaughter, Stan Musial, Johnny Mize, Allie Reynolds, and Pee Wee Reese. As it happened, I felt kind of awkward knowing I made the Hall of Fame in my first year of eligibility while poor Enos Slaughter, a lifetime .300 hitter, had not yet made it. Therefore, I was particularly pleased to learn of his election to the Hall of Fame in 1985.

Great ballplayers. Perhaps if I had been around when Babe Ruth was playing, he would've been my idol. I was like him in many ways. No, not the home runs. I mean the staying out all night. And boy, how often I've thought about being on the same team with him. Many a night Billy and I would stay late in the clubhouse and listen to Pete Sheehy, who'd been with the Yankees since the twenties, and he'd tell us some real nutty stories about Ruth.

And to give you an idea how much I worship Ted Williams, after I retired I went down to the Florida Keys for a vacation. Ted has a house in Islamorada and several mornings I slowly drove by, hoping he would come out. I didn't have the nerve to ring his door bell, figuring I might disturb him.

In May 1968 I went ahead of Williams in home runs. All I remember is the roar of the crowd and being dimly conscious of the ball sailing off my bat, a blur of faces peering at me from the third base box seats, the stadium scoreboard flashing: "522 . . . 522 . . . 522." Another milestone came in late September. But I have to share some of the glory.

The Tigers were playing us and I was struggling to pass Jimmie Foxx at 534. By then, what with my right leg as shaky as a wet noodle, when I got up to hit against Denny McLain, the Detroit crowd thought this would be my last turn at bat.

So we're losing, 6–0. McLain strolls toward the plate, beckons his catcher, Bill Freehan, then says loud enough for me to hear, "I'm gonna let him hit one."

Freehan comes back and I say, "Did I hear that right? He's gonna let me hit a pitch?"

Freehan grins. "Yeah." He snaps down his mask.

The first pitch is a fastball for a strike. I let it go by. Denny gestures as if to say, "What's going on here?"

I look at Freehan. "Don't shit me, Bill. Is he setting me up for something?"

"No, Mick. He wants you to hit one."

The next pitch is another juicy fastball. I foul it off. Freehan gets a new ball, rubs it up, throws it to Denny, crouches behind the plate, and says to me, "Here comes another one."

Sure enough, it's another fastball, right down the middle. This time I hit it as well as I ever hit a baseball—my 535th home run into the upper deck. I shake hands with Joe Pepitone, the next batter, and run into the dugout.

Joe steps in and holds his hand out in the strike zone, about waist high. "Right here!" he says.

And Denny knocks him down.

That year Denny won 31 games, followed by 24 more in 1969. A couple of years later I read about his suspension for gambling, consorting with bookmakers, and packing an unlicensed firearm. Later still, stories went around that he doused a couple of sportswriters with a bucket of ice water.

Tragic. Just this past year I watched a news clip of Denny walking up the courthouse steps to face a bunch of federal charges—all kinds of underworld stuff. I only know he had it all, then it was gone. I'm grateful that he gave me a lot of laughs— and a most generous gift.

I got my final career home run on September 20, 1968. No. 536. It was my 373rd from the left side and my 266th at the stadium, 7 more than Ruth's total, which established a new stadium record.

A week later at Fenway Park, I came up in the first inning, made an out, and returned to the bench. Ralph sent Andy Kosco in to replace me. I sat back and watched the kid limber up. I knew I had reached the end of the line. After a few moments I headed through the runway into the locker room, took off my uniform, and went home.

Chapter 28

One day in Cleveland during the summer of 1968, my legs were so sore I could hardly get out of the dugout. I would have pinch-hit, but we were too far ahead or too far behind, I don't know which, so they didn't use me. After the game, as we were getting on the team bus, a man grabbed my arm.

"Mickey, I brought my kids four hundred miles today just to see you play. Now they're really disappointed." A real nice guy. Not mean, not angry, just sorry. And I felt bad.

Right there I decided that if I didn't get much better before the next year, I'd quit.

The following year I had to convince myself that it was really over. So I went down to Fort Lauderdale a few days ahead of the regulars and tried to work out—just a little running—but I couldn't do it. I was convinced. There was no putting off my retirement.

The night before the announcement Merlyn and I went out for dinner with Harold and Stella Youngman. The press conference was coming up the next day, March 1, 1969. Baseball was all I had ever known. I wasn't in much of a mood for celebration.

After the press conference Harold and I drove out to the ballpark. I packed my duffel bag, probably hung around for an hour or two, and then we left. The rest is a blank. I might have stayed in Florida for a week. I have no idea what I did for the next few months.

Gradually, the realizations hit me. Baseball was over. The $100,000 a year salary was gone. My bowling alley in Dallas had closed years before. I was thirty-seven years old with a family to support. I had to start making a new life. But what was I going to do?

There was one good prospect. People then were talking about the booming restaurant business: McDonald's, Kentucky Fried Chicken, Burger King—all of those chains were growing fast and there was money to be made for those who got in on the ground floor.

In the summer of 1968, I got together with a group of investors to talk about a restaurant venture. People knew that I was a big fan of country home cooking: chicken-fried steaks, biscuits, gravy, that sort of thing. I could really get enthusiastic about promoting restaurants that offered really good country food—and we decided to start a chain, opening our first store in San Antonio: Mickey Mantle Country Cookin'. By the time I retired, we had opened several other outlets and we were doing a pretty good business. I thought I would be set for life. Several franchises for further restaurants had been sold to investors.

We went public in June 1969. I was chairman of the board. I had 110,000 shares of stock. At an offering price of $15 a share, I immediately became a millionaire—on paper.

Since March I had been going around cutting the ribbons and glad-handing the locals who'd come marching in for the big meal. We served the best chicken you ever ate, not to mention the beans and hamhocks, chicken-fried steak, creamed gravy, beef stew, and iced tea in mason jars. Delicious fare, reasonably priced.

When I look back on it, I think our chain should have been successful. We had good publicity, good comments on the way things were run, and eventually we expanded to thirteen restaurants.

Prior to this I had no involvement with a major business outside of baseball. But now I was becoming a tycoon, right? Soon the money would be rolling in and our little restaurant chain would expand from coast to coast.

When I realized that I was leaving baseball and going into the business world, I decided to get my own attorney. Roy True, now a senior partner with the Dallas law firm of True & McLain, came highly recommended. After a few months of discussion in March 1969, he took me on as a client.

Thank God.

Among other things, one of his jobs was to look over the Country Cookin' Restaurant paperwork for me.

After we had gone public, the restaurant began to decline. The profit outlook wasn't as rosy as it seemed. In fact, our franchise operation was headed for trouble. Roy settled in for months of eighteen-hour days before he untangled the mess. The company stock changed hands several times. The restaurant side of the business was closed down.

Thanks to Roy, I narrowly escaped a brush with the SEC.

The important thing is, he saved my reputation and prevented a catastrophe for me. From that day forward I haven't made a move without his approval. He's my business manager, my lawyer, my family counselor, my friend. What more can a man ask for?

In June 1969 the Yankees retired my number. I was supposed to make a speech in front of an overflow crowd at the stadium. I said to Roy, "It's gonna be tough. I've been up all night and still don't know what to tell them."

"That's your problem, Mick. You've been thinking about it too much. Be yourself. Just say whatever is in your heart."

The next day started with a ceremony at home plate. Joe DiMaggio presented me with a plaque that they were going to hang on the center field wall. Later I presented him with one that would hang alongside mine.

I made a speech. Straight from the heart, every word. Then I rode around the stadium for the last time in a golf cart; Yankee pinstripes were painted on the side; on the front and back were license plates reading MM-7. Little Danny, the groundskeeper, a good pal who'd been there as long as I had, drove the cart. Sixty thousand people stood up and applauded, really pouring it on as I slowly went by, waving and smiling. I was deeply touched.

Afterward, I expected to rest on my laurels for a while, then get into a routine of golf at Preston Trails, a little fishing, a little hunting, a whole mess of idle stuff before getting back to my business interests.

From the year I started making $100,000, about five years before I retired, I had been deferring half of my income. So in

1969 I had a nice income. Mike Burke had immediately approached Harold with the suggestion that I do some coaching for the Yankees upon my retirement, but I wasn't very interested. The notion of going on the road again for eight months a year didn't have much appeal.

But by February 1970 I was getting the itch to see my old friends. I just couldn't break away from baseball completely. Later that spring I attended an Old-Timers' affair. Among the participants was Ralph Houk. He asked me, "How are you getting along?" I said, "It's a great life. I can't wait to get up every morning and watch the leaves fall." He said, "I'd love to have you back. The coaching offer still stands. Say the word, Mick, and you've got it." I said, "That's very nice of you, Ralph. I'll let you know."

In August the restaurant deal was behind me and I joined the Yankee coaching staff. I agreed to try it out. I came to New York and they gave me a suite at the St. Moritz. A double door separated the sitting area from the bedroom. It had six glass panes. One day I couldn't open the door, so I punched it, intending to hit the metal strip. I hit the glass and sliced my hand real deep. I went to a doctor to get it stitched.

We were playing Minnesota, my hand was hurting, and the fans were cheering like hell when I took my position as first base coach. I wasn't naïve. It put extra people into the stands, that's all. There I was, pacing back and forth in the box, and saying, "Let's get it going now!" and feeling like a fool when Bobby Murcer drew a leadoff walk in the fourth inning, called time, and asked me what the signs were. I said, "Mine look good. I'm a Libra." Well, I was nothing more than a public relations gimmick. The old Brooklyn Dodgers used it to their advantage by luring Babe Ruth out of retirement in the late thirties. They had him on exhibition, hitting home runs in batting practice. A spectacle of faded glory. It wasn't for me. To sign autographs at golf tournaments or show up at father-and-son banquets to give a talk and shake a few hands, that's fine. But to put on a uniform and pretend I was still in baseball, no thanks. As a coach, I felt more like a sideshow attraction at the circus. It didn't take me but a week to find out I didn't care for it.

Elston Howard was the regular first base coach. They kept him on the bench while I filled in during the middle innings and he might have felt I was trying to grab his job away. He never talked about it and I certainly didn't want him to think it.

Not only did I realize that I had no real responsibility, it was also clear to the players. They treated the whole thing as a lark. Thurman Munson, for instance. This was Thurman's first year up and he showed the makings of becoming a super ballplayer. I liked him and we would tease each other. I'd give him stupid tips. I'd say, "Now, Thurm, what you have to do is hook your spikes in your socks to keep your front foot from flying out." Or "Thurm, put your foot here and hold your back foot with your hand." He went along with it. When he got a hit, he'd come by me and say, "Coach, did I do it right?" And I'd say, "Perfect." After that, whenever he had a good year, I'd tell everyone, "I taught that guy how to hit." If he had a subpar year, I'd explain it away with: "Well, he just didn't want to work with me."

It was a joke, my coaching career.

I understand that now. I was still dreaming of making a comeback in baseball. If I stayed home longer than a week, I'd begin to feel like a caged animal, thinking that by some miracle I would be turned loose, exactly as I used to be—strong, vital, running on sound legs again. Then I'd sink my head down on a pillow, thinking I could escape through sleep . . . I would dream of me punting the football at Commerce High and it wouldn't travel as far as it should. And there's another dream about basketball, about jumping up for the dunk, only to find myself frozen in space high above the basket, looking down at the net from an incredible height.

I had a recurring nightmare: coming to Yankee Stadium in a cab, wearing my uniform. Trying to crawl through a hole. I can see Whitey and Billy and Casey and my other teammates. I'm supposed to be with them, but I can't squeeze through the hole in the wall. I'm stuck. I hear the public address speaker blare out my name: "At bat . . . number seven . . . Mickey Mantle . . ." That's when I'd wake up, drenched in sweat.

I don't have that dream anymore. Yet sometimes I dread

going to bed at night, thinking it might come back. It hasn't, not for a while.

Until recently I've been having another bad dream. I have died and I'm buried. But somehow I'm floating above my grave, reading the words on my tombstone: HERE LIES MICKEY CHARLES MANTLE. BANNED FROM BASEBALL.

I guess I won't have that dream again either.

In the earlier days I was only concerned with Mickey Mantle. I worried about hitting the baseball. I worried about my career. I had little room for anything else, so a well-rounded family life was missing, to the detriment of my kids. I never pushed them. I didn't even make them finish high school. Whatever they liked was good enough for me. As a result, they were sheltered all their lives. And Merlyn wouldn't talk much about the daily strife at home. For the most part, she kept the bad news away from me.

My son Billy is twenty-seven years old. As a little boy he had dyslexia, a reading disability. We enrolled him, as we did all our kids, at the Lamplighter's School in Dallas, where special teachers gave Billy remedial help.

Then, at nineteen, something else happened. A small lump developed behind his ear. He went to the hospital for tests. It turned out to be Hodgkin's disease, the same illness that killed my father. There were times when Merlyn and I would sit together silently, unable to comfort each other.

I often wondered why the disease had skipped me after it had felled so many in my family. I had been expecting it all my life. For that matter, why had it spared my brothers, my sister, and their children? Why had it picked Billy?

He went for radiation treatments, but they weren't effective. His spleen was removed. For a few months, the disease seemed to slow, then it came back. Billy was put on chemotherapy.

Two years ago we took him to Houston, to the M. D. Anderson Clinic. They were using an experimental drug on cancer patients and getting good results. Merlyn drove Billy down to the clinic and after a CAT scan he was told to wait while the doctors talked with Merlyn. The cancer had spread all over his body and there was only a 25 percent chance of survival for our boy.

She called me from the clinic, her voice breaking. "We're going back in the morning . . . a new drug . . . Maybe it'll work . . . I don't think Billy knows how bad off he is."

I remember staring at the phone, wishing it was me instead of him.

The days passed. I saw him after the third or fourth treatment. He looked terrible. His face was clouded by the pain and nothing is more awful than to watch your own son struggling to appear happy when in your heart you know his life is slipping away and there's little you can do or say to make things better for him.

Finally I sat with him on the sofa. "Billy, you've got a chance. It's a lot better than none at all. Believe me, we can win."

"I'll try, Dad."

Looking back, I can see a parallel between that trip to Houston and the one my father took to see me in Kansas City so long ago. I had just about given up then. Now so had Billy. I know that Dad turned me around and I prayed that my words would do the same for my boy.

Anyway, that night in our hotel room across the street from the clinic, as Merlyn and I talked, I realized—she had showed her love for me and the kids in so many different ways. Just looking at her, just knowing this, I knew I would be lost without her.

There were trips back and forth, the months piled up from January to July. Then Billy went into remission. A miracle. He's better now and I think he's getting some confidence.

So there's no need to say more.

Chapter 29

Satchmo Armstrong once said about jazz: "If you have to explain it, you shouldn't be playing it." Evidently I had a similar problem while trying to explain baseball on "The Saturday Game of the Week" shows for NBC. It happened around the same time I accepted the part-time coaching job with the Yankees. Between the two, I was locked into a pattern. I was excess baggage.

On the NBC games I worked with Curt Gowdy and Tony Kubek. If our limo was ordered for 10:30 A.M., Tony and I had to be in it at 10:15. There were producers, directors, assistants, writers, all kinds of people. There were regular meetings that I rarely attended. With the network, as with the Yankees, I was just around.

On the opening segment, Gowdy would do the intro: "Here we are in beautiful Anaheim Stadium for a game between the New York Yankees and the Los Angeles Angels." Me and Tony would just be standing there, grinning. Gowdy would talk a while, then hand the mike to Tony. Perhaps he'd ask me one question, but mostly I'd just keep on grinning. After a while I thought about getting a sweatshirt with FILL written on it. That's "fill" as in "fill-in."

Of course, Tony went on to prove that he was born to be an announcer. Nowadays you also have guys like Drysdale, Snider, Rizzuto, Richie Ashburn, Ralph Kiner, Jim Palmer, Tim McCarver, and so many others who are doing great as sportscasters.

All things considered, my experience at NBC wasn't bad for a week or two. Then I realized I'd be stealing their money if I continued in that line of work. So I just finished out the season.

In 1973 I joined the Reserve Life Insurance Company in Dallas to help with public relations. The company has many salesmen and field offices across the country. I go out to the regional meetings, the award presentations, sales contests, annual conventions, and other such functions. I also help recruit agents. It keeps me busy throughout the year and I'm getting better at what I do all the time.

In 1983 I signed a $100,000-a-year contract to do basically the same thing for the Claridge Hotel in Atlantic City. Bill Dougall, the president and general manager, used to be with the Sahara Hotel in Las Vegas when Del Webb owned it. That's how I first met him.

Across the street from the Claridge is Bally's Park Place. Willie Mays works there as a public greeter and Bill must have said to himself, "If Willie is helping the Bally, why don't I get my friend Mickey to help us?"

Of course, Willie was banned from baseball when he took the Bally job. Commissioner Bowie Kuhn didn't want the game "tainted" by anyone who got involved in the gambling business. To him, the Atlantic City hotels were just that and nothing more. So, on the day Lee MacPhail found out I was thinking of signing up with the Claridge, he called me and said that Kuhn would ban me as he had banned Willie if I accepted the offer.

Some threat. What would I be banned from? Since my retirement I had been a Yankee batting instructor during spring training. What it really amounted to was a two-week paid vacation for me and Merlyn. The guys with whom I associated the most at spring training were Thurman and Graig Nettles. I didn't give them much instruction, we just kidded around.

Once, when Billy was the manager, he told me, "If we want somebody to learn to strike out, we'll call you." On the other hand, some of the young guys would come up to me and say, "Listen, Mick, you're the greatest drag bunter in the world. Could you show me how to do it?"

"Hell yes."

I remember outfielder Roy White asking me that very same question. He was the type who always looked for ways to improve his batting average.

I said, "Roy, you're trying to get away from the plate too fast. You have to hang in there longer." Roy was starting out on his left foot, running away from the pitcher toward first base. "What you're supposed to do, hitting right-handed, is start with your right foot aimed straight at the pitcher. Then try to drag the ball past the pitcher to make the second baseman field it. That way you're on a dead run immediately. That's how I was able to run to first in 3.1 seconds."

And sure enough, the next time I saw Roy he was dragging bunts for hits instead of outs.

I also know that the Yankees would have kept me on indefinitely. I had fun being around the guys and I got a little sun and exercise.

The big blowup with Kuhn came in New York, immediately after we held a press conference at the Waldorf Astoria to announce I had signed with the Claridge. A messenger walked over and handed me a letter. The commissioner himself wrote to say I had been banned from the game due to my casino employment. Kuhn was sorry that I had not taken another job, like Joe DiMaggio's with Mister Coffee.

Of course, I had been out of baseball for quite a while, doing all kinds of public relations, and nobody like Mister Coffee had offered to hire me.

Also, for the last fifteen years I've been getting invitations to the Hall of Fame Golf Tournament sponsored by the Riviera Hotel in Las Vegas. One of the co-chairmen of the tournament was Joe DiMaggio. I've gone to those tournaments at least four or five times. So it seemed to me there was a double standard somewhere because that's exactly what I do for the Claridge. I don't hang out in the casino. I go to public relations parties, I play golf with customers and at four golf tournaments each year. The hotel sends me to charitable events, such as the Jimmy Fund benefit dinner in Boston, the Save-A-Heart tournament in Baltimore, the Special Children's Olympics in Philadelphia. Good stuff, all worthwhile, all of it done in behalf of the Claridge.

If they plan to make a donation to a charity like the United Way, I go to the dinner and present the check.

I guess the commissioner had to do it because he had already banned Willie. In Willie's instance, he had a good job with the Mets. They were paying him something like $50,000 a year as batting instructor for their minor league teams. With the suspension he lost out on some pretty good money. I never lost a dime because the Yankees weren't paying me anything to speak of.

As for the commissioner, I understood his position. He was voted in by the owners. They hired him. They wanted someone to protect their interests and in case after case their business priorities superseded the game of baseball. Now, as in the past, we see where the big money comes from: the communications field, real estate, oil, food and beverage companies, shipbuilding, race tracks, and, yes, even gambling casinos.

Look around and you'll find owners like George Steinbrenner. He's into ships. But among his other profitable enterprises are racetracks. In my day, a major portion of Del Webb's income was generated by his land holdings, hotels, and gambling casinos in the state of Nevada.

There was no doubt in my mind about that double standard. For nearly two years I stayed away from baseball. I remember the Old-Timers' game in 1983 especially. I was at home in Dallas, watching the game on television. During the ceremonies I heard the fans chanting my name. "We want Mickey! We want Mickey!" I would have loved to have been there to see my old friends, but I wouldn't have felt right. I decided that I would never go back to Yankee Stadium or any major league promotion, not as long as I was banned from the game.

Peter Ueberroth took over as baseball commissioner in October 1984 and in the months that followed I began to hear rumors that a change might be coming. Mr. Ueberroth himself called me on the afternoon of Sunday, March 17, 1985, to invite me to New York for an announcement. And on March 18 Willie Mays and I appeared at the Astor Salon of the Waldorf Astoria with the commissioner and were officially welcomed back to baseball. The ban had been lifted and I was part of the great game of baseball again.

I am proud to have been a Yankee. I was in there with some of the greatest outfielders of all time: Willie Mays, Hank Aaron, Ted Williams, Joe DiMaggio, Stan Musial, Duke Snider—I was among them, a Hall of Famer. To think of it sends chills up and down my spine. Since I was four years old that's all I ever worked for. And I had people behind me who pushed me along almost as though I was on a production line. My dad stuck with me till high school. He molded the frame. Then Barney Barnett put on a hubcap or something. Harry Craft put on the hood. Casey added the polish. Ralph Houk took the finished car and drove it off. Then Yogi wrecked it.

(Just kiddin', Yog.)

I stood in the sun that morning in August 1974 in Cooperstown, New York. Beside me was Whitey. My buddy. We were together again, both of us admitted to the Hall of Fame on the same day. It seemed right. We had been together for so many years. As players we laughed a lot together, won and lost together. Now this, the thrill of our lives.

We had chartered a bus in New York City and took off for Cooperstown. There was Merlyn and my four boys, Mom, Phil Rizzuto, his wife Cora and their boy Scooter, Roy True and his wife Pat, Harold and Stella Youngman, George Scanlon and his wife June, and my friend Joe Warren and his wife.

The ceremony was held on the back porch of the museum. Little snow fences were erected to keep the crowds back. (These didn't do much good. There were about 10,000 people there and they just walked right on through.) On the platform there were a bunch of past Hall of Famers, an array of baseball dignitaries, and the four other inductees: Cool Papa Bell, Sunny Jim Bottomley, Sam Thompson, and umpire Jocko Conlon.

At the microphone, I introduced my mother, Merlyn and my boys, Harold and Stella. I don't remember if I introduced Phil or not, but I hope I did. And if I didn't I should have. I wanted to give a decent speech. I thanked all of my Yankee teammates and Casey for sticking with me through the tough times. I looked over and Casey was sitting there in a blazing yellow shirt, a red jacket with a red tie, his face jutted up at the sun, looking satisfied, content.

As I travel around these days, people often ask me about the biggest thrill I ever had. Along with having my number retired on Mickey Mantle Day, going into the Hall of Fame with Whitey has to be the biggest moment in my life.

Chapter *30*

It's impossible for me to think about baseball without thinking of Casey. That he was fired from the Yankees after the 1960 season is of course a scandal and I haven't forgotten the way he went on to breathe new life into the game with the New York Mets. To me, he lived and died a complete success.

I also think the major leagues have the same spirit going today. Baseball is still the greatest game, but there are changes I'd like to see.

The ballparks, for instance. Every other sport has a uniformity of playing fields; football, basketball, soccer, track, tennis— standard dimensions. Not baseball. The distances down the foul lines and out to the fences vary from park to park. Make them conform to standards and then you can tell who your home run hitters really are. I know one thing. Yankee Stadium was the worst park for me to hit in. Ask any power hitter and he'll tell you the same. Harmon Killebrew hated it. I used to stand back there and catch balls on him all day. One time I caught three balls off him that went 450 feet. He was standing on second base when I came in with the last one and he yelled, "How the hell can you play here?"

I also wish they'd get rid of artificial turf. A whole lot of players who are hitting .300 wouldn't be near that average if they played on grass. Take the Cardinals. Whitey Herzog teaches his team to swing down at the ball. They can all run like rabbits and all they have to do is make the ball bounce high and straight through for a hit. On grass the ball has a tendency to run smooth, therefore it's easy to pick off by the infielders for an out.

The biggest rap I have is against the damage artificial turf can do to a ballplayer's legs. In 1965 they opened the Houston

Astrodome. A magnificent ballpark, no question. We played an exhibition game there and I hit the first home run ever in the Astrodome. But when we went on to New York, I could barely play on Opening Day. My leg had swelled up from all the pounding. The next day there I was taking whirlpool baths, diathermy, cortisone, whatnot. I was hurting for a week. So you can have your AstroTurf. I'll take grass anytime.

I'd also like to see the farm club system strengthened. In my early days of professional ball, there were literally hundreds of minor league clubs operating. Today only a scattered remnant exists. A lot of people say you can't draw crowds in the minor leagues. My friend A. Ray Smith from Tulsa, who is now with the Louisville Redbirds, has drawn over a million people in the last two years. It just proves that if you work hard enough people will come to see baseball anywhere.

Today A. Ray Smith is an exception. The minor leagues are suffering. The best players are being pruned from colleges and baseball schools. And most of these kids know they should go to school, where they'll get great coaching. Modern technology helps. TV has advanced baseball all over the world. So I'm in favor of kids going to college. Go, get an education, play a couple of years at a good school. If you don't cut it as a ball-player, at least you'll have something to fall back on.

But I still think there's nothing better than having minor league experience under your belt. I know it helped me. With all the things I've said about George Weiss, now I'll admit he was absolutely correct in his assessment. He *knew* I wasn't ready for the majors. As it turned out, going down to Kansas City made the difference. Because playing there toughened me. No spoon-fed instructions, no pampering, no special favors. I realized it was either make the grade or end up in the mines.

I'm still a baseball fan and some of the guys that I love to watch are Steve Garvey, Tommy John, George Brett, and Pete Rose—guys that I know must be hurting some days, just like Lou Gehrig must have been hurting when he played in 2,130 consecutive games.

I still get a kick out of the long ball hitters. Dave Kingman, for one. He disappears once in a while, then comes back. Recently he resurfaced in Oakland, had a bunch of home runs, hit for good average, and played regularly. Maybe the change in scenery reinstilled his pride. I hope so. I once saw him get a home run off Mel Stottlemyre in St. Petersburg. A shot. It rippled the water in Tampa Bay. He's like me. Swings from his ass.

Reggie Jackson. Another home run hitter. I used to kid him that he'd break my record of 1,710 Ks. And of course he did. What pisses me off, I watched him on television one day. He had just tagged a pitch and the announcer said, "Well, folks, that puts Reggie ahead of Mantle for post-season home runs." The graphic showed Reggie on top and me second. False reporting. What they did was combine his post-season *and* World Series home runs. I got so mad watching, I almost threw a shoe at the set.

But the game goes on.

Two of the questions I'm asked in my travels around the country are: "What's the difference between baseball now and when you played?" and "Why aren't there any superstars today?" When I came up in 1951, if we were playing the St. Louis Browns and knocked out the starting pitcher, we could have a field day. Nowadays, if you knock out a million-dollar starter, a two-million-dollar reliever comes in. I'm not one of those old-timers who thinks baseball isn't as good as it used to be. I think it's probably as good or better than ever. These kids today are so evenly matched no one stands out that far above the others. They are all six-foot-four or thereabouts and can run a hundred yards in ten seconds and throw the ball 100 miles an hour.

Today's Little Leaguers—and there are millions of them each year—pick up on how to hit and throw and field just by watching the game on TV. By the time they're out of high school, the good ones are almost ready to play professional ball.

I hope I've covered some of the things you all have wondered about. I guess we're on the same team now. And it's the greatest team ever put together in the history of the world. It's even like Casey is running it. I might not know what he's saying all the time, but if he tells me to bunt, I'm going to bunt. If he tells me to swing away, I'm going for the fences.

Until I see y'all around again, I'll just say so long for now.

Your teammate,

Mickey Mantle